Performed Imaginaries

In this collection of essays, performance studies scholar and artist Richard Schechner brings his unique perspective to bear upon some of the key themes of society in the twenty-first century.

Schechner connects the avant-garde and terror, the countercultural movement of the 1960s and 1970s, and the Occupy movement; self-wounding art, popular culture, and ritual; the Ramlila cycle play of India and the way imagination structures reality; the corporate world and conservative artists. Schechner asks artists to redeploy Nehru's Third World as a movement not of nations but of like-minded culture workers who must propose counter-performances to war, violence, and the globalized corporate empire.

With characteristic brio, Schechner urges us to play for keeps. "Playing deeply is a way of finding and embodying new knowledge," he writes.

Performed Imaginaries ranges through some of the key moves within Schechner's oeuvre and challenges today's experimental artists, activists, and scholars to generate a new, Third World of performance.

Performed Imaginaries

Richard Schechner

 Routledge
Taylor & Francis Group

LONDON AND NEW YORK

First published 2015
by Routledge
2 Park Square, Milton Park, Abingdon OX14 4RN

and by Routledge
711 Third Avenue, New York, NY 10017

Routledge is an imprint of the Taylor & Francis Group, an informa business

British Library Cataloguing in Publication Data
A catalogue record for this book is available from the British Library

Library of Congress Cataloging in Publication Data
A catalog record for this book has been requested

ISBN: 978-1-138-78868-8 (hbk)
ISBN: 978-1-138-78869-5 (pbk)
ISBN: 978-1-315-74751-4 (ebk)

Typeset in Sabon
by Taylor & Francis Books

MIX
Paper from
responsible sources
FSC
www.fsc.org   FSC® C013604

Printed and bound by CPI Group (UK) Ltd, Croydon, CR0 4YY

Contents

A Foreword Looking Back

An aged man is but a paltry thing,
A tattered coat upon a stick, unless
Soul clap its hands and sing, and louder sing
For every tatter in its mortal dress,
Nor is there singing school but studying
Monuments of its own magnificence;
And therefore I have sailed the seas and come
To the holy city of Byzantium.
                    (William Butler Yeats, "Sailing to Byzantium," second stanza, 1928)

Yeats sailed to Byzantium, I flew to Abu Dhabi. I don't feel tattered yet, nor old hanging from a stick, but I desire my soul to sing and clap its hands. Byzantium was once a great city, heir to Empire and prologue to Islam in the modern world. Istanbul stands in Byzantium's place; Abu Dhabi, one of Islam's possible futures, rises from a sea of sand covering an ocean of oil. "Tribal modern," Miriam Cooke calls it and the whole enterprise known as "The Gulf" ... fringing Saudi Arabia, facing Iran, hinging Africa, importing labor from south and southeast Asia, emulating American dreams, Japanese ingenuity, and European banking ... sailing into a future not quite in its own hands, but trying (Cooke 2014).

My book, like all, attempts to capture "monuments of its own magnificence," as a necklace of writings composed between ... when? ... it's hard to say, exactly. *Performed Imaginaries* has been in my bodymind since I first dipped in the Ganga river at Varanasi, India, in 1971. Known as Kashi to devout Hindus, Banaras to Buddhists and British, and a plenitude of other names depending on why one goes there to live or die, Varanasi "is one of the oldest living cities in the world [...] its present life reaches back to the sixth century BCE in a continuous tradition" (Eck 1982: 4–5). Abu Dhabi, where I am writing this Foreword, is Varanasi's identical opposite, rising like a postmodern Athena fully made from the brain of its creator, "our father" (as a huge billboard in Abu Dhabi proclaims) Sheikh Zâyed bin Sulṭân âl Nahyân (1918–2004). But, of course, Varanasi is always changing, and the Gulf's history can be traced back thousands of years. The difference is that Varanasi's residents try to keep this holy city on the banks of India's holiest river "the same," while the rulers of the United Arab Emirates prize their own unfolding future as signaled by eye-candy architecture, global-brand shopping malls, and a smorgasbord of cultural "attractions" (the Louvre, the Guggenheim, NYU, the Sorbonne, the Abu Dhabi Grand Prix, the Dubai Desert Classic … and many more). I write in "Performed Imaginaries" (chapter 5) about how the Ramlila of Ramnagar, Varanasi, literally embodies the Hindu divine. Here in Abu Dhabi I teach "ritual and play" at NYU, not yet knowing how to factor in much of what I am experiencing.

The writings appear in a different sequence in the book from the order I discuss them in this Foreword. That's because the book follows a thematic logic while the Foreword follows the logic of my associations.

The newest essay in this book, "Can We Be the (New) Third World?" (chapter 1) spoken in 2012 and revised ever since, is my musing on the deleterious doings of the past half-century as prologue to, maybe, a brighter future led by understanding what "performance" is and what "performing" can do. I teeter between the optimism of my belly and the pessimism of my brain. Around me, ecological catastrophe, willful human ignorance, deprivation, oppression. Enacted daily, Kurtz's "The horror! The horror!" in our own heart of darkness. And yet, surging moon-driven tides of lunatic hope. Global warming? Well, if the Arctic had not once been tropical where did all that oil come from? What can be wrong with more ocean and a Greenland that is really green? OK, don't remind me of the apocalypse that must accompany the submerging of coastlines.

With those thoughts in mind, and afflicted by having seen with my own eyes the second plane mash into the World Trade Center in New York the morning of September 11, 2001, I wrote "9/11 as Avant-Garde Art?" (chapter 4) – the question mark being a most important punctuation. Don't we humans usually get what we ask for, whether we know we are asking for it or not? Yeats's "every tatter in its mortal dress" are the fragments of still smoking steel next to photos of the dead and missing taped to fences along with notes pleading for information. All this wishing shredded by days of wind, unable to sink into memory.

Memories linked to the 1960s, the decade when my academic life began amidst street demonstrations and avant-garde theatre. It was then that I, and others, formed the ideas that would become performance studies. That story I tell in "The 1960s, TDR, and Performance Studies" (chapter 3). I totally reshaped my responses to a 2009 interview for this book because I realized that my academic project is unfinishable. "Self-Inflicted Wounds" (chapter 6) is an outlier – except at a Freudian level, where we, as a collation of cultures, are always cutting ourselves, making art from injury, and enjoying the blood. "Self-Inflicted Wounds" began as lectures, was incorporated into my seminars, and underwent a series of rewritings, most recently in 2014. I both seek and abhor violence: So many of my night dreams are scary.

In "The Conservative Avant-Garde" (chapter 2), I rehearse themes that go back to "Restoration of Behavior," conceived in the early 1980s. What is "new" is already recycled, "a widening gyre," to quote Yeats again ("The Second Coming," 1919). And, finally, circling back on myself, "'Points of Contact' Revisited" (chapter 7), a rethinking of the now of the then. I mean: in the 1980s, refracting my work and intimacy with Victor Turner, I turned over in my mind and my artistic work how "anthropology" broadly conceived could affect, shape, and interact with performance studies. Then, in 2012, invited to address the annual meeting of the Brazilian Anthropological Association in São Paulo, I realized how current my "old" thoughts still were, if properly imprismed by some of what I learned over time.

What do all these writings share? Why put them in the same book? Sitting here at 4:46 in the predawn Abu Dhabi stillness ... not yet quite time for the first call to prayer ... I wonder how a man's life as sampled by his writing matters. "An aged man is but a paltry thing," Yeats wrote in the sixty-third of his seventy-four years. Premature debility, I'd estimate; and probably not entirely sincere – but poets will be poets. I am soon to turn eighty, well over my biblical allotment. Yet I do not feel paltry, but well-abled and entitled to share with you these writings.

Abu Dhabi, United Arab Emirates
April 2014

References

Cooke, Miriam (2014) *Tribal Modern* (Berkeley, Calif.: University of California Press).
Eck, Diana (1982) *Banaras: City of Light* (Princeton, NJ: Princeton University Press).

Acknowledgments

The six essays and one dialogue that comprise this book have been revised for this volume. My writing often begins as lectures or seminars. Writing for me is editing and revising – like rehearsing a theatrical production. Though nothing can be said to be "definitive," the work in this book is as close as I can get to finished.

"Can We Be the (New) Third World?" began as a talk to the 2012 Performing the World conference in New York. A revised version is in Atay Citron, Sharon Aronson-Lehavi, and David Zerbib (eds.), *Performance Studies in Motion: International Perspectives and Practices in the Twenty-First Century* (London: Bloomsbury, 2014), pp. 42–58. It is further revised here.

"The Conservative Avant-Garde" appeared in an earlier version in 2010 in *New Literary History*, 41 (4): 895–913.

"9/11 as Avant-Garde Art?" appeared in an earlier version in *PMLA, a publication of the Modern Language Association*, 124 (5) (2009): 1820–1829.

"The 1960s, *TDR*, and Performance Studies" is based on an interview conducted in 2009 by Ana Bigotte Vieira and Ricardo Seiça Salgado. That interview was published in Portuguese in 2012 (see indanca.net/uma-tarde-com-richard-schener [sic]). What appears here is thoroughly revised and updated.

"Performed Imaginaries: The Ramlila of Ramnagar" has not appeared in English. Earlier versions were published in German and Romanian.

"Self-Inflicted Wounds" has not appeared in English. It began as a talk in 2002 at the University of Maryland. I revised it in 2004 for a seminar at Cornell University's School for Theory and Criticism and again in 2009 for the Performance, Art, and Anthropology conference at the Musée Quai Branly, Paris. It is revised again here.

"'Points of Contact' Revisited" has not appeared in English. It began as a keynote lecture to the Brazilian Anthropological Association in 2012. A Portuguese version was published in Brazil in a journal in 2013 and in a book in 2014.

Permission

Figure 4.1 © Telegraph Media Group Limited 2001/Getty Images.

Chapter 1

Can We Be the (New) Third World?

I sit here this morning (does it really matter which morning?) trying to be optimistic. I want to write how performance studies and the performing arts can save the world, or at least help to save the world. I am typing while rockets and bombs are exploding in Gaza and Israel; Egypt is in turmoil, Syria in the throes of civil war; M23 rebels are closing on Goma in the Congo, putting a million people under threat; suicide bombings and assassinations continue in Iraq and Afghanistan; the Somali civil war is ongoing. Sunnis and Shias have warred against each other since the martyrdom of Hussein in 680 CE; in India, Hindus murder Muslims and vice versa; anti-Semitism is rife in many places; and not long ago Catholics and Protestants were murdering each other in Northern Ireland a few centuries after religious wars decimated Europe. The Shoah is not ancient history.

I am more than halfway through my seventy-ninth year. For seventy-one of those years, the USA has been at war. Big wars, small wars, long wars, short wars, good wars, bad wars, just wars, greedy wars, invasions, incursions, missions, actions in Europe, Asia, Latin America, the Middle East, Africa. From World War II and the Korean War to Grenada ("Operation Urgent Fury") and Lebanon (twice, 1958 and 1982–1984); from Vietnam to Iraq and Afghanistan; from Serbia to Libya. And: Panama, Cambodia, El Salvador, Colombia, Liberia, Egypt, Zaïre, Kosovo, Bosnia, East Timor, Yemen, the Philippines, Congo, Ivory Coast, Haiti, Dominican Republic, Nicaragua, Honduras. ... And where America has not sent troops it has sent arms, trained soldiers, created alliances, and supported proxy armies. Sometimes with grotesque paradoxes such as helping Saddam Hussein invade Iran, precipitating a bloody stalemate from 1980 to 1988, a half-million dead, and then, barely three years later, turning against Saddam with "Operation Desert Storm," and after that, in 2003, "Operation Iraqi Freedom," where the USA led the "Coalition of the Willing." (Who's kidding who?) Plus untold covert actions and wars waged by surrogates with American "advisers"; the "dirty wars" in Latin America fought in the name of anticommunism; the Cold War with its nuclear buildup still not substantially dismantled. What about the close calls from the Cuban Missile Crisis to the US Seventh Fleet "patrolling" the strait between mainland China and Taiwan? The continuing "showdown" against North Korea and Iran over their nuclear arms programs? The US Congressional Research Service, in its "Instances of Use of United States Armed Forces Abroad" reports that from 1950 to 2006 there were 153 occasions when American forces went on missions outside the borders of the USA. No year was without its particular military excursion; many years had several. Yes, some were for just causes or humanitarian reasons; but most were applications by force of US policy. In addition to active armed intervention is the US "presence" (troops stationed in bases around the world) and multiple covert operations. Covert means "classified," secret, kept from public view and accountability – even in a self-professed "open" society with its "free press." Who knows how many secret actions there have been and how many continue today? These "operations" (surgery?) involve "intelligence" (what a weird name for spying and dirty tricks), terror, and torture in camps such as Guantánamo and secret "black sites" around the world. Even the seven years of peace, my infancy and early childhood, from 1934 to 1941, were gloomed by the 1937 Japanese invasion of China, the Nazi and Soviet invasions of Poland in 1939, and the preparations for the USA's entry into World War II. And what about the wars within American borders – "war" being used only partly metaphorically? The House Un-American Activities Committee (1938–1975), the anticommunist "witch hunt" led by Senator Joseph McCarthy (in the 1950s), the violent responses to the African-American Civil Rights Movement and gay liberation, the PATRIOT Act, the War on Drugs ... the list goes on and on.

American society and culture – and, through their influence, global societies and cultures – have been deformed by a plague of wars, threats of war (national wars, civil wars, insurrections, "actions," "operations," ... the war family has plenty of members). Continuous war both creates and requires a political-cultural-social-educational-economic paranoiac system underpinning weapons research and testing, large standing armies, and a spidery stealth apparatus. In the USA, we are bombarded (yes, I am aware of the metaphor) by messages telling us that we can enjoy the benefits of (un-)peace – consumer goods, leisure, an open society – while waging (note the metaphor) wars or, rather, crafting on a "volunteer army" to fight for us (in quotation marks because economic necessity and, to some degree, racism and sexism determines who volunteers). The message is disturbingly schizoid: Live "normally," but "if you see something, say something." This specific War on Terror slogan-instruction is posted everywhere in New York, and elsewhere I suppose; it is displayed and uttered in a soft voice and reinforced with omnipresent signage and surveillance cameras. Surveillance has been normalized, the panopticon has arrived. Go on vacation, but take off your shoes before passing through the metal detector. The war machine needs both jingoism (America is the best, the greatest, the freest) and paranoia (America is under attack, our "way of life" threatened, "they" are crossing our borders actually and figuratively). The military-industrial complex and its concomitant "disastrous rise of misplaced power" that General and then President Dwight D. Eisenhower warned of in his 1961 farewell address has come to pass. The universities are not exempt but are closely knit into the fabric.

The global outcome of all this is that billions of people live on less than $1 per day; billions have no clean water or adequate sanitation. Twenty years ago, people in the top 20 percent of the world's population were thirty times as rich as those in the bottom 20 percent. Now they are seventy times as rich. Of the 1,233 drugs developed in the past decade, only eleven were for treating tropical diseases and, of these, five cured livestock, not humans. The richest three persons in the world have more wealth than the GDP of the forty-seven poorest nations; the richest fifteen persons have more wealth than the combined GDP of all sub-Saharan Africa, 550 million people. The Occupy Wall Street movement in the USA became famous for pointing out that the top 1 percent of Americans earned more than 20 percent of total income.

All the military "engagements" (married to war?) cost plenty. The expenditure for arms can be averaged out to $330 billion (in 2012 dollars) a year from 1940 to the present. That adds up to about $23.5 trillion ($23,430,000,000,000). Can you even imagine such a pile of gold? What it would buy if put to constructive uses? Health care, education, public works, arts, housing? Maybe it doesn't make sense to unilaterally disarm. But neither does it make sense to be the world's number one military spender for years, decades, generations, forever. Not since Rome – and remember what happened to Rome, from republic to imperium to decay – has an empire so extended-expended itself. And the cost is not just dollars. The cost is cultural, personal, and spiritual.

So what is it about war? Is it all greed and power? No, culture – deep culture, historically reinforced – loves war. Think of it: the foundational Indo-European and Middle Eastern myths are war stories: the *Iliad*, *Odyssey*, *Mahabharata*, *Ramayana*, *Gilgamesh*, the Old Testament. Yes, there's a lot happening that is not war, but the core narratives celebrate battle, conquest, and heroism – more the glory than the gory of war. These myths admire and even worship the warlike person or deity, male usually but not always because ferocity and valor in battle trumps gender – think Athena and Enyo, Durga and Kali. The Old Testament is warlike, from the Plagues (God's war against Pharaoh) to the tumbling down of Jericho's walls, from the ethnic cleansing of Canaan to David's bloody expeditions, and more. In the realm of literature, the Greek theatre brings against war the claims of women: witness the *Oresteia*, *Antigone*, *The Trojan Women*, and *Lysistrata*. But heroism is always honored, and war is sometimes celebrated as in *The Persians*. Shakespeare is no pacifist, nor is Milton, Hemingway, or even Joseph Heller. Pop culture from video games to contact sports is driven by violence and saturated with metaphors of war.

When leaders want to focus people on a task, war is a chosen metaphor. Not only the jihads and the War on Terror but also the War on Cancer, the War on Drugs, the War on Poverty, the War on Violence, etc., etc. World War I was "the war to end all wars." War is what people do, along with sex, death, and taxes. Can we change this? Competition for land, hierarchy (power), reputation, honor, mates ... overlapping each other ... drives human action and, some say, all of nature. Ironically, even the opposite of competition – generosity, sharing, and "love" (in quotation marks because the concept is so malleable) – often is a rivalry of who or what can do the most good. Is war natural, is it cultural – or what mix of both?

There is a counter-narrative to this history of violence. In *The Better Angels of Our Nature* (2011), Stephen Pinker deploys impressive statistical and social analysis to show that for centuries violence has declined globally, and continues to do so. Violence in terms of war, genocide, terror, murder, torture, slavery, capital punishment, domestic mayhem, infanticide, and child abuse. He attributes the decline to a set of interwoven causes: the rise of civil societies, democratization, decline in superstition, global trade and affluence, and, decisively, the increasing power and influence of women, what Pinker terms "feminization," where "female-friendly values" prevail over the "manly honor" of violent retaliation – on individual, family, tribal, and national levels, where contraception allows women to determine if and when to have babies. In summary:

> The declines we seek to explain unfolded over vastly different scales of time and damage: the taming of chronic raiding and feuding, the reduction of vicious interpersonal violence such as cutting off noses, the elimination of cruel practices like human sacrifice, torture-executions, and flogging, the abolition of institutions such as slavery and debt bondage, the falling out of fashion of blood sports and duelling, the eroding of political murder and despotism, the recent decline of wars, pogroms, and genocides, the reduction of violence against women, the decriminalization of homosexuality, the protection of children and animals. [...] All these developments undeniably point in the same direction.
>
> (Pinker 2011: 672)

How can Pinker be right, given everything I asserted previously? There are two ways of understanding Pinker's data. As statistics, trends, and overall developments, clearly the proportion of violent acts – individual, societal, national, international – has declined relative to the number of people alive. But the absolute numbers of people who suffer or die has not decreased because there are so many more people alive today than previously – and the world's population will go up a lot more before it levels off or declines. To put this another way, humans may be regarded as parts of a group – the statistical person, relative to all the others – or as absolute individual "souls," or "beings," each endowed with her or his own particular self. From the perspective of unique beings, the number of individuals who suffer or die has increased, even as the proportion of these relative to the whole population has declined. Second, violence is not limited to what happens between and among people. Violence is also done to animals and plants, lands and seas – the world as "Gaia," a unified living thing. This violence against species and habitat, against the planet, is definitely approaching the level of – what words do I need? – specicide and globacide. We are presently living through earth's sixth great extinction, driven by homo sapiens, us.

It didn't have to be this way. I won't speak about nations other than my own, the USA, but I know that blame also belongs elsewhere. However, the USA has been the leading entity – the "American Century" and all that – economically, militarily, and, after the collapse of the USSR, ideologically. Think for a moment where the world might be if the USA supported the Cuban revolution, opposed the military regimes of Latin America and embraced the democratic socialism of Salvador Allende (instead of being complicit in his murder). What if the USA helped Patrice Lumumba in the Congo, worked to overthrow apartheid in South Africa and instituted an African Marshall Plan enabling the continent to recover from the horrors of colonialism? What if the USA refused to take up the cause of defeated French colonialism in Vietnam, worked for the peaceful reunification of Korea and demanded a just settlement of the Israel–Palestine conflict? What if the USA recognized sixty years ago that dependence on Middle Eastern oil distorted American foreign and domestic policy and therefore launched an all-out moonshot-type effort to develop non-fossil energy sources? What if, instead of automobile mania, big industry and government collaborated in constructing networks of bullet trains and local mass transit? What if the USA rejected McCarthyism and the hunt for "un-American activities," which continues under the auspices of the PATRIOT Act? Some things have been accomplished, but not nearly swiftly or thoroughly enough: an end to racism, sexism, and homophobia; comprehensive health-care reform. Other urgent items await action: immigration reform, because millions of undocumented are an exploited underpaid underclass; real protection for the environment, the fisheries, the water supply; meaningful support for education and the arts. Meanwhile, corporations gain more power, increasing the wealth imbalance, keeping or transporting millions to poverty (exactly what the Occupy Wall Street movement protests).

"What if?" is a loser's game. However, I am not dreaming when I say that all the possibilities I've just listed were on the table in America, supported by a considerable number of people and debated in more or less mainstream media (as well as by progressives and radicals). Why were these programs and reforms not successful? Why were those who actively supported progressive policies wiretapped, hounded, imprisoned, shot, and ground to dust? I am not a conspiracy-theory-type thinker. I don't believe American policy-makers are being controlled by a cabal. I do think that policy-makers didn't fully comprehend the world they were shaping when they made the decisions they made – and continue to make. What they wanted was and is to stay in power in Washington and to expand the new American corporate empire. Even scarier, some American leaders – like the colonialists of former times – believed they were and are doing good. How Brecht would wince and then laugh.

Sometimes clichés and platitudes are useful. So here're some: Ignorance is the plague. Xenophobia is the plague. Hatred of others is the plague. Greed is the plague. Disrespect for nature is the plague. Eradicate the plague. Performances are – or at least can be – model utopian societies. Workshops are ways to destroy ignorance; rehearsals are ways to creatively relate to others not by submerging or ignoring differences but by exploring differences as the group devises a generous common way forward; performances can hold up to public view the outcome of such active research. The broad spectrum of performance studies offers critical lenses to understand societies, groups, and individuals who embody and enact their personal and collective identities. Performance studies develops from the axiom that we live in a performatized world where cultures are colliding, influencing, and interfacing with each other and are hybridizing at a swift and increasing rate. These collisions are not always politically correct or pleasant. Populations and ideas are on the move, pushed by ideologies, religions, wars, famines, disease, hopes for improvement, government intervention, and global trade. The outcome, if there is to be "an" outcome, of all this circulation is neither clear nor certain. Some argue that change will be radical, stemming from the list I just listed and from almost unimaginable technical progress – robots, nano-computers, colonizing the moon and Mars; others see a new medieval epoch of circulating stasis. I myself shuttle between these alternatives – and all the stops in between.

Performance studies is a particular response to this global circumstance. Performance studies arises from the premise that everything and anything can be studied "as" performance. The tools of performance studies are drawn from other disciplines and have not yet coalesced into a coherent singularity. Perhaps that's good – it keeps performance studies practitioners alert to what's happening around us. Some of the disciplines that performance studies borrows from, steals, adapts, and makes use of in our own way include the social and biological sciences, history, gender studies, psychoanalysis, social theory, critical race studies, game theory, economics, popular culture studies, theatre, dance, film and media studies ... and more: performance studies is wanton, promiscuous, and bold – even as we try to get organized and arrive at consistency and coherence.

There is a problem at the heart of all this. If anything can be studied "as" performance, if any tool can be used (performance studies being the ultimate disciplinary bricoleur), then what "is" performance, what "is" performance studies? As I theorize it, something "is" performance when, according to the conventions, common usages, and/or traditions of a specific culture or social unit at a given historical time, an action or event is called a "performance." I know this is a squooshy definition, shape-shifting, and unreliable in absolute terms. But it is also useful, throwing the performance theorist back into the concrete social realities she is studying. Over the past seventy-five years (at least), what performance "is" has been stretched, twisted, and expanded. This expansion was at first driven by the avant-garde and by interactions between non-Western and Western cultures. Later, the expansion was also driven by the internet, with a resulting blurring of boundaries between the actual and the virtual, between so-called "art" and so-called "life."

Performance as distinct from performance studies (except in the dizzying circumstance where performance studies is studied as a performance) – and here I mean performance in its various realms, in social life, in the arts, in politics, in economics, in popular culture, and so on – realms that overlap each other, sometimes reinforcing sometimes subverting each other – performance marks identities, bends and remakes time, adorns and reshapes the body, tells stories, and provides people with the means to play with, rehearse, and remake the worlds they not merely inhabit but are always already in the habit of reconstructing.

Having written such sweeping generalizations, I must qualify by saying that every genre of performance, even every particular instance of each genre, is concrete and specific, different from every other. Not only in terms of cultural difference but also in terms of local and even individual variation. No two film showings of the same film are exactly the same as every other. At the same time, that which carries over – which is "not for the first time" – is the preponderance of every event, even once-only events. This paradox must be understood and accepted. The tension among permanence, repeatability, ephemerality, and originality is what constitutes the process of behavior and the representations of behavior at all levels and all instances. Understanding this is powerfully important in a period of accelerating digitization where reproducibility, interchangeability, and sameness seem to have the upper hand. But even cloned performances are different from each other when experienced by different audiences or by the same audiences at different times. The Heracletian river cannot be bathed in twice.

If we take into account the myriad artworks, personal interactions, rituals, media exchanges, pop-culture events, and so on, that go on every day all over the world, then both production and reception are incalculably varied, even as they appear to become more the same. Ironically, performance and performance studies, as they participate in an increasingly digitized world culture, resist that which they produce. As I noted earlier, what "is" performance cannot be decided a priori. The same event can "be" a performance in one instance and not in another. We, as theorists, artists, and teachers, must not only live with this indeterminacy but devise effective ways to theorize it. The development of performance as a category of theory as well as a fact of behavior and action makes it increasingly difficult to sustain the distinction between appearances and facts, surfaces and depths, illusions and substances. More than that: appearances are actualities, appearances drive actions. In modernity, what was "behind," "beneath," "deep," and "hidden" was (often) the "most real." But in postmodernity – and whatever will come after – the relationship between depths and surfaces is fluid and dynamically convective. What was hidden is tossed upwards; what was skim is plunged to the interior.

In 2011, Occupy Wall Street had taken over Zuccotti Park (appropriately located at the corner of Broadway and Liberty) in the financial district of Manhattan. Other "Occupys" sprang up around the USA and in other countries. Their driving slogan was "We are the 99 percent," meaning that the vast majority do not control the wealth of nations. In Zuccotti Park, when I visited, a set of related performances were taking place. The community encamped there were mostly younger people. The mood was performative and academic. Seminars, speeches amplified by call-and-response instead of loudspeakers, drumming and dancing, art displays, petitions circulating, food-sharing, and many other indications of creativity, goodwill, activism, and even irony. The Occupiers knew they were enacting an evanescent utopian moment. Unlike the Weather Underground of the 1960s and 1970s, they did not believe that they could overturn the social order by blowing up the symbols of the powers they detested. They knew that Zuccotti Park was surrounded by police and infiltrated by undercover agents. The park was quarantined. Then, on November 15, in the wee hours of the night, the New York police swept the Occupiers from their camp. Over the next few months, other Occupiers were assaulted and evicted from other sites globally.

Nothing physical remains. What lessons can we learn?

In the Occupy movement, I and others hear loud and clear echoes of the great freedom, student, and antiwar movements of the 1960s and 1970s and links – conceptual and strategic – to the Arab Spring, from Tunis through Cairo, on to Yemen, Libya, and Syria. Links also to the protests in Greece, Spain, and elsewhere against austerity programs and to violent labor uprisings in South Africa and China. None of these uprisings and protests is yet "finished." Some have turned authoritarian. In terms of economics, politics, the environment, human rights, and health – all the items I began this essay with – the powers are not making changes, or are not making them deeply, broadly, or swiftly enough. The 99 percent is angry, dissatisfied, and restless. But is it revolutionary? And if so, what form should revolution take? Armed struggle, as in the past? Cultural reformation? Something not yet articulated?

In the 1950s, as a way of finding a new path, the "Third World" was imagined. The Third World was not communist, it was not capitalist; it was not allied with the Soviet Union nor with the USA: it was "non-aligned." The Third World comprised mostly poor nations, in Africa, Asia, Latin America, and Oceania. On a global scale, the Third World was the 99 percent, the vast majority of people, excluded and exploited by the Great Powers. India's Jawaharlal Nehru was an eloquent spokesperson for the Third World. In Bandung, Indonesia, in 1955, Nehru addressed representatives of the Third World:

I speak with the greatest respect of these Great Powers because they are not only great in military might but in development, in culture, in civilization. But I do submit that greatness sometimes brings quite false values, false standards. [...] I submit that moral force counts and the moral force of Asia and Africa must, in spite of the atomic and hydrogen bombs of Russia, the USA or another country, count. [...] Therefore, are we, the countries of Asia and Africa, devoid of any positive position except being pro-communist or anticommunist? Has it come to this, that the leaders of thought who have given religions and all kinds of things to the world have to tag on to this kind of group or that and be hangers-on of this party or the other carrying out their wishes and occasionally giving an idea? It is most degrading and humiliating to any self-respecting people or nation.

Today, artists, activists, and scholars are a New Third World. Nehru's Third World had a specific geographical location. Today's New Third World is a proportion of people present everywhere with a majority nowhere. What unites the New Third World is a community of purpose, a mode of inquiry (the experimental, if you will), and a sense of being other – of not being hangers-on. The New Third World is incipient, seeds, not yet fully self-aware. The New Third World needs to organize itself as "non-aligned," neither capitalist, whether of the USA or Chinese brand, nor knee-jerk communist/socialist, nor fundamentalist religious, whether Islamic, Christian, Jewish, Buddhist, or whatever. The vanguard of this New Third World are – and here I hope you won't think me too arrogant – performance theorists and artists who practice collaborative performance research, persons who know that playing deeply is a way of finding and embodying new knowledge, renewing energy, and relating on a performative rather than ideological basis.

What would be a manifesto of this Performance Third World?

1. To perform is to explore, to play, to experiment with new relationships.
2. To perform is to cross borders. These borders are not only geographical but emotional, ideological, political, and personal.
3. To perform is to engage in lifelong active study. To grasp every book as a script – something to be played with, interpreted, and reformed/remade.
4. To perform is to become someone else and yourself at the same time. To empathize, react, grow, and change.

I am asking "you" – whoever is reading this – to consider the almost unimaginable because it is so hard for people to take seriously those who are not doing business, making war, or enforcing the will of God. To take seriously those who play, those who create playgrounds and art spaces. To take seriously the personal, social, and world-making force of performance. We must reject ideological, economic, and religious rigidity in favor of flexibility and fluidity.

All well and good. But can I offer some examples to substantiate my four-point manifesto? There is a lot going on in art, scholarship, and social action – especially where these three spheres interact and overlap. Let me offer a very few examples from a very long repertory of possibilities, and, in doing so, urge more synergy, more connections among various actions, artists, and scholarly pursuits.

Take Eve Ensler's project, "A Billion Women Rising." In the aftermath of the rape-murder of Jyoti Singh, a twenty-three-year-old in Delhi in December 2012, women (joined by many men) mobilized to insure that action is taken, not only in India but globally too. This action begins as artworks, manifestations, demonstrations, and petitions – all strong performatives – and continues as constant pressure for legislation, the enforcement of laws protecting women and guaranteeing them equality on all levels, and a raising of consciousness among women and men. Take for example, "One Billion Rising for Justice," coordinated by Eve Ensler's V-Day movement, in its sixteenth year in 2014, and continuing:

> Today, on the planet, a billion women – one of every three women on the planet – will be raped or beaten in her lifetime. [...] one billion rising for justice is a global call [...] to survivors to break the silence and release their stories – politically, spiritually, outrageously – through art, dance, marches, ritual, song, spoken word, testimonies and whatever way feels right. The campaign is a recognition that we cannot end violence against women without looking at the intersection of poverty, racism, war, the plunder of the environment, capitalism, imperialism, and patriarchy. Impunity lives at the heart of these interlocking forces. [...] one billion rising for justice is an invitation to break free from confinement, obligation, shame, guilt, grief, pain, humiliation, rage, and bondage.
>
> (http://www.onebillionrising.org)

This is not a movement with a known endpoint – except finally the end of violence against women.

On February 2, 2013, the BBC World Service broadcast "Sita, Draupadi and Kali: Women in Hinduism," exploring the need for a radical rethinking of Indian religion. Ensler was part of the conversation. A few excerpts:

VANDANA SHIVA: We've got to reform religion in its ancient exclusions. With all the slokas and mantras saying the woman is secondary, the woman is to serve the husband and all, and in its new virulent forms that is reinforced plus those forces that are new and are not part of religion in its ancient form but part of a new religion of the market, the religion of greed, the religion of commodification – because these are new forms of religion. And if we don't address the two patriarchies together and deal with them as one process of social reform we will never be able to get safety for women and women's rightful place in society.

Two hundred years of a particular kind of thinking about earth, about nature, about resources has created this false idea, totally false at the scientific level, that the earth is dead matter and therefore you can't violate her – because how can you violate something that's inert. But the earth is living, and the best of science teaches us that. And the same mindset that allows the objectification commodification ownership torture of women is the mindset that allows the commodification ownership torture of the earth.

ROMILA THAPAR: And it's not just religion in this country, but in any country in the world. There is in all religions moments when there are crises, when the religion is being questioned by social custom. Now, the question is: Who is going to be the victor in this confrontation? Social custom, social justice, gender equality, or religious tradition? This is a battle that has to be fought.

EVE ENSLER: It is not about asking now, or waiting, it is about rising.

The "woman question" is as vital today, maybe more so, than when American women assembled in Seneca Falls in 1848 to press for their rights; the injustices as palpable as those Ibsen portrayed. It's not just a matter of equality but of changing the history of violence. Pinker notes the strong correlation – a cause–effect system, I'd say – linking the rise of women, the decline of rape and battering, and an overall fall in violence:

> We are all feminists now. Western culture's default point of view has become increasingly unisex. The universalizing of the generic citizen's vantage point, driven by reason and analogy, was an engine of more progress during the Humanitarian Revolution of the 18th century, and it resumed that impetus during the Rights Revolution of the 20th. It's no coincidence that the expansion of the rights of women followed on the heels of the expansion of the rights of racial minorities. [...] What about the rest of the world? [...] Worldwide, it has been estimated that between a fifth and a half of all women have been victims of domestic violence. [...] I think it's extremely likely that in the coming decades violence against women will decrease throughout the world. [...] Among the grassroots, attitudes all over the world will almost certainly ensure that women will gain greater economic and political representation in the coming years.
>
> (Pinker 2011: 404, 413, 414)

Performance supporting women's rights is part of "social theatre," itself closely related to the project of performance studies. As James Thompson and I wrote in our introduction to *TDR*'s 2004 special issue on social theatre:

> Taken as a whole, social theatre stands alongside of, and sometimes in place of, "aesthetic theatre" (including art theatres, experimental theatres, university theatres, regional theatres, and commercial theatres). We do not

deny either the social aspects of aesthetic theatre or the aesthetic aspects of social theatre but rather point out differences of purpose, audiences, venues, and production values. [...] Social theatre may be defined as theatre with specific social agendas: theatre where aesthetics is not the ruling objective; theatre outside the realm of commerce [...] and the cult of the new. [...] Social theatre takes place in diverse locations – from prisons, refugee camps, and hospitals to schools, orphanages, and homes for elderly. [...] Social theatre often occurs in places and situations that are not the usual circumstances of theatre, turning "nonperformers" into performers. [...] Social theatre activists often are artists, but they need not be. The varieties of social theatre [...] can be put into four groups that have a logical and sequential relationship to each other: 1. Theatre for healing; 2. theatre for action; 3. theatre for community; 4. theatre for transforming experience into art. [...] Performance studies as a discipline promises to lead theatre studies out of its parochialism and into a necessary and powerful interdisciplinarity. Performance studies recognizes all areas of social life as topics for the performance theorists. Social theatre carries this banner into practice by going to hospitals, prisons, and war zones and proving that performance itself is a method for understanding what goes on there; for intervening, participating, and collaborating in positive ways with people who live in these sites.

(Thompson and Schechner 2004: 11–12, 15–16)

Of course, understand "theatre" in the above to include all of the performing arts. The theoretical underpinning of social theatre – beyond Thompson's writings and those of Guglielmo Schinina – include Paolo Freire's "Pedagogy of the Oppressed" and Augusto Boal's expansion of Freire into performance, the "Theatre of the Oppressed."

But, of course, aesthetic theatre – aesthetic performances of all kinds – is crucial if my proposed Third World of Performance is to become a reality. The number of progressive avant-garde and experimental artists is too great to list even a fraction of them. *TDR* has for decades championed the work of these artists. For example, Rabih Mroué's *The Pixelated Revolution*, about which Carol Martin writes:

The work demonstrates the ways in which theatre of the real can explore and exploit tensions between fact and fiction, aesthetic innovation, and political ideas. Its interpretive intentions are less about literal truth and more about the self-conscious use of materials to question the conventions of the representation of truth. [...] He notes at the outset that both professional and freelance journalists are absent from the Syrian revolution, making it impossible to know what is going on [...]. Born out of a detailed and forensic analysis of the Syrian protestors' uploaded images, like something one might see in a spy film, his performance is a provocative commentary on the aesthetics of post 9/11 warfare and revolution. [...] *The Pixelated Revolution* reveals a strange paradox. Everyday recordings can suddenly become acts of resistance and treated as transgressions that have to be eliminated. Surveillance here is not constant and panoptic. The surveillance of and by both the Syrian Ba'athists and their opposition is a surreptitious pop-up surveillance. There is not one eye scanning the landscape but many eyes, all looking for and trying to capture other eyes. The target of security forces is no longer people with guns with intent to kill, but people with mobile phones with intent to record. The target of people with mobile phones is people with guns, and their intent is to stop the killing by recording it. [...] Mroué participates in an aesthetic and analytical discourse that claims to represent the real and to tell the truth while openly acknowledging the simultaneous use of fiction to do so. He straddles fiction and nonfiction, performance and documentation, entertainment and edification in a performance in which acting, video, photographs, stage design, and text all operate together as equal partners in the creation of meaning.

(Martin 2012: 22, 24)

Mroué's approach is close to that of many others: synthesizing, multimedia, combining fiction and "real," acting and nonacting, seriousness and parody, scholarship and entertainment – a post-postmodern performative bouillabaisse. I need to stop here, though I could list groups and individuals from Forced Entertainment and the Yes Men to Gob Squad and the TEAM, from Nature Theatre of Oklahoma to the Assembly and Builders Association, and many more, who are making concrete the Performance Third World. Added to these are scholars and teachers – for this performative Third World fuses the academic in the noblest sense (Socrates living and dying for his ideas) with the artistic; the reflective with the active; the critical with the celebratory. Ironically, what's needed now – even in this epoch of hyper-connectivity – is for individuals and groups, movements and tendencies, artists and scholars, to coalesce into a single, unstoppable force for positive change.

A PS for PS

PS means "performance studies," and it means "postscript," what is written after. So this, at the last.

In his masterful *Identity and the Life Cycle*, papers written in the 1940s and 1950s, collected in 1959 and republished in 1980, Erik H. Erikson declares that the crisis of old age (the phase of life I am now entering), is "integrity/wisdom vs. disgust/despair" (1980: 104–105, 129). Integrity meaning "gaining a view of the whole," what poet Yeats called "an old man's eagle mind." So, I am trying to hold things together, to not surrender to "facts," but struggling to imagine alternatives. I have often said that my brain is pessimistic while my belly is optimistic. That is, what I know reinforces the world I described at the start of this essay. But what I feel urges me toward the New Third World. Doing yoga – the very word means to tie together, to yoke as oxen are yoked – keeps my brain and belly in some kind of deep commerce. Every crisis – personal, public, artistic, global – involves choice; choice – a turning this way or that. And, at my age, the turning is a Janus-look peering both forwards and backwards at the same time. More than a half-century ago, Erikson wisely and prophetically wrote:

> Ideologies seem to provide meaningful combinations of the oldest and the newest in a group's ideals. They thus channel the forceful earnestness, the sincere asceticism, and the eager indignation of youth toward that social frontier where the struggles between conservatism and radicalism is most alive. On that frontier fanatic ideologists do their busy work and psychopathic leaders their dirty work; but there, also, true leaders create significant solidarities. All ideologies ask for, as the prize for the promised possession of a future, uncompromising commitment to some absolute hierarchy of values and some rigid principle of conduct; be that principle total obedience to tradition, if the future is the eternalization of ancestry; total resignation, if the future is to be of another world; total martial discipline, if the future is to be reserved for some brand of armed superman; total inner reform, if the future is perceived as an advanced edition of heaven on earth; or (to mention only one of the ideological ingredients of our time [sic]) complete pragmatic abandon to the processes of production and to human teamwork, if unceasing production seems to be the thread which holds present and future together. [... W]hen established identities become outworn or unfinished ones threaten to remain incomplete, special crises compel men to wage holy wars, by the cruelest means, against those who seem to question or threaten their unsafe ideological basis. We may well pause to ponder briefly the fact that the technological and economic developments of our day [sic, again!] encroach upon all traditional group identities and solidarities such as may have developed in agrarian, feudal, patrician, or mercantile ideologies. [...] In large parts of the world, this seems to result in a ready fascination with totalistic world views, views predicting millenniums and cataclysms, and advocating self-appointed mortal gods. Technological centralization today [sic, one last time] can give small groups of such fanatic ideologists the concrete power of totalitarian state machines.
>
> (Erikson 1980: 169–171)

Performance studies scholars and performance artists need always to remain actively critical of "self-appointed mortal gods." We must imagine, invent, and perform alternative ways of becoming.

References

BBC World Service, "Sita, Draupadi and Kali: Women in Hinduism," episode of *Heart and Soul* broadcast on February 2, 2013. Available online at http://www.bbc.co.uk/programmes/p013vqxs (accessed June 9, 2014).

Erikson, Erik H. (1980) *Identity and the Life Cycle* (New York: W. W. Norton). First published 1959.

Martin, Carol (2012) "Introduction to *The Pixelated Revolution* by Rabih Mroué," *TDR*, 56 (3): 18–35.

Nehru, Jawaharlal (1956) "Speech to Bandung Conference Political Committee, 1955," in G. M. Kahin, *The Asian-African Conference* (Ithaca, N.Y.: Cornell University Press), pp. 64–72.

Pinker, Steven (2011) *The Better Angels of Our Nature* (New York: Viking).

Schinina, Guglielmo (2004a) "Here We Are: Social Theatre and Some Open Questions about Its Developments," *TDR*, 48 (3): 17–31.

——(2004b) "'Far Away, So Close': Psychosocial and Theatre Activities with Serbian Refugees," *TDR*, 48 (3): 32–49.

Thompson, James and Richard Schechner (2004) "Why 'Social Theatre'?" *TDR*, 48 (3): 11–16.

Chapter 2

The Conservative Avant-Garde

We are in the midst of a period of excellent new and impressively "reper-formed" avant-garde works wholly able to hold their own with any and every earlier period of artistic fecundity. If that is true, then how wrong I was when in 1982 I decried the "decline and fall of the American avant-garde" (Schechner 1982: 11–76). But, from a different vantage, how wrong was I thirty-five years ago? Not entirely. The paradox of being both right and wrong is because the avant-garde has fundamentally changed from the period of the 1950s–1980s to the second decade of the twenty-first century. The middle ground – the 1980s – saw a shift from "avant-garde" to "avant-gardes." I explored that plurality in "The Five Avant-Gardes … or None?" which began as part of my intro-duction to *The Future of Ritual* (1993) and which I have subsequently updated several times, most recently in 2009 (unpublished). In "The Five Avant-Gardes … or None," I asserted that the avant-garde was no longer a single phalanx moving ahead of anything but was rather a set of styles or ways of making performances, standing next to and to some degree in competition with other styles such as realism, surrealism, epic theatre, and so on. I also discussed the idea of an "intercultural avant-garde," defined not so much as trying to invent the new but rather as a means of performatively exploring, coping with, and resisting globalization. I am still chewing over the questions raised in these earlier writings.

Mike Sell defines the avant-garde as "a minoritarian formation that chal-lenges power in subversive, illegal or alternative ways, usually by challenging the routines, assumptions, hierarchies and/or legitimacy of existing political and/or cultural institutions" (2011: 41). Accepting Sell's definition, I wonder how today's avant-garde, so often funded by governments, corporations, and universities – or, if not yet so funded, seeking money from these sources – can be called anything but mainstream. Certainly this is true politically.[1] In terms of art, of style, is today's avant-garde "experimental," "alternative," "new," or "ahead of" (the vanguard from which it draws its name)? So-called avant-garde ways of making performances have been around for a century or more.

James Harding has also been chewing over these problems. In his 2013 *The Ghosts of the Avant-Garde(s)*, Harding argues for a plurality of avant-gardes and against any single definition of the avant-garde. He forcefully critiques the classic theories of Peter Bürger, Renato Poggioli, and their acolytes even as he notes these theories are still widely accepted and taught. In 2006, Harding wrote that the avant-garde should not be regarded "as a European but as a fundamentally global cultural phenomenon" (2006: 19). Harding locates the practices and theories of the avant-garde within specific political as well as aesthetic contexts. He writes that these practices and theories change according to historical period, geo-cultural location, and individual practice. They are processes, not genres; doings, not objects.

With these assertions in mind, I call attention to CIFET, the Cairo International Festival of Experimental Theatre. In 2013, CIFET held its twentieth edition where sixteen Arab and twenty-seven non-Arab nations were represented.[2] I attended CIFET in 2009. Some participants surprised me – "experimental theatre" from Saudi Arabia, Algeria, Sudan, Libya, and Yemen? Others, I expected: Lebanon, Egypt, Jordan, and Palestine. The productions I saw were not avant-garde as I have defined and practiced it. But they were avant-garde within their own cultures and sociopolitical circumstances. The same relativity ought to be applied to other festivals, such as the Fadjr Festival in Iran, in its thirty-first year in 2013. Productions from Tehran, other parts of Iran, and from a number of countries around the world compete for prizes. During the nearly two weeks of the festival, a lot of sharing and opening-up goes on. As Fadjr's website states: "This important cultural and artistic event provides a venue for the exchange of new experiences of Iranian and international theatre troupes in Tehran."[3] Given the religious-political censorship in Iran, one can only speculate what is meant by "exchange of new experiences."

Indeed, with the turmoil in Egypt, I wonder how CIFET's producers figure "experimental theatre," what role it plays, how "independent" can it be from government or Islamicist influence, themselves currently in conflict? Before those of us living in glass houses throw stones, I ask that we consider the perhaps more covert but equally pervasive control exercised by producers, festival-tour bookers, and funding agencies in the so-called "free world." To put it bluntly, manipulation and even outright censorship – external and directly imposed or internalized and "accepted" – is not a problem restricted to authoritarian regimes in China, Egypt, Iran, North Korea, Kenya … and counting. Everyone who makes art, or any kind of engaged and embodied speech, lives under both surveillance and restraint.

Granting all that, what the categories-labels-practices-theories "avant-garde" arise from is what poet John Keats labeled a "negative capability," the avant-garde's penchant for delighting in contradiction and doubt, for being always already in opposition to the "mainstream" and the "normative."[4] But what is mainstream and normative varies widely, even wildly, from place to place, time to time. What I will now turn my attention to is an avant-garde in the USA mainly (but in USA-influenced places wherever) that stands in opposition to Broadway commercial theatre, humdrum regional-provincial theatre,

Hollywood film, and mass-media television. I wonder if opposition is any longer a "position," a place to take a stand? It once was that mainstream categories were dominant. No longer. The mainstream categories have been skewed (but not yet satisfactorily theorized) by the rise of the internet making available millions of performances of hugely different kinds and qualities on such platforms as YouTube, Facebook, Vimeo, and the rest, and on a multitude of individual, group, and commercial homepages. What we have today is a triangular, surprisingly stable, trilectical tension among the avant-garde, the mainstream, and the social media. Works of a particular kind can and do show up under any of these categories, sometimes sliding easily from one to the other.

I am writing about this relatively new stability as it operates in the avant-garde understood as the works of, for example, the Wooster Group, the Builders Association, Marina Abramović, Robert Wilson, Richard Foreman ... and many younger groups and artists who are following (more or less) the path of these older "masters." By the mid-second decade of the twenty-first century, artists draw on "performance art" along with theatre, dance, music, film, and digital media.[5] In fact, performance art has taken its place alongside the other categories. Performance art is an umbrella term referring to works in the tradition of what began about a century ago in Europe with Futurism, Dada, Constructivism, Surrealism, etc., and was greatly elaborated on in the post–World War II USA by John Cage, Anna Halprin, Allan Kaprow, Andy Warhol, Suzanne Lacy, Carolee Schneemann, Robert Rauschenberg, Michael Kirby, Alejandro Jodorowsky, Yvonne Rainer, Fluxus, some of the work of the Living Theatre, and other innovators of Happenings and performance art. These New World pioneers were, of course, helped by the influx of artists and theorists from Europe – the transplanted Frankfurt School, Bauhaus to Black Mountain College, Brecht's American years, Xanti Schawinsky, the translated *Theatre and Its Double* of Antonin Artaud, and more. In Japan, a parallel impulse of syncretization and energy gave rise after World War II to the Butoh of Hijikata Tatsumi, Ohno Kazuo, and, somewhat later, the theatre of Suzuki Tadashi. Europe has its own rich performance-art history – interrupted by the Nazis and Stalin's repressions – but resuming after World War II, first in the West, then in Poland, and, since the collapse of the Soviet Union in 1989, just about everywhere.

Because digitization means not only that we collectively and individually can and do access past performances – not clearly, not without lapses and elisions – very few of these earlier "movements" or "practices" have vanished. Some thought over the horizon of recoverability have been recuperated. And incomplete recovery can be an even more powerful prompt to new work as total and accurate archiving. Inside the lacunae of imagination, new works arise like mushrooms in the dark. So many past masters of the avant-garde are visible in the twenty-first century. "Masters of the avant-garde." What a delightful paradox. This coexistence of old and new avant-garde work is, I think, unique. Usually, a particular style rises, flourishes, fades, then vanishes. But we no longer live by the rules of linear history. We live by Wikipedia and YouTube.

I am writing here from the perspective of New York. Most of my examples are from my own New York experiences. Whether or not the patterns I analyze with reference to New York are also true in other parts of the world – Asia, Latin America, Europe, Africa – depends on what one is paying attention to. Certainly, the global touring circuit has created a unified field analogous to the way that airports and shopping malls are the same in many hubs around the world. The main contrast these days is not between cultures defined as East, West, North, South; or First, Second, Third, or Fourth World; but between the urban and the hinterlands (note that one is singular, the other plural); the cosmopolitan and the provincials. These may be "regions of mind" or "regions of imagination" or, if you are so-minded, "regions of neo-liberal capitalism" rather than regions of geography and politics.[6]

I do not deny the enormous differences separating rich and poor; or the fact that the industrialized sectors of nations are far ahead of the rural areas in terms of concentrated wealth and technical advantage. The kind of avant-garde I am writing about here is a creature of an urban, cosmopolitan world. I know very well that there are plenty of performances going on that are not part of this urban, cosmopolitan world: theatre for development, social theatre, applied theatre, religious and/or ritual performances – and, of course, the vast network of performances in/of everyday life, business, medicine, sports, musics, popular entertainments, etc.[7] I have called these the "broad spectrum" of performance, the objects of performance studies.

What I am writing about here is something much more limited: the work by established artists, well known in New York and globally, such as the Wooster Group, Marina Abramović, Elevator Repair Service, the Builders Association, Robert Wilson, Richard Foreman, Lee Breuer, Anne Bogart … we all know the names … and also brilliantly realized pieces by still not so widely known groups such as the TEAM, LEIMAY, Gob Squad, the Nature Theatre of Oklahoma, The Assembly, Witness Relocation, Pig Iron, Big Art Group, National Theatre of the USA … and many more.[8] The questions are: What kind of avant-garde is this? Is it avant-garde at all? And, if not, so what? Also, what is the relationship of today's performance world to increasingly successful assaults on the values, practices, and ideologies of humanism – the "rights of man," "reason," and "democracy"?

The current state of the avant-garde is of a circulating stasis. Not in advance of anything and more a "niche-garde" than an "avant-garde," this art has for a long time been settled in its various places geographical and conceptual. "Niche-garde" because groups, artists, and works advertise, occupy, and operate as well-known brands. The younger groups fall into line behind their forebears in a familiar pattern of tradition and marketing: take a lot, change a little, and make something old look excitingly new.

This art is conservative. But what is "conservative"? There are at least two kinds. One is encapsulated in catchwords such as "reduce, reuse, and recycle," "sustainability," and "make a smaller footprint" – respect for and conservation of earth's ecosystems and its myriad cultures, both human and animal. This kind of conservatism is noninterventionist – except for intervention on behalf of the endangered. The very different Tea Party right-wing conservatism can be traced back in the USA to the pre–Civil War "Know Nothing" party, officially the "American Party," whose membership was reserved exclusively for white Protestant men. Tea Party Know Nothing conservatism is actually radical, in tune with the antiauthoritarian avant-garde of the nineteenth and twentieth centuries. The "historical avant-garde," in both its artistic and political incarnations – from, say, Futurism and Dada to Surrealism and the Situationists; from Jarry to Artaud to the Living Theatre; from Trotsky to Mao, Che Guevara to Frantz Fanon – strongly advocated disruption, overthrow, and anarchy – a revolutionary cathartic as prelude to a new world order. This species of avant-garde, I have argued elsewhere (and included in this book), was performed by those who made the 9/11 2001 terror-spectacle attack on New York's World Trade Center.[9]

As for a new world order, it is arriving in the form of the global corporation, an interlocked system of businesses, governments, ideologies, and religions. Paradoxically, amidst and despite economic imbalances and fluctuations – many of which are arranged, the better to profit by – and in harmony with unending yet limited wars, terror, and virulent religiosity, what is emerging is a neo-medieval stasis based on the interdependence of the system's information and financial infrastructure. Everyone from jihadists to the CIA, from WikiLeaks to the cybernet warriors who go by the name of Anonymous share the same tools and systems. Adversaries are codependent in a way analogous to the system of criminals, police, and judiciary. Distance no longer matters; netspace trumps geospace. The affinity (dare I say comradeship?) of those who think or believe alike rather than live together brings the nichedom into existence. I am not enthusiastic about this emergent world order. But I am not knee-jerk against it either.

Today's niche-garde enacts social, cultural, and political circumstances far different from the historical avant-garde which would not be imaginable without the philosophies of the Enlightenment which invented "art" as something that could be thought of in its own terms, "framed" and detachable from other kinds of processes and things. What can be framed and detached can be evaluated and sold, more "art for the market's sake" than "art for art's sake." Today, what is framable-detachable are not only "things," *objets d'art*, but behaviors. This framing of behavior is what drives the spate of reperformances, such as the 2007 redoing of Allan Kaprow's *18 Happenings in 6 Parts*, the 2009 simulation of Brian De Palma's film of the Performance Group's *Dionysus in 69*, or the Museum of Modern Art's 2010 *The Artist Is Present*, the museumification of some of Marina Abramović's most famous performance-art pieces along with her weeks-long enthronement on a chair at the center of MoMA's large ground-floor atrium, where people, after waiting in line for hours, sat opposite her, their eyes fixed on a being somewhere between Queen Elizabeth and Our Lady of Lourdes.[10] The Kaprow, Performance Group, and Abramović – and many other recent redoings – are fundamentally different from, say, Robert Lepage's 2012 restaging of Wagner's Ring Cycle at the Met, where what is prized is a "new" vision of an old score or text. What is asked of the Kaprow, the Abramović, and such are events as close to possible to the "originals," as if performances were not ephemeral but the *Mona Lisa* or the *Demoiselles d'Avignon*, "things" available for experiencing in their pristinity – again.

All this redoing depends on branding, the advertising and marketing that makes a product instantly recognizable and felt to be needed. David Savran noted this in 2005 when he wrote that the avant-garde develops "distinctive logos and brand identities" in keeping "with major changes in the marketplace [just] as Calvin Klein, Nike, Starbucks, Martha Stewart, and the Body Shop (among many others)" do. "Ironically enough, the production of the avant-garde as brand, collective hallucination, and endlessly alluring and prestigious commodity, signals less a modification than a complete reversal of its original meaning" (Savran 2005: 36). Far from being unpredictable, or even repulsive, today's avant-garde inhabits the already known. Spectators, scholars, funders, and festival-bookers know what to expect when they dial the Wooster Group and other "classic" avant-garde masters. Along with identity politics, political correctness, and academic orthodoxy, today's avant-garde depends on its being known before it is experienced.

In my decades of experience, the quality of niche-garde performances has never been higher. Some groups and artists provide formalism; others take realism-naturalism to its quotidian limits; some lay out complex political and social histories; some celebrate alternative lifestyles and sexual orientations; some promote collective creativity and group-devised works; others enact the unique visions of auteurs. This diversity and quality is as true of the newer groups and artists as of the more established. New artists arrive on the scene already well-trained, thoughtful, and equipped to deliver superb work that deserves attention and applause. Groups often premiere their work far from New York, even if the city remains the companies' home base and destination. Ironically, given the hype that nothing could be further from Broadway than the avant-garde, the touring circuit and overseas commissions function like Broadway's "out of town tryouts," playing on the road before opening on the Great White Way. Beginning out of town gives avant-garde groups the chance not only to polish their work but also to collect the critical acclaim and internet buzz needed to promote "new" pieces to those willing to pay a pretty penny for tickets. For example, Elevator Repair Service's *Gatz* – a deservedly praised six-hour performed reading of F. Scott Fitzgerald's *The Great Gatsby* – arrived in New York in 2010, as the Elevator Repair Service website put it, "at long last, five years after its creation and ten years after its conception."[11] Once the domain of the young, today's niche-garde is inhabited by people in their sixties, seventies, or older, showing few signs of slowing down: Breuer, Mnouchkine, LeCompte, Wilson, Malina, Foreman, me … [12] It's not only that older artists are producing new works, that's often the case, but also that these artists are embraced and emulated by the young. The point I am laboring is that the brand avant-garde is not "avant" but a tradition replete with identifiable styles, themes, and lineages.

Innovation and excellence are in an inverse relationship to each other. When innovation is high, excellence is low, and vice versa, as with a see-saw. This is not always true, but an overall tendency that makes sense because when people experiment, much of what they try fails. In science and engineering, the failures rarely reach the market, but in the arts – in performance, because it is an art that needs an audience and an art whose works cannot be tucked away awaiting more receptive times as novels and paintings can, failures are enacted publicly. But, over time, as experimental processes are honed and new forms, new venues, and new styles are tested, improved, and accepted, success replaces failure. Today's fecundity of excellence is also a paucity of originality. Every brilliant use of media or mixed media, each unorthodox use of space or site-specific work, every attempt to involve the audience, each knitting together of the performers' real lives and fiction, every – you name it – has been done before, but maybe not as well. More "bad" or "unacceptable" performances would signal an avant-garde actually "in advance of."

Alongside the emergence of the avant-garde tradition is a strong return to the written text. And here, ironically, may be the only really new thing about today's niche-garde. Rejection of the written text and what it stood for, authors and authority, was a hallmark of the historical avant-garde. Avant-garde manifestos called for burning libraries and wrecking museums. In theatre, I was not alone in advocating rejecting words as written by playwrights, deconstructing, twisting, and collaging texts. The Wooster Group, in a series of well-known works from the mid-1970s through the 1990s,[13] *Nayatt School, Route 1 & 9, LSD: Just the High Points, Fish Story*, and *To You, the Birdie!*, had its way with T. S. Eliot, Thornton Wilder, Arthur Miller, Anton Chekhov, and Jean Racine. But, in the 1990s, the text-as-text reasserted itself. Even as one part of *LSD* deconstructed Miller's *The Crucible*, the piece opened with Wooster performers holding books in their hands and reading some of their own favorite passages about mind-altering drugs. Wooster-influenced Elevator Repair Service took the text-as-text theatre further by staging parts of William Faulkner's *The Sound and the Fury* and then reading every word of F. Scott Fitzgerald's *The Great Gatsby*. These performances were not theatre in the orthodox sense, nor were they "staged readings," such as new plays-in-development get in order to attract producers. Wooster and Elevator Repair Service put the physical-object book-as-object-as-text at the center of their performances. Performers uttered every "she said" and "he said," every descriptive phrase. Reading aloud was combined with acting whereby the characters emerged both as "living" beings (theatre) and "literary" objects (reading). This practice, which I think we will see a lot more of, is part and parcel with cell-phone "texting," another blurring of the distinction between visual speech and heard objects.[14]

Rather than tearing everything down and starting from scratch, the niche-garde, in line with ecological conservation, recycles and circulates techniques, texts, and performances. The tendency to conserve and recycle is hugely helped by the easy availability of what amounts to an infinite archive, digitally preserved. The explosion of access to information and the ease with which this information can be processed creates a respect for the past. First, a personal past – my work, my family, my archive – then next a shared set of domains always increasing as time marches on and technology reaches further back as retrieval skills, software, and mainframes improve. Older works formerly locked in difficult-to-view archives are increasingly available digitally. The "was" enters into an ongoing and ever-expanding circulation with the "is," the "will be," and the "could be." These relations are both liberating and binding: There is so much that can be "done" to the data; yet also this abundance of information reminds anyone who cares to examine it that there is nothing new under the sun – except new ways to access and circulate information. Nothing is anymore permanently shut nor absolutely open.

Additionally, since Duchamp and Warhol at least, the avant-garde has converged with popular culture. A urinal and the art object called *Fountain* or the labels on Campbell's soup cans and Warhol's rendition of same are distinguishable by nothing except where and in what context each is displayed – plus the opinions of art scholars. The same items, ideas, and techniques go around and come around. The festival circuit adheres to world markets, with North America–Europe and Asia–Australia dominating. Smaller markets link the Americas and penetrate the Middle East and Africa. As artists make it in smaller markets, they are recruited for the larger; for example, Rabih Mroué of Lebanon is now a presence in Europe and the USA. Despite this inequality of circulation, the niche-garde is increasingly intercultural in personnel, themes, and techniques. The audiences, tiny compared to pop music, film, sports, video and DVDs, and the internet, know what they are in for and are generally in support of the work they see. The *épater la bourgeoisie* of the historical avant-garde no longer wounds spectators but, if at all sharp, lances governments, corporations, and other operators on the "dark side." These attacks are in bad faith because the attackers appeal to the very governments, rich individuals, corporations, and foundations they attack. Niche-gardists – like stand-up comics (and some are stand-up comics) – seek acceptance and money from those they mock. Festivals are often supported from the public purse, not out of respect for art but because art is a tourist attraction. In relation to this larger world of which it is a part, the niche-garde plays the role of being apart.

Go a little deeper into the circumstances that converted the avant-garde from radical to conservative. Nineteen-sixty-eight was a watershed year with confrontations between youth rebels and conservative authorities in Mexico

City, Paris, and Chicago. The conservatives defeated the students in the streets but not (at that time) in their minds. In the USA, the assassinations in April and June 1968 of Martin Luther King, Jr. and Robert F. Kennedy brought an end to optimism with regard to real change coming from or being forced on the ruling classes. Many intellectuals and artists took shelter in academia, where they created a powerful "avant-garde of theory." The displacement from the streets to seminar rooms accelerated during the 1970s and 1980s, two decades formative of performance studies.

Parallel to this, from the late 1970s through to the early 1990s, meaningful opposition to capitalism collapsed: in Europe, the fall of the Berlin Wall in 1989 and the collapse of the USSR in 1991; in China, the reforms of Deng Xiaoping ("socialism with Chinese characteristics") was accompanied by the bloody put-down of the Tiananmen Square democracy movement. Marxism as an economic system and liberatory ideal was dead, even though Communists were still in power in China, North Korea, and Cuba. The tenured radicals who lived through, participated in, and were stirred by these events made post-structuralism and performance studies scholarly reperformances of the defeated Leftist student-and-artist-led upheavals. As the world accepted or had forced on it a capitalist market economy, academic Marxists and deconstructionists imagined a world shaped by speech acts and performatives, upended hierarchies, reversed binaries, and no more master narratives. What was not – could not be – accomplished by direct political action was "thought about" and "theorized" by us professors and our students. In this world, actual change in favor of ordinary people was no longer enacted – how could it be, given the rise of globalization? Instead, change was "figured" as scholarship, imagined and theorized inside the corporation. Academic radicals exchanged ideas at conferences (academia's version of the touring circuit).

At present in the USA, corporation-minded universities are ditching tenure in favor of adjuncts and part-timers. They are developing online courses where star professors appear as authors of online "lessons" while lesser lights, graduate students often, teach the in-person sections of these courses. Or there may be no face-to-face sections. In this insecure environment, most students and their parents get the message and turn to business, the sciences, law, or engineering. For those in the arts, the majority seek careers in mainstream theatre and dance, media, or film. Relatively few train in niche-garde performance or in its partner in theory, performance studies. Many of those who are performance studies students are also performance artists and/or are active in social theatre in schools, prisons, hospitals, shelters, refugee camps, and the like, working with the oppressed or sick but not with the proletariat identified as such. In fact, the word "workers" sounds quaint in a world where so many want to be rich. In this downsizing, outsourcing economy, workers are no longer an organizable category. Labor is another example of circulating stasis.

The system that is settling in is conceptual as much as it is economic and political. It shows itself as the niche-garde I referred to earlier: the parsing of formerly big ideas into smaller packages of interlinking entities subsumed into the corporation. The corporation is a neo-medieval system so opaque that its operators do not, cannot, understand it. We are of it, in it, and governed by it without being able to comprehend it. Seen this way, the avant-garde – as a definable entity – lasted for about 100 years, roughly from Ibsen's *Et Dukkehjem* (*A Doll's House*) in 1879 to the Wooster Group's *LSD* in 1985. Avant-garde artists prided themselves on originality, innovation, and the rejection, if not outright destruction, of the past. The avant-garde was populated with ideas and actions clustering around such words (in English with counterparts in other languages) as "new," "revolutionary," "alive," "aggressive," "anti-," and so on, with the clear intent (rhetorical if not actual) to destroy both the existing aesthetic and sociopolitical order. Indeed, in the aesthetic sphere, the newest new opposed and swallowed the new that came before, from Futurism, Cubism, and Constructivism through Surrealism and Dada and on to abstract expressionism, conceptual art, environmental theatre, pop art, and the abolition of hierarchies. The avant-garde was divided roughly into what Allan Kaprow called "artlike art" and "lifelike art."[15] The dynamic tension Kaprow theorized provided the energy for avant-garde burst of 1960s and 1970s. This activity raised deep questions: What is performance? Where does it take place? Can anyone perform? Can a performance event – no longer a play or concert, no longer theatre, dance, or music as such, but an "event," a "piece," a "work" – proceed in a nonlinear way, and, if so, what gives it unity? Does it need unity? What is the relationship, or relationships, among the performing arts, popular culture, politics, rituals, therapies, sports, and play? And the performances of everyday life, business, law, and medicine? By the second decade of the twenty-first century, these questions seem settled. Of course, performance can take place anywhere and can include anything. "What's next?" is no longer a relevant question – because anything can happen, will happen, and can be absorbed.

Theory's role in the formation of the conservative avant-garde is demonstrable. Restored behavior, surrogation, ghosting, haunting, citation – repetition and/or the deferral of meaning – all indicate the impossibility of defining, no less finding, "originals." In the late 1960s, I began the thinking that led to various versions of "Restoration of Behavior" which achieved its definitive shape in 1985 in *Between Theater and Anthropology*. Although I didn't know it then, I see now that I was undermining the ruling ideas of the historical avant-garde as expressed in my own theatre works.

"Restoration of Behavior" preceded and paralleled the thinking of feminist performance theorists such as Judith Butler, Peggy Phelan, Jill Dolan, and Sue-Ellen Case whose works took off in the late 1980s.[16] The feminists often drew on the earlier thought of Foucault, Derrida, and Lacan: notions of iteration, citation, and historiography. A little later, in *The Archive and the Repertoire* (2003), Diana Taylor took up the problem of the unstable relationship between embodied practice and the archive. From the perspective of queer theory, José

Muñoz explored similar themes in *Disidentifications* (1999) and *Cruising Utopia* (2009). All these scholars, and many others in the same vein, emphasize the performative construction of social identities, gender, sexual orientation, and daily life roles and the tension between embodiment and "recordings" (in that word's various meanings). Some refer to the "deadness" of performance – not as an inactivity but as an uncanny "presence-as-absence."

Many artists-in-the-making studied with these and like-minded scholars. In earlier epochs, emerging artists were trained by apprenticeship, not at school. Today, the Performance Studies Department at New York University which I helped conceive in the late 1960s and 1970s, and which took its current name in 1980, is populated by artists taking a dip in the scholarly river. What began at NYU about thirty-five years ago is increasingly the norm at many schools where young artists learn the "post" theories undergirding the niche-garde. "Starving artist" and "waiting-to-be-discovered" have been replaced by "applying for grants," "landing a teaching gig," and "being invited to festivals."

The TEAM, Rimini Protokoll, Gob Squad, Nature Theater of Oklahoma, Vivarium Studio, Forced Entertainment, Witness Relocation, and many more too numerous to list, are steeped in theory. Are these groups "avant-garde"? Yes, insofar as the avant-garde is a style or an embodiment of theory. And no, insofar as the practice of these groups is "ahead of" anything. What are the sources of the circulating stasis that defines the niche-garde but is not limited to it? Taking a long view of history by reintroducing the often criticized but useful notion of the "master narrative," I propose that the peoples of the world are engaged in a tripartite struggle pitting Adam Smith's free-market economy against Karl Marx's socialist-guided economy against religious fundamentalisms – Islamic, Christian, Jewish, and Hindu. Yes, these domains overlap, and individuals can belong to more than one domain; it is even possible, perhaps inevitable, that a considerable number of persons are split inside themselves. But despite these overlaps and ruptures, human societies – and the individuals who comprise those societies – are in the midst of a centuries-long struggle about how to imagine and accomplish a "better society," whether by means of Smith's "invisible hand," Marx's "from each according to his ability, to each according to his needs!" or divine guidance (but under the aegis of which god?). When the narratives contradict one another, persons must choose which action to take, or to refrain from taking. However, such choosing is not a matter of individual choice alone. Leaders, elected or imposed, make choices that affect multitudes. These choices are neither determined nor the result of free will: There is as yet no means (and probably never will be) to determine what "guides" this kind of decision-making. I place the verb in quotation marks because the systems in play appear to operate of their own accord, even as they are also clearly a function of human intervention and choice. Again, the corporation operates seemingly autonomously. Most of today's intractable problems and flash points are at the fault lines of these thoroughly interlocked yet mutually contradictory systems. The American "War on Terror" has the quality not only of the Cold War but also of the Crusades – on both sides. This crusaders' war is also a struggle for the control of markets. The War on Terror is Janus-faced, looking backwards to the European medieval epoch and forward to advanced capitalism. The Chinese leadership has devised its own version of a free-market economy while actively suppressing dissension and worrying about the disintegration of the nation (Tibet, Taiwan, the Falun Gong, and other internal tensions). All this conflict without resolution keeps things moving – not moving forward but around and around.

And here is where the niche-garde comes in. With some notable fascist or fascist-leaning exceptions, the historical avant-garde was anarchist or on the left – self-identifying as "radical," "progressive," or "alternative" and fiercely "against." Niche-gardists are not against. Using New York as an example, young artists wait in line to clamber up the ladder from performances in lofts to small theatres like the Collapsible Giraffe to PS 122 or La MaMa and on to where very few arrive: the Lincoln Center Festival or the Brooklyn Academy of Music's Next Wave Festival. From the mid-levels on up, many of the artists and groups go international. They premiere their work wherever the money is, wherever sponsors can be found. Like Lexus or Sony, the niche-garde has been tested and branded in the global market, acquiring a following in the press and public. New York, actually, is home to relatively few premieres of the older, more expensive, groups. Even mid-level groups such as the TEAM look outside the USA for sponsoring venues where the creative core can devise new works. *Architecting*, its themes as American as can be, premiered in Scotland. One cannot speak of a radical politics at the level of Robert Wilson, the Wooster Group, Elevator Repair Service, Sasha Waltz, Heiner Goebbels, Sankai Juku, etc. Many of these artists are on the left personally, but in their artistic practice, in terms of venues, audiences, and effects on the political world, this left is apolitical, a style left rather than a workers' left.

For sixty-five years, since the end of World War II, humanity has suffered incredibly but not generally. There has been no World War III. Instead, there is always a "small" war here, a genocide there, an ecological catastrophe somewhere else, a terrorist attack, a reprisal. We live in an atmosphere of impending doom forestalled by promises of huge technological "breakthroughs." Will the icecaps melt, species diversity plummet, deserts expand ... and so on; and will genetic engineering, electric automobiles, windmills, and solar panels save us ... etc.? Even though their power is decreasing, states remain strong enough to cause mayhem. The internet is impossible to govern – a fact both glorious and fearful. Terrorists operate outside of state control. Some regions such as Afghanistan, Iraq, Palestine–Israel, and parts of sub-Saharan Africa suffer for decades with no end in sight.

American media create and export an obsessively repetitive infotainment by splicing human-made and natural disasters: a war, a tsunami, a famine, a spate of tortures, a car bomb, a plague, an assassination, a murder, an economic depression. In the American media, real events are dramatized and fictions are presented as real. It's all arranged in sequences that allow for maximum commercial exploitation. After genocide, Mylanta; and after the News, *The Simpsons*. These strips of behavior are rebroadcast over and over. Because of media – especially TV news and the internet – events no longer seem to take place uniquely in specific times and places. Images-actions recall or replicate a host of others – as if everyone were attending the Wooster Group's *Hamlet*, where the attention swivels from Scott Shepherd's meticulous simulation of Richard Burton to the ghostly tremulous video of Burton, who seems to be dissolving into his own ghost as we watch him. For Wooster, Shakespeare-as-such is not important, only the hard-to-pin-down … the rendition, the ghosting.

Increasingly, artists respond to the global situation and their own need for branding by redoing avant-garde classics. MoMA's Abramović retrospective drew record crowds – to what? To a famous artist sitting in state? To see safely museumified performances that were so edgy when first done? A few months later, in September 2010, the Whitney Museum redid several of Trisha Brown's pieces from the 1960s and 1970s, including *Man Walking Down the Side of a Building*. Except that it was not a man but dancer Elizabeth Streb walking down the building, which was not the backside of a fire-escape-cluttered building in SoHo before SoHo was a fancy district, but the sleek exterior of the Whitney on classy Madison Avenue uptown. I stood in the crowd and felt a thrill of recollection. I said to *TDR*'s Associate Editor, Mariellen Sandford, who was next to me, "This is good, it really is good. It hasn't aged." I was wrong: It had aged. We all have. And not even the most meticulous redoing can be the same as the first time. Circumstances change, audiences are different, memory itself deprives the reperformance of its shock of the new.

In the reperformances of the niche-garde, the audacity of the original gives over to the nostalgia of the repeat. This nostalgia is as reassuring as it is depressing. When a big chunk of the avant-garde no longer lives in the future, but in the past, while another chunk is a brand, we as people – not just as artists – know that we live in a time of lost opportunities. In the twenty-first century even more than in the twentieth, we know what ails the world, but our leaders, and, by proxy, ourselves, are unable to effectively address, no less heal, what's wrong. Much of the niche-garde answers not by blasting those who are corrupt, inept, and evil but by repeating itself.

Yet these cautious conservative enactments, so unlike what the avant-garde used to be, are in line with what, possibly, is the best, the wisest instruction: reduce, recycle, and reuse. Why shouldn't art go green and make a smaller footprint? Is it "bad" that the avant-garde is conservative? That it excellently recycles its own best ideas and techniques? Is the way forward under the circumstances not moving at all? Are we, like Gogo and Didi … waiting?

This is not what many younger people feel and believe. Take, for example, Rachel Chavkin, of the TEAM:

The work I was seeing while I was an undergraduate [at the turn of the century] was often aesthetically and politically miraculous but also very often steeped in irony. I don't mean off-the-cuff ironic. There was a profound sense that change was not possible in human beings. The politics of the country at that time reflected this sensibility. [...] My generation is the product of a new youth movement that I think – I hope – has been reinvigorated. It seems like political change is possible again and that the country believes in this possibility again.

(Martin 2010: 110)

Show me.

Notes

1 Unless we regard actions such as the 9/11 attack on New York's World Trade Center as an avant-garde act. Sell thinks so. For my opinion, see "9/11 as Avant-Garde Art?" (chapter 4 in this book).

2 For a complete list, go to http://www.sis.gov.eg/En/Templates/Articles/tmpArticles. aspx?CatID=659 (accessed June 10, 2014).

3 For more on Fadjr, go to http://www.fadjrtheaterfestival.com/en (accessed June 10, 2014).

4 In a letter to his brothers, George and Thomas, on December 21, 1817, Keats observed, "it struck me what quality went to form a Man of Achievement, especially in Literature, and which Shakespeare possessed so enormously – I mean Negative Capability, that is, when a man is capable of being in uncertainties, mysteries, doubts, without any irritable reaching after fact and reason" (Keats 1899: 277).

5 In Europe and elsewhere outside of the USA, performance art is often referred to simply as "performance." I find this confusing because I posit "performance" as an overarching category including not only the aesthetic but many kinds of social, political, and personal performative behaviors.

6 Each political regime has its own ways of coping with, trying to control, tolerate, or (maybe) encourage "alternative" artistic expression. All regimes recognize that artistic expression is very close to political expression and that artworks can be disruptive. The lines between free expression in the agora, in the press, in legislative bodies, and in the arts – particularly the performing arts, whose lingua franca is behavior – is wavy, always shifting. For the situation in second-decade twenty-first-century Beijing, see Cheng (2014).

7 With regard to "social theatre" and "applied theatre," see Thompson (2013, 2009a, 2009b, 2005, and 2003) and the 2004 special issue of *TDR* on social theatre edited by Thompson (48 [3]). Of course, Thompson is not the only person working this field whose practices can be traced back to Augusto Boal's Theatre of the Oppressed and, before him, to the Federal Theatre Project in the USA in the 1930s and the activities in the Soviet Union from the 1917 Revolution through much of the 1920s. See chapter 3 in this book.

8 The name Nature Theatre of Oklahoma is taken from the final episode of Franz Kafka's *Amerika*. Today's Nature Theatre is very New York, no Oklahoma in sight. The National Theatre of the USA is an ironic title. This tongue-in-cheek stance is held by several newer groups who have grown up media-savvy, suspicious of big promises and grand designs pumped up by hyperbole. An excellent look at this work in New York is in *TDR*'s special issue "Caught Off-Garde," 54 (4) (2010).

9 See chapter 4 in this book.

10 There are many accounts of the MoMA Abramović show. I recommend Thurman's "Walking through Walls" (2010) in the *New Yorker* and Rebecca Schneider's "Remembering Feminist Remimesis" (2014) in *TDR*.

11 See https://www.elevator.org/shows/gatz (accessed June 10, 2014).

12 See http://www.livingtheatre.org/about/history (accessed June 10, 2014). The founding dates of the others: Wooster Group, 1967 (as the Performance Group, with the name Wooster Group appearing for the first time in 1980); Richard Foreman/ Ontological-Hysteric Theatre, 1968; Robert Wilson/Byrd Hoffman School of Byrds, 1969; Lee Breuer/Mabou Mines, 1970.

13 This work began when what was to become the Wooster Group in 1980 was still part of the Performance Group, which I founded in 1967 and was Artistic Director of until 1980.

14 The TEAM's 2008 *Architecting* is related but not identical in its bringing the text-as-text to the fore. In *Architecting*, Margaret Mitchell – her *Gone with the Wind* physically in hand – is presented as a consultant for a new film version of her novel, this time directed by an African American. Mitchell argues that the new film – full of politically correct rhetoric regarding "enlightened" race relations – is as false to her novel, and to history, as was the David O. Selznick–Victor Fleming 1939 movie. All this in the context of post-Katrina New Orleans and in the shadow of a man silently constructing a large model of Chartres Cathedral: a model of a model of collective creativity. For nuanced discussions of the TEAM in general and *Architecting* in particular, see Martin (2010), Chavkin (2010), Wickstrom (2010), and Daniel (2010).

15 See Kaprow (1983: 201–218).

16 To name a few key texts of these writers from the period I am discussing: Case, *Feminism and Theatre* (1988); Dolan, *The Feminist Spectator as Critic* (1988), *Presence and Desire* (1993); Butler, *Gender Trouble* (1990), *Bodies That Matter* (1993), and *Excitable Speech* (1997); Phelan, *Unmarked* (1993) and *Mourning Sex* (1997).

References

Butler, Judith (1990) *Gender Trouble* (London and New York: Routledge).

——(1993) *Bodies That Matter* (London and New York: Routledge).

——(1997) *Excitable Speech* (London and New York: Routledge).

Case, Sue-Ellen (1988) *Feminism and Theatre* (Basingstoke: Macmillan).

Chavkin, Rachel (2010) "Five Years and Change with the TEAM: Moving Fast Past the Apocalypse," *TDR*, 54 (4): 108–117.

Cheng, Meiling (2014) *Beijing Xingwei: Contemporary Chinese Time-Based Art* (Kolkata [Calcutta]: Seagull).

Daniel, Rachel Jessica (2010) "Art in the Age of Political Correctness: Race in the TEAM's *Architecting*," *TDR*, 54 (4): 136–154.

Dolan, Jill (1988) *The Feminist Spectator as Critic* (Ann Arbor, Mich.: University of Michigan Press).

——(1993) *Presence and Desire* (Ann Arbor, Mich.: University of Michigan Press).

Harding, James (2006) "From Cutting Edge to Rough Edges: On the Transnational Foundations of Avant-Garde Performance," in James Harding and John Rouse (eds.), *Not the Other Avant-Garde: The Transnational Foundations of Avant-Garde Performance* (Ann Arbor, Mich.: University of Michigan Press), pp. 18–40.

——(2013) *The Ghosts of the Avant-Garde(s): Exorcising Experimental Theater and Performance* (Ann Arbor, Mich.: University of Michigan Press).

Kaprow, Allan (1983) *Essays on the Blurring of Life and Art* (Berkeley, Calif.: University of California Press).

Keats, John (1899) *The Complete Poetical Works and Letters of John Keats, Cambridge Edition* (New York: Houghton, Mifflin & Company).

Martin, Carol (2010) "What Did They Do to My Country! An Interview with Rachel Chavkin," *TDR*, 54 (4): 99–107.

Muñoz, José (1999) *Disidentifications* (Minneapolis, Minn.: University of Minnesota Press).

——(2009) *Cruising Utopia* (Minneapolis, Minn.: University of Minnesota Press).

Phelan, Peggy (1993) *Unmarked* (London and New York: Routledge).

——(1997) *Mourning Sex: Performing Public Memories* (London and New York: Routledge).

Savran, David (2005) "Death of the Avantgarde," *TDR*, 49 (3): 10–42.

Schechner, Richard (1982) "The Decline and Fall of the (American) Avant-Garde," in *The End of Humanism: Writings on Performance* (New York: Performing Arts Journals Publications), pp. 11–76.

——(1985) *Between Theater and Anthropology* (Philadelphia, Pa.: University of Pennsylvania Press).

——(1993) "Jayaganesh and the Avant-Garde," in *The Future of Ritual* (London and New York: Routledge), pp. 1–23.

——(2003) *Performance Theory*, rev. edn (London and New York: Routledge).

Schneider, Rebecca (2014) "Remembering Feminist Remimesis: A Riddle in Three Parts," *TDR*, 58 (2): 14–32.

Sell, Mike (2011) *The Avant-Garde: Race Religion War* (London: Seagull Books).

Taylor, Diana (2003) *The Archive and the Repertoire: Performing Cultural Memory in the Americas* (Durham, NC: Duke University Press).

Thompson, James (2003) *Applied Theatre: Bewilderment and Beyond* (New York: Peter Lang).

——(2005) *Digging Up Stories: Applied Theatre, Performance and War* (Manchester: Manchester University Press).

——(2009a) *Performance Affects: Applied Theatre and the End of Effect* (Basingstoke: Palgrave Macmillan).

——(2009b) *Performance in Place of War* (Kolkata [Calcutta]: Seagull Books).

——(2013) *Humanitarian Performance: From Disaster Tragedies to Spectacles of War* (Kolkata [Calcutta]: Seagull Books).

Thurman, Judith (2010) "Walking through Walls," *The New Yorker*, March 8, pp. 24–30.

Wickstrom, Maurya (2010) "The Labor of *Architecting*," *TDR*, 54 (4): 118–135.

Chapter 3

The 1960s, *TDR*, and Performance Studies

From a 2009 interview by Ana Bigotte Vieira and Ricardo Seiça Salgado, revised in 2014 by Richard Schechner

Revisiting the 1960s

ANA BIGOTTE VIEIRA: Why do so many people seem to be interested in revisiting the 1960s now, and why did you decide to teach "USA experimental performance: the 1960s to the 1980s" now?

RICHARD SCHECHNER: Well, I decided to offer the course because people seem to be revisiting the 1960s, which really started in the 1950s and went on to include much of the 1970s.[1] I'd say that the 1960s began with the US Supreme Court's 1954 ruling outlawing racial segregation in the public schools.[2] There was a straight line from the courtroom to the streets. So many people are interested in finding out what happened, and to do that we need to revisit the 1960s. I look at myself both as an effect and as a cause. I effect things but also, because people listen to me, I also cause things. I was active in the 1960s. I did the course because I could teach from what I lived. The world doesn't repeat itself, but it doesn't not repeat itself either. Things go around and around in a gyre. A gyre is a spiral, or a cone, where something circles back on itself but at a different level or position; a repeat and not a repeat at the same time. William Butler Yeats wrote about history's gyre in his 1919 poem "The Second Coming," which starts:

> Turning and turning in the widening gyre
> The falcon cannot hear the falconer;
> Things fall apart; the centre cannot hold;
> Mere anarchy is loosed upon the world,
> The blood-dimmed tide is loosed, and everywhere
> The ceremony of innocence is drowned;
> The best lack all conviction, while the worst
> Are full of passionate intensity. [...]
> Surely some revelation is at hand;
> Surely the Second Coming is at hand.

From that poem, way back in college at Cornell in the 1950s, I learned "gyre." I can put it more colloquially, "What goes around comes around." So maybe the 1960s are here again, the same but different. The 1960s went around, and now they are coming around. There are certain fascinating parallels.

Today's students weren't alive then. Someone born in 1970 would be more than forty today; if you were born in 1980, you'd be more than thirty years old now. If you were born in 1960, you'd be more than fifty years old today and still have missed the 1960s. To really have lived the 1960s, you have to have been born in the early 1950s or before. People today who want to learn about the 1960s are reaching back over the horizon of their lives. But even if they don't have memories of it, they've heard about it. Maybe their parents were active, maybe even their grandparents. Yes, it's that long ago.

Today's students hear about the 1960s not only from their parents and grandparents but from popular culture. The echoes of Woodstock are still being replayed, are still reverberating. Today's youth are curious about this period.

And also I think people think of the 1960s as a time of great hope, of intense activity, of utopian dreams – and of violence and conflict. The Vietnam War. The Civil Rights Movement. Dogs and police with fire-hoses in the streets of Birmingham; soldiers sloughing through jungles, napalm decimating villages. Hopes and atrocities, possibilities and betrayals, all jumbled together. And, of course, "sex, drugs, and rock 'n' roll," too.

Most students of today don't think they're living in a time of great hope, a jumping-off place from where they can change the world for the better. They don't believe in revolution. They hardly believe in anything beyond the pale "Yes we can!" of mainstream political campaigns. Radical change is no longer thinkable. Everything is "step by step." "Will I get a job?" "Where can I afford to live?" "How will I pay my student loan debt?" Necessary things, of course, but clearly limited horizons. The corporations are in charge: corporate thinking. The neoliberal system is deeply entrenched. So today's young people, especially in the West, are fascinated by a generation and a period where people actually felt that the world was going to be transformed by actions that they themselves undertook. So many people felt they were engaged in a meaningful struggle. Not a struggle for individual survival – how am I going to get a job, who will fund my art, where should I go to live? And not Ronald Reagan's master narrative, the struggle between what George W. Bush called the "axis of evil" and the West, between communism and capitalism, and not American exceptionalism. But the utopian struggle between unjust authority and liberation, between oppression-repression-poverty and freedom-openness-fair-distribution-of-wealth.

A time – so near and yet so distant – when people believed in this kind of idealistic struggle fascinates people today. And because media is what it is, people today can relive that earlier struggle as "re-enactment" and "reperformance." They can go there without going there, without enacting their own revolution. For so many of today's younger people, "revolution" is not only archaic and romantic, it is downright crazy. I mean youth not only in Europe and North America but also, from those I encounter by travel and other means, even young people in Latin America, Africa, and Asia. It's a global phenomenon I am talking about.

Also, I think, as I've found out by going back over it during the course, the artworks of the 1960s were really very good. Many pieces hold up in time. There are many people still interested in experiencing these works insofar as they can be experienced via the archive or by means of reperformance. The art of the 1960s isn't very dated. Some of this work is "canonical," "classical," even. In 2009, *Dionysus in 69* was "reperformed" by the Rude Mechanicals of Austin, Texas. The Rudes used Brian De Palma's movie of the Performance Group's 1968 production, which I directed, as the basis for their reperformance. It was a big hit in Austin, then toured to Princeton in 2011 and to New York in 2012, where it was nominated for a Bessie for "outstanding revived work."[3] Shawn Sides, the production's co-director, with Madge Darlington, earned her MA from NYU's Gallatin School in 1997. She took a bunch of classes in performance studies.

In earlier times, people would stage plays or scores of music or choreographic notations and reinterpret these. A "new" production of a Shakespeare, the Greeks, or *The Rite of Spring*. But what's happening today is different. The key works of the 1960s were videotaped and later digitized. So people today can look at those performances in detail and re-enact them, the performances themselves, not just the texts, the words. This is not true of earlier periods, of the works of Brecht, Meyerhold, Stanislavsky, and so on. We have photographs, some film clips, but not anything approaching a full set of productions, digitized and available. Even Brecht, who took great pains to document his productions in *modelbuchs* – portfolios of photographs detailing the staging scene by scene – did not make a record that is as full as the performance videos we are used to today. Today, so many of the "classics" from the 1960s have been digitized. The rage to record and archive has been in full throttle for decades. This has given rise to a spate of reperformances, for example, Allan Kaprow's *18 Happenings in 6 Parts* (1959, 2006), Anna Halprin's *Parades and Changes* (1965, 2009), Trisha Brown's *Walking on the Wall* (1971, 2010), the 2010 MoMA show of Marina Abramović's signature early performance-art works … and so on, many more than I can list. These are not new interpretations but re-enactments. Of course, the re-enactments cannot duplicate the first time because audiences change, social circumstances change – everything changes except the "work itself." Even the work itself changes because individual bodies and mentalities are different. No matter, the reperformed works open a window onto an imagined past. And what people experience is stuff that is very vital.

And, finally, I think it's important that in the USA – I'm talking mostly in USA, although I know a little bit of what's happening in Japan, China, Europe, and India – so many of the people who were active in the 1960s are still active today. The new avant-garde has not pushed the old avant-garde out of the way. I've been directing steadily on into the present. Lee Breuer, Richard Foreman, Robert Wilson, JoAnne Akalaitis. Who's retired or been pushed offstage? Such continued vigorous activity is unusual from the perspective of earlier historical periods, because usually after a person passes a certain age – especially if one earns a reputation as an "experimental" or "avant-garde" artist – you are forgotten or regarded as out of date. Picasso was an exception, not the rule. The rule is that after you reach a certain age nobody but your friends and people too uninformed to know better go to see your works, nobody "important," nobody among the new Young Turks cares. But that's not true with the generation who arose in the 1960s. Today's youth and also more mature trendsetters (critics, scholars, teachers) are fascinated by these survivors from the 1960s. People see the work they make now and know about the work they made forty or even fifty years ago. So why are the artists of the 1960s still respected? Why are they still active? Why am I still invited to direct works, both new and old? That's both good news and bad news. The good news is that I think we're good at what we do; the bad news is that we haven't been pushed offstage. The world has not progressed so far that the works and thoughts of the 1960s are irrelevant.

Europe and America

RICARDO SEIÇA: What was the background of these experimental groups? What kind of artistic education influenced them?

SCHECHNER: When the Nazis came to power in Germany, a lot of intellectuals and artists left Germany, Jewish ones especially. Many came to New York, some joining the progressive New School for Social Research, temporarily renamed the University in Exile, and some going to Columbia University and other US schools. This accumulation of left-leaning intellectuals formed an American version of the Frankfurt School.[4] Among the émigrés – some temporary, some who stayed in the USA after the end of World War II – were Herbert Marcuse, Erich Fromm, Max Wertheimer, Theodor Adorno, Max Horkheimer, Roman Jakobson, Hannah Arendt, Leo Strauss, and Claude Lévi-Strauss. Walter Benjamin probably would have ended here too, but he committed suicide in 1940 while fleeing the Nazis. Not only intellectual Marxism but leftist theatre too were taught at the New School. Between 1940 and 1949, Erwin Piscator led the New School's Dramatic Workshop. In the 1920s, Piscator coined the phrase and pioneered the practice of "epic theatre." (Brecht took the term from Piscator.) Piscator's students in the Dramatic Workshop included Stella Adler, Elia Kazan, Tennessee Williams, Harry Belafonte, Marlon Brando, and Judith Malina, whose deep impact on the performing-arts scenes in New York and Hollywood are undeniable. On the academic front, the theories of the Frankfurt/New School spread to hundreds of American universities. From the Actor's Studio to the Living

Theatre; from neo-Marxism to Woodstock Nation, the Frankfurt/New School lived in the 1960s and beyond. In the early 1960s, I read Marcuse's *Eros and Civilization* (1955), a liberatory book if there ever was one.

Let's trace out a couple of intersecting lines of influence. Malina enrolled in Piscator's Dramatic Workshop in 1945. Then, inspired by what she learned from Piscator,[5] in 1947 Malina and Beck co-founded the Living Theatre. The Living Theatre, in turn, directly spawned Joseph Chaikin's Open Theatre and impacted many other performing-arts groups and individuals. About two decades earlier, in 1923, a few year after the Russian Revolution, the Moscow Art Theatre (MAT) performed in New York. In 1923, MAT actress Maria Ouspenskaya defected to the USA. She teamed up with Richard Boleslavsky, a Polish-born member of the MAT's legendary First Studio, who defected from the USSR in 1922. Together, they started the American Laboratory Theatre, where Harold Clurman, Stella Adler, Lee Strasberg, and Francis Fergusson, an important performance theorist, were students. The impact of these American students of the Stanislavsky system – as interpreted and modified by Ouspenskaya and Boleslavsky, then reinterpreted by Lee Strasberg at the Actor's Studio as "The Method" – is incalculable. Another First Studio veteran is Michael Chekhov, nephew of playwright Anton Chekhov. Michael Chekhov emigrated from the USSR to Germany in the late 1920s, from Germany to Lithuania and Latvia in the early 1930s, then to England in 1936, where he started the Chekhov Theatre School at Dartington Hall. He moved his school to Connecticut in 1938 and finally to Hollywood in 1942. Chekhov devised what he called the "psychological gesture," a much more physical approach to acting than what Strasberg was teaching as the "Method" at the Actor's Studio. But, of course, there was lots of cross-fertilization. Marlon Brando, Stella Adler, and Elia Kazan were all important to the Actor's Studio as well as were Piscator's students at the New School. What all this adds up to is that the American theatre of the 1960s was saturated by influxes of people, ideas, and techniques from Europe from the 1920s through the 1940s. Somewhat later, with the USA waging three wars in Asia from 1941 through to the mid-1970s, waves of influence came from Asia. The pervasive African influence has been here all along but inherent American racism meant it was less recognized academically before the 1960s. Ditto for the Latina/Latino influence from the Caribbean, Mexico, and further south.

All this granted, still by the 1960s we thought that what was avant-garde in the 1930s was old hat. We worked against the former radicals of the 1930s. The wheel had turned.

Or, back up a little bit still further: Duchamp emigrated to the USA in 1915. The work of Dada and other radical new art movements was known here at least from New York's Armory Show in 1913. Surrealism gained a large audience with the 1936–1937 show at MoMA, "Fantastic Art, Dada, Surrealism." From 1941 to 1947, Brecht lived and worked, or tried to, in America.

He wrote or revised some of his greatest plays during his American exile including *The Good Person of Sichuan, Galileo, The Resistible Rise of Arturo Ui, The Caucasian Chalk Circle*, and the screenplay for *Hangmen Also Die*. His *Antigone*, written in 1947–1948, was staged in 1966 by the Living Theatre with Judith Malina translating and playing the title role. Brecht despised much about America, partly of course because he was blacklisted and harassed. On the day before Brecht left America for good, he testified before the House Un-American Activities Committee. He told the Committee that he was not a member of the Communist Party. The Committee Co-chairman Karl Mundt thanked the German playwright for his cooperation.

Ironic, isn't it, that Europe in a certain sense got rid of its most adventurous minds – and why? Because of Stalinism, Nazism, and the war. Ironically, if Hitler had not been a Jew-hater, he may have got the atom bomb and won the war. If Hitler and Stalin had not existed, the arts explosion in America in the 1950s and 1960s might not have happened. And the 1930s would have been very different too. All those immigrants stimulated what went on here. Just as the USA was becoming the world's most powerful military and economic force – a force not often enough used for good – the USA also became enormously intellectually powerful. What made the USA powerful was a combination of homegrown and immigrant artists and theorists. America thrived on high-level immigrant minds in the years around World War II. From Einstein in the sciences through to the faculty at Black Mountain College, which is a continuation of the Bauhaus, to the New School/Frankfurt School, and so on. Even the soldiers who went to war in Europe and Asia returned to North America with a whole lot of new "foreign" ideas that soon were thriving in the USA. From new foods to yoga and Zen. Foreign cultures educated us – I mean, my generation.

People were able to accomplish here what they couldn't accomplish in Europe. Europe just after World War II was devastated. So what happened here is a continuation of the European avant-garde – and a big change in that avant-garde, too. It became Americanized. Because just as the Europeans – and, to some degree, the Asians too – changed us, we changed their thinking, we Americanized it. What emerged in the 1960s was not Europe-in-America or Asia-in-America so much as a powerful fusion of Europe–America–Asia. It was both very new and very American, because America has been built on imported and then transformed ideas and people. Yes, the Native Americans have suffered horribly. Paradoxically, they who were here first have been the most left out of all Americans.

Foundational Artists and the Living Theatre

VIEIRA: In your course, we revisited some artists and groups that you called "foundational": John Cage, Allan Kaprow, Anna Halprin, Jack Smith, the

Living Theatre, the Open Theatre, the Performance Group, the Wooster Group, the Judson Church groups, Bread and Puppet Theatre, El Teatro Campesino, feminist theatres, Robert Wilson, Richard Foreman. ... Why are these foundational?

SCHECHNER: Well, I can't go through them all here one at a time. That's what we did in the course. Speaking generally, I can say that each of these groups, individuals, trends – the list is very varied, not really consistent – "started something." Of course, as I just outlined, they "continued something" too. But if you look at the list, you see that each made a pathway that others followed. So, whether you call that "foundational" – what is underneath, what is built upon – or "path-finding" – showing the way forward – doesn't matter. The metaphors are different, but the process is the same.

Take the Living Theatre for an example. One of the ways the Living is foundational is in its practice of taking political theatre into the streets. The Living crossed ʰe boundary separating "art" from "action." They went beyond Brecht, whose political involvement was as representation, as dramaturgy, as what happened on the stage. The Living drew on Dada's interventionist tradition and welded that to Brecht's political convictions. With a difference: Brecht was Marxist, and the Living was anarchist. Brecht himself, finally and superbly, was a man of the theatre who stayed in the theatre. When, in 1954, he had the chance to pick a theatre as the Berlin Ensemble's permanent home, he chose the Theater am Schiffbauerdamm, a bourgeois edifice with a history. It opened in 1892 with Goethe's *Iphigenia in Tauris*; Gerhardt Hauptmann's naturalistic masterpiece *The Weavers* premiered there in 1893; for four years, 1902–1906, Max Reinhardt managed it. More important for Brecht was that his *Threepenny Opera* premiered there in 1928. The theatre itself, both outside and in, looks bourgeois and ornate, not at all what I expected from Brecht and his celebration of the working class. The Living Theatre went beyond Brecht by taking the theatre into the streets, insisting that theatre be direct action. This was both noble and naive. Often once in the streets – especially with *Paradise Now* – the Living, and the audiences they incited, seemed out of control. The youth they stirred up didn't know what to do after the immediate street action with the Living was over. And, in my opinion, the Living's members were too stoned too often. Being high and getting things done politically don't go together. Maybe it was because the Living was truly anarchic – they lived what they preached. They waved the black flag of anarchy and lived by its principles.

Don't think I am dismissing the Living. They were both a barometer measuring what was happening in the 1960s and an instigator, making things happen. The Living rolled up into one ball the African-American freedom movement, the anti–Vietnam War movement,[6] the youth radicalism of the Students for a Democratic Society, sexual liberation, LBGT rights, and Artaud's call for martyrs "signalling through the flames." Julian Beck and Judith Malina made a great team: his ethereal Jewish Buddhism, his quiet slightly European-sounding voice, and his not-of-this-world transparent visage – you could see his blue-green veins right through his pale skin. Judith, on the other hand, is salt of the earth, direct, loud, forceful, peda-gogical, intellectual, no-nonsense. Julian and Judith fused theatre, politics, and their private lives into a single thing. Well, not so private actually; they lived very openly, were seemingly always on display – a showing of their principles.

The Living was also foundational in the sense of constructing performance texts rather then staging dramas. Of course, the Living also staged plays, such as Jack Gelber's *The Connection*, Brecht's *Antigone*, and Kenneth H. Brown's *The Brig*, especially after 1964, when they lost their 14th Street theatre and went into exile.[7] In Europe, the Living devised three extremely powerful performance works: *Paradise Now*, *Mysteries and Smaller Pieces*, and *Frankenstein*. When the Living brought these back home to the USA in 1968, the performances electrified audiences, outraging some, inciting others, and pleasing many. These pieces, theatrical and political simultaneously, were closer to Happenings than to orthodox theatre. But, unlike many Happenings, which were usually small-scale and apolitical, the Living's works were enormous and fully politically engaged. Beck was a visionary designer in the line of Vsevolod Meyerhold–Lyubov Popova Constructivism.

Away from Drama, Going toward Environmental Theatre

My own work at about the same time, both in New Orleans from 1963 to 1967 with the Free Southern Theatre and the New Orleans Group and then in New York from the fall of 1967 onward with the Performance Group, conformed to and diverged from the Living. I was insistent on staging "works," "events," and "environmental theatre" – not plays. I thought about it thoroughly and published those thoughts as my 1968 "Six Axioms for Environmental Theatre." What I summarized and theorized there had been developing in me for several years previously. I was influenced by the African-American Civil Rights Movement which I participated in; by the Free Southern Theater, of which I was a producing director, by Artaud, by Happenings, and – after 1963 – by Grotowski. What environmental theatre did was challenge the notion that a theatrical production was the "staging of a play," the "realizing" or "interpreting" of a text. I, and those who thought like me, didn't really care what the author intended, or even if there was an author. We shifted the center of theatre to the performance, to what hap-pened, to behavior and body language, to action, to stage language – what I later called the "performance text." The performance text completely superseded the dramatic text, the play-as-play. Yes, words were important, but not as abstractions or things on a page but the words spoken or sung or chanted or mumbled by the performers. I, and those who thought as I did, didn't care what Shakespeare might have intended. How was anyone to

know that anyway? And where there was a living writer to voice her intentions, or someone like Shaw, who wrote it all down, or O'Neill, whose stage
directions are massive – well, mostly I didn't read these prefaces or stage
directions. And, if I did read them, I took them on as auxiliary information,
not *obiter dicta*. I didn't think that the director existed to serve the playwright. We threw all that out. We didn't care what Shakespeare might have
wanted, or what Euripides might have wanted, or any writer: Chekhov,
Shaw, Pirandello, O'Neill, Williams, Miller, Brecht … even Beckett, who
was so careful about seeing to it that his plays were done exactly as he
wanted them done. We needed to ask, "What does my group want? What do
the spectators want?" Not to pander to them: sometimes we gave the spectators not what they said they wanted but what we thought they should want.
Each production had to answer the question, "What's relevant now?" I know
that sounds arrogant, and doubtlessly it was. But it also was a declaration of
independence, freeing the theatre from the tyranny of the playwright, the
demands of an absentee landlord, a distant authoritarian-author.

This approach was political on several levels. First, it restored power to the
people who were there working on making the performance: the director,
the actors, the designers, the technicians. The playwright, too, if the playwright was in the rehearsal room working with the rest of the group.
Otherwise, the playwright was regarded as an absentee landlord. We seized
his property, the play, and we used it for the benefit of the people who were
there present to each other day in and day out. And for the benefit of
the audience, who were also asked to participate. We took "authority" – the
power of being the author – away from the playwright and gave it to
the directors, actors, designers … the people there doing the work. Even to
the audience.

I wanted to take Brecht one step further than he had taken himself. I followed
Brecht's maxim: "You want to build a house, use the bricks that are there."
That is: make something with what you have on hand; be responsible to the
people that are actually doing the work. The workers should control the work.
We rejected the idea that the "person who owns the land" has the power to
determine what to do with it. Instead, we proclaimed that "the people who
work the land" have the power to determine what to do with it. It was our
own kind of ideal socialism. That was very important, that political feeling.
We asked Marx's kind of question: "Who owns the means of production?"
We wanted the workers in the theatre to own the means of theatrical production. I liked the fact that in English the word "production" means a
theatre piece.

Later on, I retreated a little from such a radical and total rejection of the
playwright. I staged plays according to the principles of environmental
theatre and still remained "true" to a text such as Brecht's *Mother Courage
and Her Children* or Chekhov's *The Cherry Orchard* and *Three Sisters*. But
I did these plays in ways they had not been done before. I very radically

changed how these plays looked, how they were experienced – maybe, even, what they meant. I won't go into details about that here. There is plenty written about those productions and others of mine in a similar vein.

Collective Work, the Streets, Lofts, Galleries, and Stages

SEIÇA: How was this kind of work collective?

SCHECHNER: It was collective in the daily process of working, but it wasn't without leaders. And there were struggles among the workers and between the workers and their leaders. I was a leader; Beck and Malina were leaders. Some avant-gardists were very insistent on determining everything that went onstage. Richard Foreman, Robert Wilson, for example. But, for me, the work in the rehearsal room was collaborative, if not collective. The capitalist "I hire you. You work for me. I fire you" didn't operate. Once, when I fired people from the Performance Group – after *Makbeth* in 1970 – the Group blew up. A number of Group members thought I worked very hard to reconstitute it for *Commune* in 1971. That "second" Performance Group was different than the first, the ones who made *Dionysus in 69* and *Makbeth*. Paradoxically, in the second Group, I was both more in charge and also more willing to share power. I talk about that situation in my book *Environmental Theater*.

At the same time, things were taking place all around us: the Freedom Movement and other political actions in the streets, art installations – Happenings were becoming more common but weren't yet called "performance art" or "site-specific." Things were happening in storefronts, lofts, on the streets, in many "found spaces." Visual artists were making performance pieces in their "AIR" lofts (artist in residence) in what later became known as SoHo, South of Houston Street. The Performing Garage at 33 Wooster Street was the first non-theatre theatre in SoHo. The Performance Group moved into the Garage in the winter of 1968. We owned shares in the Grand Street Artists Co-operative. Next to us, Norman Taffel, an avant-garde dancer, had his studio-performance space. The Performance Group was its own landlord, we could do what we wanted in and with our space. How liberating and empowering that felt!

The boundaries separating visual artists, dancers, musicians, and theatre people were blurring and even vanishing. The word "performance" became current because it could indicate all of these individual-genre kinds of artists doing ... what? ... actions, events, Happenings. The art world was quickly becoming performatized. Artists didn't need to rely on galleries or theatres. They didn't want gallery owners or theatre landlords controlling them. In today's world, the internet functions in roughly the same way. YouTube and Facebook, blogs, and self-postings – these are ways of getting around the restrictions of the authorities, ways of doing and showing work without money, or with less money. Of course, the authorities are also smart. They reoccupy the liberated spaces; they reinfect them with money, and so Facebook and the rest become not only or even mostly a social network so much as a money-making machine. Or maybe it's both, the collapse today into each other, making money and making society. Too bad that Marxism exists only as nostalgia or an academic theory. Will it come back? Maybe someday, but don't hold your breath.

SEIÇA: This new sense of artistic encounter, people living in the same neighborhood, gave rise to an ethos of community?

SCHECHNER: Exactly. Lofts, galleries, storefronts, streets: performances were taking place everywhere.

The Birth of Performance Studies

SEIÇA: How do you relate this cultural, social, and artistic context with the need for doing theory, how do you relate it to the birth of performance studies?

SCHECHNER: Well, you know, I've always done theory along with practice. I think of myself as "scientific" rather than "artistic." The theatre rehearsal space is a laboratory. And to conduct effective laboratory research you have to integrate theory and practice. The theory feeds the practice, the practice feeds the theory. I am not, strictly speaking, a scientist. I do not test theories; I do not do mathematics. But I am, to some degree, a "social scientist," working in two arenas: by participant-observation in several cultures; by means of artistic creativity through the training and rehearsal processes. This combined interest in, and practice of, theory and art has been part of my life since my college student days, and maybe before. As a little boy, I went to the beach on the New Jersey shore facing the Atlantic Ocean and spent many hours building sand structures, literally, and then observing the wind, the tide, the waves come up and wash what I made away. I was both sad to see my work destroyed and awed by the ineluctable power of "nature." Maybe I couldn't put it then in the words I am using now. I was only six or eight years old. But I wondered about the relationship between large-scale natural systems and human cultural behavior. Definitely I couldn't articulate this in such a sophisticated way when I was a little boy. But this kind of thinking has been part of me from as far back as I can recall. I like to fantasize, to build things from my fantasies, and to see what happens to those things, and then to generalize based on my observations. I like to develop systems, patterns, theorems. I like to read scientific literature. I pay for a subscription to only one magazine, *Science*, the weekly publication of the American Association for the Advancement of Science. A lot of what's in there is too technical for me to understand fully. But I get the drift, I appreciate the process, I suck up the information, I learn. I am curious about human behavior, about archaeology, about neurology, about ethology and biology, about cosmology – everything from the origins of human culture in animal behavior to string theory and the notion of multiple universes, from Newton to Darwin to Einstein to Hawking.

VEIERA: And why the word "performance"?

SCHECHNER: Oh! Hmm ... Now, when did I first use the word "performance" in the ways we are talking about? Here, look at this *TDR* from 1966, volume 10, number 4. See this essay, "Approaches to Theory/Criticism," where I discuss what I called "the public performance activities of men." Yes, I wrote "men" instead of "human beings." Back then I wasn't very sensitive to the language of gender. In a footnote, I offer a definition of "performance" which I still basically subscribe to. This definition helped guide my theories and, through them, performance studies. Let me quote from that note:

> Performance is an extremely difficult concept to define. From one point of view – clearly stated by Erving Goffman in *The Presentation of Self in Everyday Life* (1959) – performance is a mode of behavior that may characterize any activity. Thus, performance is a "quality" that can be "applied" to any situation. This is true [...] However, I choose to mean something much more limited by performance: the doing of an activity by an individual or group largely for the pleasure of another individual or group. Thus, while performance in its larger sense may characterize any activity, performance in the smaller sense is part of the form of many kinds of play, games, sports, theatre, and ritual.[8]

Later, I refined this into studying things "as" performance or "is" performance. I won't go into that distinction here. It's spelled out in *Performance Studies: An Introduction*. I just want to note here that I wrote about "performance" more or less in the performance-studies sense back in 1966. Probably in my classes at Tulane, where I taught from 1962 to 1967, I was discussing "performance" even earlier.

The Turner Connection

SEIÇA: That curiosity for science was what led you to work with Victor Turner?

SCHECHNER: By the mid-1970s I had read Turner's *Ritual Process*, which was published in 1969, and also I think some of his essays which were gathered in his 1974 *Dramas, Fields and Metaphors*. Turner's work, and that of a few other social scientists too – Goffman and Lévi-Strauss especially – impacted me a lot. I used Turner's ideas about social drama, liminality, ritual, and communitas. Those ideas are still important and alive for me. I first met Victor face to face in 1976.

One day, in the fall of that year, Turner phoned me. He was in New York to introduce a talk at Columbia University by Clifford Geertz, another very important anthropologist. Victor told me over the phone who he was, but of course I knew who he was. I went up to Columbia, and, after Geertz's lecture, Victor and I went to a seedy bar near the university, had a couple of beers, and talked for hours. We really hit it off. And over the years, until his death in 1983, Victor and I worked together very intensely. He invited me to participate in a ten-day symposium on "ritual, drama, and spectacle" he was planning for August–September 1977.[9] Victor asked me to suggest people to invite. I named poet-theorist Jerome Rothenberg, who linked oral poetry and shamanism. Grotowski didn't attend, but I brought some of his ideas. I showed the De Palma movie of *Dionysus in 69*, discussed the process of making that performance and delivered a paper that I later reworked into "Restoration of Behavior." The symposium opened a door between theatre and anthropology. But I was not able to stay for the whole ten days. At the moment of the symposium, Joan MacIntosh (to whom I was married at the time) was eight-months-plus pregnant. I went to Austria with the understanding that if Joan went into labor, I would come home. She did, I did – leaving the symposium two days before it ended. Our son Sam was born on September 6. My experience at the Burg was my initiation into how Turner and his group were exploring the many complex relationships between ritual and performance. To this day, that Burg Wartenstein Symposium is the finest conference I ever participated in or attended.

VIEIRA: And how did your work with Turner lead you to performance studies as a discipline?

SCHECHNER: At the Burg I met Barbara Myerhoff, Paul Bouissac, John MacAloon, Roberto DaMatta, Alfonso Ortiz, and Bruce Kapferer – all of whom later accepted my invitation to lecture to my large "Performance Theory" course at what was then the Graduate Drama Department, NYU – in 1980, renamed the Performance Studies Department. After lecturing on Monday night, on Tuesday morning my guest led a seminar with a small number of PhD students. Over four or five years I offered this course – roughly from the mid-1970s through the early 1980s – many scholars and artists foundational to what was becoming performance studies came to NYU.

Before Turner

Of course, the suite of ideas that would grow into performance studies (as I and my NYU colleagues conceived it) began a long time before I met Turner. Remember my 1966 *TDR* article written while I was at Tulane? And remember too that performance studies is not only about scholarship but about practice. What I was doing in New Orleans from 1960 onwards – and to some degree before that, when I ran a summer theatre in Provincetown in 1957 and 1958 – underlay environmental theatre and from there performance studies.

Let's reach way back to 1954, when I was a junior at Cornell University. I wrote think pieces for the *Cornell Daily Sun*, and one of these was a series on the *Brown* v. *Board of Education* case before the Supreme Court. This was the landmark case that ended legal segregation in American public schools. To better understand what was going on – the case had not been decided yet – I contacted the attorney arguing that case for the National Association for the Advancement of Colored People (NAACP), Thurgood Marshall. He met me in his Harlem office and took a couple of precious hours explaining to me the case, its background, and its importance. I cannot say we became friends, but Marshall took me under his wing to some degree. Later, in September 1957, by means of a letter Marshall wrote to Daisy Lee Gatson Bates of the Little Rock NAACP, I was in the house across the street from Central High School in the same room as the nine students who integrated the school over the objection of Arkansas Governor Orval Faubus. It was a defining few hours for me. I saw rabid segregationist crowds outside near the school. I saw calm African Americans willing to risk their lives for freedom. I felt part of their struggle.

I also experienced the theatricality of the situation. Things were as they were, and they were symbolic at the same time. Simply walking up some stairs, across a street, and into a high school was an emblematic action that much of the nation was watching, a confrontation and an accomplishment that was changing American society. I was starting to grasp the importance of "performance" to politics, social life, personal life, justice, oppression ... everything. During the years that followed, both as a civilian and during my nearly two years in the army, I continued to agitate for civil rights and civil liberties.

I finished my PhD at Tulane in 1962 and was hired immediately by the Theatre Department as an assistant professor and editor of the *Tulane Drama Review*. During my years at Tulane, both as a student and as a professor, I continued to be very active participating in and leading civil-rights actions. In November 1963, I was among a mixed-race group arrested in New Orleans for asking to be served at the City Hall's cafeteria. That same year, I began working as one of the three producing directors of the Free Southern Theater.[10] Also, I co-founded, with visual artist Frank Adams and composer Paul Epstein, the New Orleans Group. The work I did with the Free Southern Theater and the New Orleans Group was really transformative for me both in terms of sociopolitical people's theatre and in terms of experimental performance.

I also led demonstrations and teach-ins against the American involvement in the Vietnam War. I must say that Tulane's president and members of its board of directors were not happy with me. I am proud of that.

From Tulane to New York University

SCHECHNER: To cut to the chase: In 1967, I left Tulane for NYU, bringing *TDR* and my activist environmental-theatre ideas with me.

SEIÇA: As a theatre professor?

SCHECHNER: Drama, actually. When I arrived, performance studies did not exist. I was part of the Department of Drama and Cinema. Later, Cinema split off, and then Drama was broken into graduate and undergraduate programs. In 1980, the Graduate Drama Department officially became the Performance Studies Department.

The man who brought me to NYU was Robert W. Corrigan, the founding dean of the School of the Arts, later the Tisch School of the Arts. Corrigan began *TDR* in 1955 at Carleton College in Minnesota. He brought it to Tulane in 1957. I took his classes. He directed my dissertation. For one term, I worked at *TDR* – but found the job, which was mostly office work, tedious, so I quit. Corrigan was only seven years older than I. He was not only my teacher at Tulane but my friend. When in 1962, as I was working on my dissertation on Eugene Ionesco in Paris, he suddenly left Tulane for Carnegie Mellon in Pittsburgh – and the Tulane faculty offered me Corrigan's job and his journal, if I finished my PhD. I scaled down the scope of the dissertation and finished it by May. It felt natural for me to succeed Corrigan as *TDR*'s editor. We shared a lot of ideas. But I was more interested in the social and political aspects of performance. I saw the experimental more in performances and less in texts. And, finally, I had a more USA-centric view of theatre than Corrigan did. He loved Europe. Another big difference between us was that he was a scholar and administrator, I am a director and scholar.[11]

Within a couple of months of my moving to New York, I continued the work of the New Orleans Group. In November 1967, during and right after four weeks I spent nightly in a workshop led by Grotowski at NYU – his first workshop in the USA – I convened a group of students and some others to share what I was learning and to continue the work I had done in New Orleans. These people, with a few additions and subtractions, became the Performance Group. Oh yeah, that word "performance" again! In the Drama Department, I taught courses mainly about the avant-garde theatre but increasingly with what was becoming the performance-studies approach. During my first thirteen years in New York I concentrated on directing plays. After two years of trying to do everything – running a theatre group, teaching, writing, editing *TDR* – I realized I had to give something up. I couldn't stop teaching because not only do I love relating to students but also I needed my professor's income; I couldn't stop writing because a writer is who I am; and I didn't want to stop directing the Performance Group. So in 1969 I resigned my editorship of *TDR*.

Michael Kirby and *TDR*

SCHECHNER: Years before that, in 1964 at Tulane, I wanted to do a special issue on Happenings. The problem was I didn't know enough about Happenings. So I invited Michael Kirby to co-edit a special issue with me.[12] I really don't remember how I met Michael. Although I lived in New Orleans, I came to New York frequently. However we met, Michael and I hit it off; we became good friends. Kirby was writing or had just finished *Happenings* (published 1965). Michael took me to Happenings and introduced me to a new cohort, including John Cage and Allan Kaprow. He was just the person to work on the Happenings issue, which was a great success. At that time, Michael, who did not have a PhD, was teaching at Saint Francis College in Brooklyn, a dead-end job. After I moved to NYU in 1967, I suggested to Michael that he earn his PhD at NYU's Drama Department. "Then we can hire you," I said, partly as a joke, partly in earnest. He did get his PhD in 1971;[13] and we did hire him, also in 1971. After Michael retired in 1991, he still taught in the department from time to time. He died in 1997.

Let me backtrack to more of the Kirby story. In 1969, when I stepped down as *TDR*'s editor, I designated Erika Munk (*TDR*'s managing editor in New Orleans and associate editor in New York) to become editor. That didn't work out. Erika left in 1971. Then I asked Michael Kirby to become editor. He accepted, bringing his own vision to the journal. In his first editorial statement, Kirby declared his policy:

> We are not interested in opinions and value judgments about what is "good" and what is "bad." We feel that the detailed and accurate documentation of performances is preferable and gives sufficient grounds for a reader to make his own value judgments. [...] We should like to present material that is useful to people who actually work in theatre – material that provokes, stimulates and enriches that work. In part for this reason, we prefer articles by people who actually work in the theatre.[14]

Michael was not averse to scripts, history, and theory – but he defined these in his own way. By history, he meant "documentation of trends and movements in theatre as well as the documentation of significant performances." Kirby defined theory mostly negatively: "Unfortunately, much writing that would like to be taken as theory either re-works old, and frequently outdated, ideas, or it is merely disguised criticism that offers opinions, appreciations and interpretations instead of attempting objectivity."[15] No value judgments and objectivity constituted Kirby's credo. I won't discuss my take on these matters; decades of editing and writing provide all the evidence you need. When Michael resigned as *TDR*'s editor, I returned in 1986 as editor. Michael and I were friends but we had entirely different views on what *TDR* should be. I hope to remain *TDR*'s editor for ... who knows how long, just shy of forever.

Jerzy Grotowski, Teaching, Asia

Jerzy Grotowski was another important influence. I first heard about the Polish master in 1963. From 1964 onward, *TDR* published many pieces by and about Grotowski. Throughout the 1960s, Grotowski loomed ever larger in my life. I met him face to face first in Montreal in 1966. In November 1967, partly through my efforts, he and Ryszard Cieślak came to NYU to lead an actor-training workshop. I was by some years the oldest student in the room. What Grotowski and Cieślak taught during the day, I brought to the fledgling Performance Group at night. Of course, it wasn't quite so simple. My version of their work was a transfer with changes. After the workshop, I and Theodore Hoffman (of NYU's acting program, and at one time the Associate Editor of *TDR*) interviewed Grotowski.[16] Later in the 1970s, as I told you, I met Turner. Grotowski's work meshed well with Turner's: the ritual process, spontaneous communitas, the aesthetic act with social consequences. Again, that interaction between practice and theory. My third dancing partner was Claude Lévi-Strauss, who I never met in person. But his ideas impacted me: the relationship between the synchronic and the diachronic, the raw and the cooked, the savage mind, the bricoleur.[17]

VIEIRA: Which avant-garde performances were you teaching?

SCHECHNER: When I first got to NYU, I taught "Trends in Modern Theatre," Corrigan's signature course at Tulane. In this course I dealt with both drama and theatre, two great intertwined lines, one of playwrights, the other of directors (and, in Brecht's case, both rolled into one). From Ibsen and Chekhov to Pirandello and Brecht on to Williams, Miller, Genet, Ionesco, and Beckett; and on the directing side, from Saxe-Meiningen and Stanislavsky to Meyerhold and Vakhtangov on to Brecht, Blin, Kazan, and Brook. Over the years, I kept updating the lists while keeping the dynamic process of the course the same. As I shifted from drama to performance, I added Happenings, the Living and Open Theatres, Richard Foreman, Robert Wilson, and Mabou Mines. You know. By the 1990s, the course's name had changed a few times. I dropped drama as such. I taught one course on "theories of directing" and another on "experimental performance." Those were two of about five or six courses I kept juggling. I also started offering summer workshops at NYU in performer training. In the 1990s, I developed "rasaboxes" in relation to my work with East Coast Artists and integrated that technique into my NYU workshops.[18] I found the dialectic between the academic and the practical to be always stimulating, always necessary.

VIEIRA: And the non-Western?

SCHECHNER: Yes, definitely. In 1971, I made my first trip to Asia. With Joan MacIntosh, I visited India, Japan, Taiwan, Hong Kong, the Philippines, Papua New Guinea, Australia, Thailand, Singapore, Malaysia, and Indonesia. I couldn't get to mainland China – it was not open to Americans. That trip ... changed my life. It made concrete for me things that I had read. And it brought into my field of experience things I simply didn't know before or knew only vaguely and abstractly. I cannot tell you here how many different kinds of performances I saw, how many people I met, how many exchanges on all levels I had. In India, in addition to everything else, I studied yoga in a serious way with Krishnamacharya, the great teacher of Madras (now Chennai).

When I returned, what had happened to me in Asia began to percolate through my being as a scholar and as a director – including the Performance Group's 1972 production of Sam Shepard's *The Tooth of Crime* and the Group's 1975 production of Brecht's *Mother Courage and Her Children*. We brought *Courage* to India in 1976. When the Group returned to the USA, I stayed on for most of a year. I saw many different kinds of performances, including a few days of the Ramlila of Ramnagar, starting what has become a lifelong study of that all-encompassing performance. In the summer rainy season, I participated in basic kathakali training in Kerala while reading the *Natyasastra* with great care, laying one of the cornerstones for rasaboxes. The next year I participated in Turner's Burg Wartenstein Symposium. In 1978, I returned to India to attend all thirty-one days of the Ramlila.

From Performance Theory to "Chaps Not Maps"

SCHECHNER: Then, in 1979, I began teaching a series of courses I called "performance theory." Each year, the basic topic would change, but the underlying idea was to radically expand the range of what was performance, to go far beyond theatre. Each course had a different subject: "Native American Performance," "Shamanism," "Play," "Ritual," "Performing the Self," "Cultural and Intercultural Performance" … and many more. NYU provided me with a budget that allowed me to invite really great people from the social sciences, the humanities, and the arts. The list is very long, including Jerzy Grotowski, Clifford Geertz, Jerome Rothenberg, Augusto Boal, Allan Kaprow, Laurie Anderson, Masao Yamaguchi, Erving Goffman, Eugenio Barba, Steve Paxton, Roberto DaMatta, Barbara Myerhoff, Alfonso Ortiz, Joanne Akalaitis, Yvonne Rainer, Meredith Monk, Colin Turnbull, Richard Foreman, Spalding Gray, Julie Taymor, Brian Sutton-Smith. Edith and Victor Turner were frequent participants.[19] The star lectured on Monday night to about seventy students, both graduate and undergraduate. Then, on Tuesday morning, the guest met graduate students in a seminar with a cap of about twenty. PhD students under my supervision met with the undergraduates in small sections. It really was a fine sequence of courses. During the three or four years I offered "performance theory," the basic contour of what was to become known as performance studies took shape. In the summer of 1979, the Turners, Goffman, Myerhoff, Alexander Alland,[20] and I co-taught a two-week workshop-seminar at the Performing Garage exploring "performing ethnography."[21]

VIEIRA: About the influences from outside Europe: It reminds me of Jameson's text "Periodizing the 60s"[22] where he sees the Third World in the First World.

SCHECHNER: For me, it was not the Third World in the usual sense of that term. I had many friends and co-workers in various parts of the world. After

I left the Performance Group at the end of 1979, start of 1980, I worked as a theatre director in India, China, Taiwan, and South Africa.[23] I conducted workshops. I did fieldwork. I started editing *TDR* again. I really didn't think in a First World, Second World, Third World way. In my ear, I heard Turner urging "Chaps not maps." Work person-to-person with people you are in sympathy with. In each place there are a few kindred spirits. Seek them out. Work with them. That's what I did.

There is a community of artists and a community of scholars. Sometimes these overlap. There are certain people in Shanghai who I am closer to than people living three blocks from where we are now. The people in Shanghai are part of my community, the people three blocks from here are not.

Performance Studies Emerges ... and Changes

VIEIRA: And the NYU Performance Studies Department?

SCHECHNER: I've already told you. But let me flesh it out. I'll start with Brooks McNamara and Barbara Kirshenblatt-Gimblett. McNamara earned his PhD from Tulane – he was a student when I was a professor there – and joined the NYU faculty in 1968. He pioneered popular-entertainment studies. In 1976, he became the first director of the Shubert Archive.[24] He was also a theatre designer: In 1969 he worked with me on *Makbeth* and in 1975 authored with Jerry Rojo and me *Theatres, Spaces, Environments*. Brooks retired from the Archive and from NYU in 1996; he died in 2009.

BKG (as everybody calls Barbara Kirshenblatt-Gimblett) was the catalyst of the Performance Studies Department when she chaired it from 1981 to 1993. She was an anthropologist specializing in folklore, Jewish studies, museums from colonial expositions to living history, tourist performances, and the aesthetics of everyday life.

Before BKG, we rotated the chair among the senior faculty. Nobody wanted to be chair. It was a burden, something we did because we had to. I was chair for one year – and I was as awful as BKG was brilliant. BKG crafted a singular department out of what had been catch-as-catch-can. We were each good in our own way, but we didn't cohere as a department. BKG insisted on regular faculty meetings where we hashed out curriculum, degree requirements, entrance standards, qualifying exams, and lots more. We debated until we reached consensus. She led us in recruiting a diverse faculty of quality: dance scholars, feminists, cultural theorists, anthropologists; Africans, African Americans, Hispanics. Her insistence on full-time students performing at a high academic level working steadily towards their degrees transformed our population. We diversified radically in terms of ethnicity, race, sexual orientation, nationality, gender ... across the board.

BKG confabbed with scholars in other departments, deans, and NYU's central administration. A tireless organizer, conference participant, keynote speaker, performance theorist, cheerleader, boss, and cook, BKG often invited faculty and friends from different disciplines to her spacious loft (shared with her painter husband Max Gimblett, whose studio was in the front part of their space on New York's Bowery). BKG's ability to squeeze money out of rocks was nothing short of magic. Her energy was unfailing and inspiring.

During BKG's tenure as chair, performance studies congealed from a related but disparate set of concerns into something that really could be called a "discipline." We moved away from theatre as a basis both theoretically and in terms of curriculum. This transformation was not an "all at once" thing. But we had our goals in sight. The first departmental bulletin with BKG as our leader under the banner "Performance Studies" proclaimed:

> The Department of Performance Studies offers a curriculum covering the full range of performance forms, from theatre and dance to ritual and popular entertainment. [...] a wide spectrum of performance traditions – for example, postmodern dance, circus, Kathakali, Broadway, ballet, shamanism – are documented using fieldwork, interviews, and archival research and are analyzed from a variety of perspectives. As a whole, the program is both intercultural and interdisciplinary, drawing on the arts, humanities, and social sciences.[25]

This mission statement was repeated almost verbatim for fifteen years.

But if the statement remained constant, what was happening in the department was changing. In 1983, performance studies students started *Women and Performance*, edited then, as today, by a feminist collective with the mission of "extending and reformulating notions of gender and performance."[26] The editorial collective and advisory board includes NYU students and faculty as well as artists and scholars from many other places too. The feminist impulse generating *Women and Performance* was given a big push when, in 1985, we hired Peggy Phelan, fresh out of grad school. In the mid-1990s, Peggy chaired the Department. In 1997, she was one of the founders of Performance Studies international (PSi), the leading performance-studies organization globally.[27] She left NYU for Stanford in 2006, and she's still there.

Throughout the 1990s and into the new millennium, the Department kept developing. Diana Taylor arrived in 1997; in 1998, she and three Latin-American colleagues founded the Hemispheric Institute of Performance and Politics. The multilingual Hemi works "at the intersection of scholarship, artistic expression and politics [... exploring] embodied practice – performance – as a vehicle for the creation of new meaning and the transmission of cultural values, memory and identity."[28] With the hiring in 1994 of a freshly minted Duke PhD, José Muñoz, queer studies moved front and center. José, a charismatic teacher and writer, chaired the department from 2005 to 2011 and was instrumental in developing our strong queer-studies focus. He passed away in 2013, much too young at forty-six years.

To back up a little. Over the roughly fifteen years from 1990 to 2005, there was considerable faculty turnover as NYU's performance studies program morphed from its BKG period to what it is now. Some professors were at Performance Studies for relatively brief times – Michael Taussig, Joseph Roach, May Joseph, Phillip Zarrilli, and J. Ndukaku Amankulor (who died in 1994). Kenyan playwright, novelist, and theorist Ngũgĩ wa Thiong'o was jointly appointed to Performance Studies and Comparative Literature before moving on to the University of California–Irvine. Others stayed for the long haul and are here as I speak: Diana Taylor, Barbara Browning, Karen Shimakawa, André Lepecki (our own PhD), Ann Pellegrini, Tavia Nyong'o, Anna Deavere Smith, and Allan Weiss. Smith and Weiss teach one course a year. BKG has been on a long leave to Warsaw where she is the Program Director of the Core Exhibition of new Museum of the History of Polish Jews. She has told us that she will retire when she returns to New York in 2015. I will sorely miss her at the Department. I myself will retire at the end of August 2017. That will mark fifty years of my being a full professor and then a university professor at NYU. Is that some kind of record? Even after I retire, I will keep editing *TDR*. The good thing about this kind of road is that it is without end.

To get back to the Performance Studies Department history. What all the changes boil down to is that from about 1990 there's been an ongoing swing from theatre and dance-based performance studies toward "performative performance studies": queer studies, critical race theory, politics and performance, post-structuralism – a move that sets NYU's performance studies more in line with cultural studies than with the social or biological sciences or with theatre and dance. I am not altogether happy with the alignment with cultural studies. I wish there were more "real performance" being studied. The only practicums are the summer workshop with East Coast Artists,[29] the Performance Composition course taught mostly by Smith, and a few other courses from time to time. I know my call for more "real performance" sounds weird coming from me because I am the champion of the "broad spectrum approach." I am not backing away from that. What I want is theory based on practice, fieldwork, participant observation, and practical experimentation.

On the bright side, because many performance-studies students and some faculty are practicing artists – more performance art than theatre or dance – there is a strong "real performance" presence in the Department. But the course work is highly theoretical, and has been so for a long time now. There is less debate than I want on questions such as: To what degree does performance studies depend on live performance? Is performance studies "performative" rather than "actual performance"? What is the place of theatre and dance studies within performance studies? What separates performance studies from cultural studies? These questions cannot be answered definitively, and that's a good thing. We ought to be always tossing them around.

In the Academy and Separate from It Too

VIEIRA: And you like teaching?

SCHECHNER: What attracts me to teaching is the ongoing interaction with people much younger than I am. When I started teaching at college as a graduate student, I was only a few years older than the students in my "communications skills" freshman course at the University of Iowa. When I first became a professor at Tulane in 1962 having just turned twenty-eight, I taught only grad students and was younger than a few of them. Now I am generations older than everyone in the room. That's both good and bad. I can't share the students' life experiences at first hand. But teaching puts me in touch with young minds, young bodies, young concerns. And I can share with these young people some of the depths of my work, the people I knew and know, where I've been and what I've seen and done. That's all to the good. The classroom is a gym for the intellect and emotions. Directing dissertations is something else again. It brings me into very close mentoring work with people who are on the cusp between being students and becoming ... whatever ... mostly young college teachers and new book authors. I edit a book series where I can place the best dissertations – and lots of other new work by more established scholars too.[30] And, of course, I am joined at the hip to *TDR*.

SEIÇA: So you maintain a kind of 1960s spirit ... ?

SCHECHNER: Even in the 1960s professors did professor things. I maintain a paradoxical spirit of being in the academy and staying separate from it too. I am at NYU but I don't think I am of NYU. I direct plays away from the university. I travel a lot, lecturing, leading workshops, and doing fieldwork. At NYU, I usually don't do committee work outside of my own department. I would never chair the Department again, not that anyone would be crazy enough to ask me. I like to do close-in work with students. I like participating in the faculty meetings of my department. I don't enjoy academic politics, writing committee reports, and things like that. People who go for that become chairs of departments, deans, provosts, and maybe even university presidents. That for me is the road not taken.

The roads I am taking reach out to me. In 2013 I went to Burning Man. Also in 2013, I returned to Ramlila. Each spring – in 2012 and 2014 through 2016 – I teach or will teach at NYU Abu Dhabi. I am developing for NYU's global network an online flipped classroom course on performance studies. In 2014, I conceived and co-directed for Peak Performances in Montclair, New Jersey, near New York, *Imagining O*, an environmental theatre piece combining Shakespeare, Pauline Réage's *Story of O*, some of my own writing, and the experiences of the performers. *Imagining O* began as a work-in-progress in 2011 at the University of Kent. In September 2014, my son Sam and his wife Mara had their first child. My first grandson. My daughter Sophia is in law school. Soon after finishing editing this life-view in the guise of an interview, my wife, Professor Carol Martin, and I will fly to Shanghai for PSi. And all that's only part of the ongoing story. *Ars longa, vita brevis.*

Notes

1 Throughout this interview, "1960s" refers to the period from the mid- to late 1950s through to the mid- to late 1970s, a "decade" that lasts about twenty years: a generation.

2 *Brown v. Board of Education.* On May 14, 1954, Chief Justice Earl Warren delivered the unanimous opinion of the Court: "We conclude that in the field of public education the doctrine of 'separate but equal' has no place. Separate educational facilities are inherently unequal." This changed everything in American society.

3 The informal name of the NY Dance and Performance Awards in honor of the Bessie Schonberg, 1906–1997, an influential choreographer and teacher at Bennington College, Vermont.

4 I am using the name "Frankfurt School" generically. More specifically, it refers to Frankfurt University's Institute for Social Research. The Institute left Frankfurt, stopped in Geneva, and landed at Columbia University in New York in 1935.

5 See Malina's *The Piscator Notebook* (London and New York: Routledge, 2012), for details.

6 The Living was 100 percent pacifist, against all wars under any and all circumstances.

7 In October 1963, during the run of *The Brig*, the IRS closed the Living's theatre on 14th Street and 6th Avenue, Manhattan. The IRS said that the Living failed to pay their taxes. Curiously, on the same day, Jonas Mekas was shooting a documentary film about the play. Soon after the seizure, The Living went first to Europe and then to Brazil. They did not return to the USA until 1968. By happenstance, I was at the 14th Street theatre when the IRS arrived and the Living temporarily barricaded themselves in their theatre. For an account of that night, including my from-the-street interview of Judith Malina and Julian Beck, see *TDR*, 13 (3): 24–107.

8 Richard Schechner (1966), "Approaches to Theory/Criticism," *Tulane Drama Review*, 10 (4): 27.

9 "Cultural Frames and Reflections: Ritual, Drama, and Spectacle" was Symposium #76 sponsored by The Wenner-Gren Foundation for Anthropological Research. The symposium convened from August 27 to September 5, 1977, at the Burg Wartenstein, Wenner-Gren's Austrian mountain castle. The symposium was not open to the public, which meant that the participants could examine issues and themes in detail. Turner, Barbara Babcock, and Barbara Myerhoff – all anthropologists – were the organizers. In addition to anthropologists, the seventeen participants included scholars of history, semiotics, performance theory, and shamanism. Participants came from the USA, Brazil, Canada, Australia, and Romania. The revised symposium papers were published as John MacAloon (ed.), *Rite Drama, Festival, Spectacle: Rehearsals Toward a Theory of Cultural Performance* (Philadelphia, Pa.: ISHA, 1984). "Restoration of Behavior," was not in the book because I had promised the essay to a journal. In retrospect, I wish I hadn't.

10 The other producing-directors were Gilbert Moses and John O'Neal. For an account of the Free Southern Theatre at that time, see Thomas C. Dent, Richard Schechner and Gilbert Moses (eds.), *The Free Southern Theater by the Free Southern Theater: A Documentary of the South's Radical Black Theater* (Indianapolis: Bobbs, 1969). See also the documents archived at the Amistad Research Center: http://www.amistadresearchcenter.org/archon/?p=collections/controlcard&id=48.

11 After leaving NYU in 1967, Corrigan became the first President of the California Institute of the Arts in 1970. During his extremely active career, Corrigan was head

of the Theatre Department at Carnegie-Mellon University, Dean of the School of Fine Arts at the University of Wisconsin–Milwaukee, and Dean of the School of Arts and Humanities at the University of Texas–Dallas.

12 *TDR* 10 (2) (1965). In 1995, Mariellen Sandford (*TDR*'s Associate Editor) edited *Happenings and Other Acts* (London: Routledge), which included the whole *TDR* issue plus additional materials. In her editor's note, Sandford wrote, "Published at the height of the Happenings and Fluxus movements, these are invaluable documents from a period that radically changed our perception of the function of the artist, the role of the observer, and the relation between art and everyday life."

13 In 1971, Kirby's dissertation "The History and Theory of Futurist Performance," appeared as *Futurist Performance* published by E. P. Dutton. The Dutton edition included scripts and manifestos translated from the Italian by Michael's wife at the time, Victoria Nes Kirby. In 1986, and again in 2001, PAJ Publications reissued *Futurist Performance* with Michael Kirby and Victoria Nes Kirby listed as co-authors.

14 Michael Kirby (1971) "An Introduction," *TDR*, 15 (3): 5–8.

15 Kirby (1971: 7).

16 "An Interview with Grotowski" was published in *TDR* 13 (1) (1968): 29–45. An edited version appeared in Grotowski's *Towards a Poor Theatre* (New York: Simon & Schuster, 1968) as "American Encounter" (pp. 243–254).

17 A term introduced by Lévi-Strauss in *The Savage Mind* (1966, 1962 in French) describing a kind of thinking and symbolization. The bricoleur is the opposite of the "engineer." The engineer creates specialized tools for specific purposes. The bricoleur improvises, playfully recombines, and deals directly with the situation on hand. The bricoleur is a "jack-of-all-trades" using a few nonspecialized tools for a variety of purposes. The bricoleur practices "the science of the concrete." Definition adapted from http://www.anthrobase.com/Dic/eng/def/bricoleur.htm (accessed June 11, 2014).

18 Go to rasaboxes.org (accessed June 11, 2014) and https://www.facebook.com/groups/436306506474754/ (accessed June 26, 2014) for more about rasaboxes and the rasaboxes community.

19 Edith, Victor's wife, was his partner in fieldwork and intellectual practice. As she writes on her University of Virginia web page: "My theoretical interests have developed from Turner's 'anthropology of experience' [...] Good anthropology rests on humanism – that is, respect for the ideas and religions of other cultures and, where possible, the willingness to experience through the eyes of others." See anthropology.virginia.edu/faculty/profile/elt9w (accessed September 15, 2014).

20 Myerhoff, theorist of secular ritual and a pioneer of visual anthropology, is known for her books *Number Our Days* (1979) and *Peyote Hunt* (1976). She and the Turners were very close friends. Alexander Alland, currently Emeritus Professor of Anthropology, Columbia University, was at that time actively interested in performance. Goffman participated in two days of the two-week workshop.

21 See Victor and Edith Turner (1982) "Performing Ethnography," *TDR*, 26 (2): 33–50.

22 Fredric Jameson (1984), "Periodizing the 60s," in Sohnya Sayres (ed.), *The 60s Without Apology* (Minneapolis, Minn.: University of Minnesota Press), pp. 178–209.

23 Chekhov's *Cherry ka Bagicha* (*The Cherry Orchard*) in Hindi in New Delhi in 1983. Sun Huizhu's *Mingri Jiuyao Chu Shan* (Tomorrow He'll Be Out of the Mountains) in Mandarin in Shanghai in 1989. August Wilson's *Ma Rainey's Black Bottom* for the Grahamstown Festival in South Africa in 1992. Aeschylus' *The Oresteia* in Mandarin in Taipei in 1996. I continue to work outside the USA – *Hamlet* in Mandarin in Shanghai in 2007 (the production toured to Poland and Romania) and *Imagining O* as a work-in-progress in the UK (the production toured to India). The "final" version of *Imagining O*, the world premiere, played as part of the Peak Performances festival in Montclair, New Jersey in 2014.

In quotation marks because nothing, actually, is final; certainly not any live performance.

24 The Shubert Archive's "mission is to preserve the business and artistic records of the Shubert Brothers and the Shubert Organization. [...] The majority of the archive focuses heavily on the first four decades of the twentieth century when the Shubert Brothers were at the height of their power and influence as producers and theatre owners." See http://www.shubertarchive.org/index_flash.htm (accessed June 11, 2014).

25 1980–1982 NYU Performance Studies Bulletin.

26 See http://www.womenandperformance.org/about-us.html (accessed June 10, 2014).

27 For information about PSi, see http://www.psi-web.org/page/about (accessed June 11, 2014).

28 See http://hemisphericinstitute.org/hemi/en/mission (accessed June 10, 2014).

29 I founded East Coast Artists (ECA) in 1992 and have directed a number of plays with ECA. In the 1990s, I devised "rasaboxes," which is the core exercise of the NYU summer workshop. I first offered the workshop in the mid-1990s. After 2010 it has been taught by others whom I have trained. There are a number of people skilled in rasaboxes by now, including Paula Murray Cole, Michele Minnick, Rachel Bowditch, Marcia Moraes, Ulla Neuerberg-Denzer, and Fernando Calzadilla. People teach rasaboxes in Europe, the Americas, and Asia. Go to rasaboxes.org for more information.

30 This is the Enactments series, published by Seagull Books. See http://www.seagu llindia.com/books/enactments.asp?cbosearch=category&txtkeyword=Enactments (accessed June 11, 2014).

Chapter 4

9/11 as Avant-Garde Art?

Nearly everyone in the world knows and has some deeply held, personal response to what happened in New York City and Washington, DC, on September 11, 2001. The extraordinary sight of wide-bodied Boeing airplanes speeding like bullets down Manhattan Island at near the speed of sound, a mere 500–800 feet above the busy morning rush-hour streets, then smashing into the city's tallest buildings, eventually reducing them to rubble – these sublime acts of terror stunned the world. In a sense, we witnessed two types of the sublime as defined by [Immanuel] Kant, the terrifying and the splendid. The terrifying arises from the great power and speed of these projectiles carrying helpless, unknowing passengers, and the dreadful toll in lost lives; the splendid results from the magnificence of the airplanes and the remarkable, gargantuan architecture of the twin towers.

(Minor 2001: 91–96)

An American general in Baghdad called Iraq a "work of art" in progress yesterday [November 1, 2006] in one of the most extraordinary attempts by the US military leadership to put a positive spin on the worsening violence. On a day in which 49 people were killed or found dead around the country, Major General William Caldwell, the chief military spokesman, argued that Iraq was in transition, a process that was "not always a pleasant thing to watch. Every great work of art goes through messy phases while it is in transition. A lump of clay can become a sculpture. Blobs of paint become paintings which inspire," Maj. Gen Caldwell told journalists in Baghdad's fortified green zone.

(Borger 2006)

[The attacks of 9/11 were] the greatest work of art imaginable for the whole cosmos. Minds achieving something in an act that we couldn't even dream of in music, people rehearsing like mad for 10 years, preparing fanatically for a concert, and then dying, just imagine what happened there. You have people who are that focused on a performance and then 5,000 [sic] people are dispatched to the after-life, in a single moment. I couldn't do that. By comparison, we composers are nothing. Artists, too, sometimes try to go beyond the limits of what is feasible and conceivable, so that we wake up, so that we open ourselves to another world. [...] It's a crime because those involved didn't consent. They didn't come to the "concert." That's obvious. And no one announced that they risked losing their lives. What happened in spiritual terms, the leap out of security, out of what is usually taken for granted, out of life, that sometimes happens to a small extent in art, too, otherwise art is nothing.

(Stockhausen 2001)

Despite the staggering violence, I doubt that too many in the field of avant-garde studies were surprised by the 9/11 hijackers' motives and methods. The attack intertwined the symbolic, the performative, the economic-infrastructural, and the ethical, in a style straight from the rule book of the avant-garde. This was "propaganda by deed" at its most audacious, terrifying and, dare I say it, traditional [...] Like the radical actors, poets, writers, and performers of the Living Theatre, the performance artists associated with Fluxus and Happenings, and the activist-intellectuals and artists of the Black Arts Movement, this was a small group of activists challenging political power through illegal, alternative, or subversive means. They materially altered the status quo by shattering the conventions of perceptions. Like Pablo Picasso or Georges Braque, [...] like the Surrealists [...] the hijackers knew that the right word or the right gesture at the right time could produce cataclysmic change. They were not artists but what they did on 9/11 resonated profoundly with what vanguard artists have done for the last century and a half.

(Sell 2011: 6–7)

In a word, hermeneutic terrorism becomes a powerful weapon, by leaving the gaps or blanks in its message available for ad-libbing. One can almost talk of an interactive terrorism, of a karaoke of sorts. I am amazed to see that so many artists or intellectuals have been ready and willing to sing in tune with the September 11 terrorists, and that the improvised statements of Gunther Grass, Arundhati Roy, Karl-Heinz Stockhausen, Jean Marie Straub, Daniele Huillet could hardly be distinguished from those of bin Laden himself.

(Dayan 2002: 71)

In the USA, dialing 911, pronounced "nine one one" is the way to call for help in an emergency. And 9/11, pronounced "nine eleven," is the universal signifier of the September 11, 2001 (terrorist) attacks on New York's World Trade Center towers and on the Pentagon. The emergency number in the USA has been "911" since 1968, so can it be that whoever coined the phrase "9/11" didn't know of its prior use?[1] Or that the date the terrorists selected was accidental? In their own view, were the attackers making an emergency call? Or forcing Americans into a horrible crisis? On October 7, 2001, less than a month after the attacks of 9/11, Osama bin Laden (1957–2011) made the following statement: "God Almighty hit the United States at its most vulnerable spot. He destroyed its greatest buildings. Praise be to God. Here is the United States. It was filled with terror from its north to its south and from its east to its west. Praise be to God."[2]

How was all of the USA – east, west, north, south – to be "filled with terror" if not by the swift and saturating dissemination of the news and images of the attack? And what was the USA's "most vulnerable spot" if not the imaginations of its people? And who, in bin Laden's view, was the attacker? Not Al-Qaeda, but "God Almighty." As with the plagues against Egypt in Moses' day, God himself is the doer of the horror.

The 9/11 attacks were a successful assault on the imagination. Americans, and the rest of the world, saw what they only dreamed of seeing. The USA severely wounded by terrorists, nonstate actors. And what kind of wound was it? Ian Boal, T. J. Clark, Joseph Matthews, and Michael Watts write:

> Spectacularly, the American state suffered a defeat on September 11. And spectacularly, for this state, does not mean superficially or epiphenomenally. The state was wounded in September in its heart of hearts [...]. [T]he horrors of September 11 were designed above all to be visible [...]. September's terror was different [than the fire bombing of Dresden or the atom bombing of Hiroshima]. [...] It was premised on the belief (learned from the culture it wishes to annihilate) that a picture is worth a thousand words – that a picture, in the present condition of politics, is itself, if sufficiently well executed, a specific and effective piece of statecraft.
>
> (2005: 25–26)

Not statecraft as we know it. Neither a treaty nor a declaration of war in the ordinary sense, 9/11 exploded Americans' sense of well-being and security. No one who saw 9/11 – and a large percentage of the world's population did see it, again and again – will forget it. From that day forward, New York's downtown skyline was marked by an absence: "There's where they were," is the common explanation accompanying a pointing finger. Absence is the motif of the Memorial which "consist[s] of two massive pools set within the footprints of the Twin Towers."[3] The massive Freedom Tower (aka 1 World Trade Center) erected near where the Twin Towers were, does not replace them so much as call to mind the ghosts of the two relatively slim structures that are no more.

And the American response to the attack? It is unlikely but possible that President George W. Bush's speechwriters knew Immanuel Kant's assertion that the "sublime is the name given to what is absolutely great, [...] what is beyond all comparison great," what is "terrifying and splendid," when they put "shock and awe" into the President's mouth to describe the American March 2003 air assault on Baghdad kicking off the second Iraq War.[4] Bush wanted the USA to answer spectacle with spectacle. Without doubt, the speechwriters knew of Harlan K. Ullman and James P. Wade's 1996 book, *Shock and Awe: Achieving Rapid Dominance*, published by the National Defense University.[5] Absolutely true is that Bang on a Can, a music group "with an ear for the new, the unknown and the unconventional" knew Stockhausen's "greatest work of art imaginable" when they designated his *Stimmung* "as the culminating piece of a twelve-hour marathon ending early on the morning of June 1, 2008 at the World Financial Center Winter Garden."[6]

Furthermore, as a military operation, as an act of (unconventional) war, the 9/11 attacks were very successful. Boal, et al. go on:

> Of course the martyr-pilots knew that bringing down the Twin Towers would do nothing, or next to nothing, to stop the actual circuits of capital. But circuits of capital are bound up, in the longer term, with circuits of sociability – patterns of belief and desire, levels of confidence, degrees of identification with the good life of the commodity. And these, said the terrorists, thinking strategically, are aspects of the social imaginary still (always, interminably) being put together by the perpetual emotion machines. Supposing those machines could be captured for a moment, and on them appeared the perfect image of capitalism's negation. Would that not be enough? Enough truly to destabilize the state and society, and produce a sequence of vauntings and paranoias whose long-term political consequences for the capitalist world order would, at the very least, be unpredictable.
>
> (2005: 26)

These observations published in 2005 proved very prophetic. Follow this causal chain: 9/11 evokes a panicked, paranoiac, and massive reaction that is harnessed to neocon/neoliberal desires both to control Iraq's oil and to "democratize" Iraq as a model for the Arab Middle East. These twin objectives could most efficiently (it was thought) be realized by an easy war symbolically capped by President Bush's May 2003 "Mission Accomplished" landing on the aircraft carrier USS *Abraham Lincoln*. Such bravado went hand in hand with contradictory instructions given to the American people. In a press conference on September 15, four days after the attack, Bush said:

THE PRESIDENT: [… T]his act will not stand; we will find those who did it; we will smoke them out of their holes; we will get them running and we'll bring them to justice. [… W]e will do whatever it takes to smoke them out and get them running, and we'll get them.

Q: Sir, how much of a sacrifice are ordinary Americans going to have to be expected to make in their daily lives, in their daily routines?

THE PRESIDENT: Our hope, of course, is that they make no sacrifice whatsoever. We would like to see life return to normal in America. […] I urge people to go to their businesses on Monday. I understand major league baseball is going to start playing again. It is important for America to get on about its life.[7]

In order to show that "they can't scare us," Americans were asked to support the "War on Terror" – "if you see something, say something" was the operative slogan – while urged to keep shopping, to expect no nationwide sacrifices such as a military draft, rationing, or higher taxes. The Iraq and Afghanistan wars were/are fought by a "volunteer" armed force whose lower ranks are disproportionately African-American.[8] As for taxes, they were cut for the wealthiest Americans. The government's doublespeak advised: We are at war but you should live as if we are at peace. Even as opposition to the war grew, the government and the people kept spending as if there were no tomorrow. The spending was a way of repressing what was happening. Soon the USA – individually, corporately, and governmentally – spent itself into unmanageable debt. And when the collapse came during the 2008 presidential campaign, the Iraq war took a back seat to the economy. But actually the wrecked economy was the outcome of the contradictions inherent in the way the War on Terror was fought – a war ostensibly waged in response to the 9/11 attacks. Thus, the terrorists accomplished their long-term objective of bringing down, or at least severely disrupting, the USA and its allied globalized economic system. Even today, as I revise this writing in November 2013 – more than twelve years after 9/11 – the US and world economy is limping rather than striding. In this regard, "The World Trade Center" is an apt name for the bombers' target. The World Trade Center means more than a cluster of buildings – it is a system of interconnected global trade with the USA at its center. Destroying the towers unfolded consequences far outreaching the spectacular initial explosions and collapses.[9]

To return to the question of art: Stockhausen aside, how can anyone call the 9/11 attack on the Twin Towers a work of art? Of what value is such a designation? Is it similar to calling the Roman gladiatorial games "sport"? Where death is dealt can art and games exist? More to the point: What does calling the destruction of the Twin Towers a work of art tell us about (performance) art, the authenticity of "what really happened," and social morality during and after the first decade of the twenty-first century? To even begin to address these questions, I need to refer to the history of the avant-garde – because it has been avant-garde artists who for more than a century have called for the violent destruction of existing aesthetic, social, and political systems.

Of French origin, "avant-garde" – cognate to "vanguard" and "van" – has been used in English since the end of the fifteenth century. The *OED* states that the avant-garde is "the foremost part of an army" (but also refers to being "ahead" or "first" in any number of circumstances). In the nineteenth century, the term was taken up by social activists, utopians, and artists to signify those ahead of the rest of society.[10] Mike Sell shows links connecting Osama bin Laden, Islamicist-jihadist thought, the 9/11 attacks, and the avant-garde. Sell notes that bin Laden called the 9/11 attackers "a blessed group of enlightened Muslims, the taliah of Islam":

> The term *taliah* [vanguard] is the tell-tale of a relationship between Islam and the avant-garde that is long-lived, complex, and virtually unremarked by critics and historians. [...] Indeed, if 9/11 means anything to the field of vanguard studies, it is exactly how far the history of the avant-garde is from being settled – and how unsettling that history can be.
>
> (2011: 18)

Among artists, the avant-garde was made flesh by manifestos: performatives calling for, even promising, violent actions. Here are a few selections from early in the twentieth century to just before 9/11:

We want to exalt movements of aggression, feverish sleeplessness, the double march, the perilous leap, the slap and the blow with the fist. [...] Beauty exists only in struggle. There is no masterpiece that has not an aggressive character. Poetry must be a violent assault on the forces of the unknown, to force them to bow before man. [...] We want to demolish museums and libraries, fight morality, feminism and all opportunist and utilitarian cowardice. [...] Let the good incendiaries with charred fingers come! Here they are! Heap up the fire to the shelves of the libraries! Divert the canals to flood the cellars of the museums! Let the glorious canvases swim ashore! Take the picks and hammers! Undermine the foundation of venerable towns! [...] For art can only be violence, cruelty, injustice.

(From F. T. Marinetti's "Futurist Manifesto," 1909)

I assure you: there is no beginning, and we are not afraid; we aren't sentimental. We are like a raging wind that rips up the clothes of clouds and prayers, we are preparing the great spectacle of disaster, conflagration, and decomposition. Preparing to put an end to mourning, and to replace tears by sirens spreading from one continent to another. [...] I destroy the drawers of the brain, and those of social organization: to sow demoralization everywhere, and throw heaven's hand into hell, hell's eyes into heaven, to reinstate the fertile wheel of a universal circus in the Powers of reality, and the fantasy of every individual.

(From Tristan Tzara's "Dada Manifesto," 1918)

True art, which is not content to play variations on ready-made models but rather insists on expressing the inner needs of man and mankind in its time – true art is unable not to be revolutionary, not to aspire to a complete and radical reconstruction of society. [...] We believe that the supreme task of art in our epoch is to take part actively and consciously in the preparation of the revolution.

(From Leon Trotsky and André Breton's "Manifesto: Toward a Free Revolutionary Art," 1938)

The religion of Christ has dominated the world. See what it has turned into: sister faiths have now begun to exploit each other. [...] Christian civilization is coming to an end. [...] The decline of Christianity will bring down with it all the people and all the classes that it has influenced, from the first to the last, from the highest to the lowest. [...] The rats are already fleeing a sinking Europe by crossing the Atlantic. However, events will eventually overtake the greedy, the gluttonous, the sybarites, the unperturbed, the blind and the deaf. They will be mercilessly swallowed up. [...] We must abandon the ways of society once and for all and free ourselves from its utilitarian spirit. We must not willingly neglect our spiritual side. [...] We accept full responsibility for the consequences of our total refusal.

(From the Québécois Artists Global Refusal, 1948)

The existing framework cannot subdue the new human force that is increasing day by day alongside the irresistible development of technology and the dissatisfaction of its possible uses in our senseless social life. [...] Alienation and oppression in this society cannot be distributed amongst a range of variants, but only rejected en bloc with this very society. All real progress has clearly been suspended until the revolutionary solution of the present multiform crisis.

(From the Situationists' Manifesto, 1960)

Dada: we eat your letters, and regurgitate our own. Dolts, Dunces, Dullards and Dumbells becoming Morons, Misfits and Multi-Media-Makers. Your Ds were deeds done in days of darkness, doom and dada de(con)struction. Our Ms are moments of MADness, a Mutually-Assured (and madder) destruction. [... O]ur Media is created at the speed of light. Where the Futurists perceived that speed, we calculate our own acceleration, and we record the measurements in virtual repositories that the unseen themselves will never see.

Now, the audience expects the spectacle:
it is not for us to put on a show,
but to show the audience that they are the spectacle.

They, we, are the spectacle: the Towers belching balls of fire and smoke; people leaping to their deaths; cameras clicking and rolling.

(From the dada2mada manifesto, 2000)

Theorizing the rhetoric of these types of manifestos, Loren Shumway wrote:

The specific form that this terror takes in the manifestoes of the avant-garde is what I choose to call "stylistic terrorism." [...] The notion of stylistic terrorism should inform our understanding of the fundamental topos of the avant-garde manifesto – the topos of the absolute necessity of a given form of cultural production as the only possible form for culture to take in the present period for such-and such reasons, and the absolutely negative character of all other forms of cultural production in the same period.

(1980: 57–58)

A Manichean world, irreconcilably split. Where there is no middle ground, there are no compromises; where there are no compromises, there is no dialogue. Only a violence as absolute as the value systems it springs from can accurately express this kind of religious-cultural war.

The attacks of 9/11 did not stop artists from issuing manifestos using the rhetoric-poetic of war:

> Art Guerrilla is an art project which is open to all the artists around the world who are ready for a guerrilla war in a multi-dimensional manner. This war has got a unique aim: recreate the soul of arts. We know that this aim is indefinite; however, if we live in an indefinite age, if our enemies use indefinite weapons against us, it is also our right to move in an indefinite and uncertain sea. [...] Are you a cynical member of the academy? Do people criticize your works in a weird way? Do you live in the periphery of the world (Asia, Balkans, Middle East, Africa, South America); or do you live in the peripheries of the center (wherever)? Are you poor economically, and, rich in imagination? Do think or imagine a kind of liberation for contemporary society? Have you got any problems with the authorities? [...] long live art guerrilla movement! long live artist-warriors of the movement! we will WIN!
>
> (From the Art Guerrilla Manifesto, 2006)

And, finally, back up sixty-eight years from 2001 to Antonin Artaud, whose importance to avant-garde theatre is canonical and who might also be writing a scenario for Al-Qaeda:

> The Theatre of Cruelty proposes to resort to a mass spectacle; to seek in the agitation of tremendous masses, convulsed and hurled against each other, a little of that poetry of festivals and crowds when, all too rarely nowadays, the people pour out into the streets. The theatre must give us everything that is in crime, love, war, or madness, if it wants to recover its necessity [...]. In the same way that our dreams have an effect upon us and reality has an effect upon our dreams, so we believe that the images of thought can be identified with a dream which will be efficacious to the degree that it can be projected with the necessary violence. [...] Hence this appeal to cruelty and terror [...] on a vast scale.
>
> (From "The Theatre and Cruelty," 1933)

Granted that Artaud stipulated that "the image of a crime presented in the requisite theatrical condition is something infinitely more terrible for the spirit than that same crime when actually committed." But, in our day, the walls between the "real" and the "virtual" have crumbled, the "theatrical" and the "actual" have merged. What 9/11 offered was an intentionally created spectacle of cruelty in the Artaudian sense, "terror on a vast scale."

Taken together, the message coming from many key avant-garde artists and theorists insistently repeated for more than a century, is clear. Destroy the current order. Create a new order, or anarchy. Are these manifestos mere ineffectual fantasies of powerless artists? Or do they set a tone that carries over from avant-garde art into popular entertainments? The pyrotechnics of rock concerts, the celebratory explosion/burning of The Man at the climax of the annual Burning Man Festival on the Black Rock Desert, Nevada, is both a sublimation of and a repetition of 9/11 (see Figs. 4.1 and 4.2). Indeed, so-called "high art" and pop have merged just as "news" has melded into entertainment. Additionally, at least since Chris Burden had a friend shoot him in the arm (*Shoot*, 1971), many performance artists have wounded themselves, opened their veins as art, suspended themselves from hooks, slaughtered animals, and in manifold ways used real violence.[11] Rituals – art's close relation – include flagellation, scarring, circumcision, subincision, and so on. Popular culture is full of tattoos, piercings, and cosmetic surgeries, which, whatever their psychological and sociological meanings, enact the desire to be beautiful or to witness the body's ability to tolerate or even enjoy pain. Aestheticizing and

Figure 4.1 The front page of the *Daily Telegraph* (London) on September 12, 2001, showing the ball of flame just after the second plane impacts the South Tower, on the left, of the World Trade Center (Twin Towers) at 9:03 a.m. The black smoke is coming from the upper floors of the North Tower, on the right, which was hit at 8:46 a.m. © Telegraph Media Group Limited 2001/Getty Images.

Figure 4.2 The Man burns on the night before the final day and night at the Burning Man Festival, August, 2013 (photo: Richard Schechner).

ritualizing violence, not as representations (as in the visual arts, theatre, or other media), but as actual acts performed in the here and now is widespread. But, you might argue, the manifestos, performance art, and violent practices of popular culture are largely a part of Western civilization, a system that Osama bin Laden explicitly despised, stood apart from, and wished to destroy. Ritual bloodletting, scarring, and cutting are another matter – these are important parts of many cultures' practices and spiritual quests, Western and non-Western.

But how separate was bin Laden from Western culture? Al-Qaeda and other jihadists are not averse to using those aspects of Western culture they find helpful. Bin Laden and his allies take advantage of the media and advanced technology from the internet to hijacked jets. The jihadists' technological sophistication debunks the ruling myth that they are primitive cave-dwellers living in "tribal areas." In fact, when bin Laden was found and murdered by US Navy SEALS in 2011, he and his entourage were living in a well-constructed, well-equipped compound in Abbottabad, northeastern Pakistan.[12] But wherever bin Laden and his allies were, or are, no location is outside the global net, not even the mountains of Pakistan and Afghanistan, and no tribe or group of people is absolutely other. Paradoxically, the West and the jihadists occupy very separate spheres from the point of view of values while sharing the same global system from the point of view of techniques. Osama bin Laden issued his fatwas over the internet, released videotapes of his speeches, and exploited global financial instruments to pay for Al-Qaeda's operations. The hijacked planes that destroyed the Twin Towers and slammed into the Pentagon were sophisticated aircrafts that the jihadists knew how to fly. In the media, where any mention is better than being ignored, jihadists and the warriors against terror jostle with each other for imagination-space on the global stage.

Almost as they were occurring, the 9/11 attacks were marketed as popular entertainment. Representations of the attacks are paradigmatic of the accelerating conflation of "news" and "entertainment," and not only in the USA. In Yueqing, a newly industrialized city southwest of Shanghai, videos showing the attacks were for sale by September 14. In larger cities, these videos probably were on the market even sooner. As Peter Hessler reported from China:

> They stocked them on the same racks as the Hollywood movies. Often the 9/11 videos were located in the cheaper sections, alongside dozens of American films. [...] All of the 9/11 videos had been packaged to look like Hollywood movies. I found a DVD entitled "The Century's Greatest Catastrophe"; the box front featured photographs of Osama bin Laden, George W. Bush, and the burning Twin Towers. On the back, a small icon noted that it had been rated R, for violence and language.
>
> (2007: 311–312)

In the USA, news programs are sponsored. That is, the news is given in small units of time, usually less than five or six minutes. After two or three items, there is a commercial. Commercials take between 25 and 33 percent of broadcast time. This format of program content alternating with advertising is the same for news, sports, drama, and various "contestant" shows (quiz shows, *American Idol*, etc.), including reality TV. A few programs – promoting a particular product – are all advertising. In the USA, the only exception to this intense marketization are the public networks, such as PBS and C-SPAN. These networks supply only a small fraction of what is broadcast. The commercials address and/or arouse the needs of the viewers. The commercials often include endorsements or testimonies from apparently ordinary people. In this, the commercials are a form of "reality TV," the appearance of apparently actual ordinary people in the midst of either their ordinary lives or, more frequently, in some real or cooked-up crisis situation. On regular reality TV, how the people deal with the crisis is the content of the show; on commercials, the product is the *deus ex machina* that saves the day or makes life easier, more profitable, or more pleasurable. All in all, the boundary between the real (including news) and the made-for-entertainment (including internet sites such as YouTube) further blurs the boundaries between the real and the fictional.

Following this tendency to conflate actuality with invention, the TV presentations of the 9/11 attacks soon took on the qualities of a made-for-TV drama series. Within hours after the planes struck the Twin Towers, the networks gave dramatic titles to their coverage. CBS: "Attack on America"; ABC: "America Under Attack"; CNN: "America's New War." A drumbeat began that led up to and into the bombing and invasion of Iraq in 2003. There was also much pathos. On September 14, NBC aired "America Mourns," heartbreaking stories mixed with calls for dedicated patriotism. On the first anniversary of the attack, the networks aired such programs as *The Day That Changed America* (CBS), *Report from Ground Zero* (ABC), and *9/11, The Day America Changed* (Fox). The 9/11 attack segued into the American-led war against Iraq, with its own titles on TV. It all went under the overall official rubric of the War on Terror.

The program titles, the style of presenting the news, the sequencing of advertising and news items, showed how television, more than the other media, marketed 9/11 and the (second) Iraq War as a made-for-television series. This series included many subplots. Reporters were "embedded" with the troops on the ground. There were daily suicide bombings and attacks of what the government and media called "insurgents." Civilians were slaughtered in these bombings and also by the Allied military. Individual stories of death and wounds, pain and pathos, were aired side by side with reports of the growing opposition to the war as well as ritualized official reports of "we're winning." The high point (or maybe the low point) of this competition for attention in the entertainment version of reality was President Bush's May 1, 2003, arrival by jet fighter onto the deck of the aircraft carrier USS *Abraham Lincoln*, where a giant banner proclaimed "Mission Accomplished." Here melodrama gave way to farce. Bush was gussied up in a flight suit though he was a passenger not the pilot. Who descended to the carrier's flight deck? Bush or a Tom Cruise impersonator? Bush's show is not the only one of its kind. These conflations of news, staged media events, and actuality do not make the 9/11 attack and the Iraq War "art," but they come very close to the melodramatic form of the serial. For performance theorists and historians, the collapse of aesthetic categories was already familiar from Marcel Duchamp and Andy Warhol. The ordinary urinal dubbed *Fountain*, the famous movie star (Marilyn Monroe), the common supermarket item (Campbell soup cans), and high art are not easily if at all distinguishable. At the far ends of the spectrum – urinal, movie star, and supermarket item at one end and the masterpieces that hang in the august galleries of the Metropolitan Museum of Art at the other – distinctions are still clear. But today most of the art world and the real world live in between these extremes. The reporting-fictionalizing of 9/11, including the broadcasting and rebroadcasting of iconic images of the explosions, fires, destruction, aftermath, and war, constitute an absorption of events not only into the popular imagination but also as *objets d'art*.[13]

On 9/11 there were four planes heading for their targets. Two torpedoed the Twin Towers of the World Trade Center, one damaged the Pentagon, and the fourth plane – probably headed for the White House or the Capitol – had its mission foiled by the resistance of the passengers and crashed in the woods of

Pennsylvania. Given four planes and three targets, why almost immediately did "9/11" mean the destruction of the World Trade Center towers? New York is a real place, but it is also Batman's Gotham and Superman's Metropolis. It is, to many Americans, simply, "The City," quintessentially American and foreign simultaneously. Weirdly, I wonder if the jihadists knew Frank Sinatra's "New York, New York":

> Start spreading the news, I'm leaving today
> I want to be a part of it – New York, New York [...]
> If I can make it there, I'll make it anywhere.

And why did the first attack occur at 8:46 A.M. Eastern time and the second at 9:03? If the planes had crashed into the Towers three hours later, many more people would have died. If the two planes hit simultaneously or nearly so, the media would not see an actual collision, but only the aftermath. I believe the jihadists timed their hijackings as a one-two punch for maximum spectacular effect synchronized to the morning news cycle in New York and midday in Europe. Their intention was not to kill as many people as possible but to reach as large a spectatorship in the West as possible. The World Trade Center was the epicenter not only of the attacks but of the imaginary that is "9/11." And what kind of imaginary is that?

When, on September 16, Karlheinz Stockhausen called the destruction of the World Trade Towers "[t]he greatest work of art imaginable for the whole cosmos," his remark was greeted by rage and disgust. Also commenting on 9/11 was the 1997 Nobel Laureate for Literature, Dario Fo, who circulated an email stating, "The economy that every year kills tens of millions of people by reducing them to poverty: faced with that, what are 20,000 [sic] deaths in New York? [...] Only one thing is certain: regardless of who perpetrated the massacre, this kind of violence is born from a culture of violence, hunger, and inhuman exploitation" (Fo, et al. 2001). Stockhausen's remarks were met with outrage, while Fo's hardly caused a ripple. Why? Because Fo left art out. His remarks were boilerplate leftist rhetoric – chickens coming home to roost. People were upset at Stockhausen because he claimed for art an importance equal to that of politics. Stockhausen saw 9/11 as "lifelike art," art as action, not representation. Theorized by Allan Kaprow in 1983, "Artlike art holds that art is separate from life and everything else, while lifelike art holds that art is connected to life and everything else" (2003: 201). Kaprow's lifelike art is sustaining, constructive, and meditative. 9/11, if it is art at all, operates destructively, on the dark side, yielding what Kant, writing in the late eighteenth century, deemed an "outrage on the imagination," a "negative pleasure."

Kant distinguishes the response to the sublime from the response to beauty:

> For the beautiful is directly attended with a feeling of the furtherance of life, and is thus compatible with charms and a playful imagination. On the

other hand, the feeling of the sublime is a pleasure that only arises indirectly, being brought about by the feeling of a momentary check to the vital forces followed at once by a discharge all the more powerful, and so it is an emotion that seems to be no sport, but dead earnest in the affairs of the imagination. Hence charms are repugnant to it; and, since the mind is not simply attracted by the object, but is also alternately repelled thereby, the delight in the sublime does not so much involve positive pleasure as admiration or respect, i.e. merits the name of a negative pleasure. [...] An outrage on the imagination, and yet it is judged all the more sublime on that account.

(1999: 202)

"Negative pleasure" and "an outrage on the imagination" was precisely the reaction of many who witnessed in real time or in replay the 9/11 attack on the WTC. But we must go further into this and give an opinion on its relation to art as we have known it, and avant-garde art especially.

Kant discusses the sublime mostly in relation to natural occurrences which in "its chaos, or in its wildest and most irregular disorder and desolation provided it gives signs of magnitude and power [...] chiefly excites the ideas of the sublime" (1999: 203). But Kant is not satisfied. He notes that if something is

great [...] without qualification, absolutely, and in every respect (beyond all comparison) great, that is to say, sublime, we soon perceive that for this it is not permissible to seek an appropriate standard outside itself, but merely in itself. It is a greatness comparable to itself alone. Hence it comes that the sublime is not to be looked for in things of nature, but only in our own ideas.

(1999: 207)

In other words, insofar as the 9/11 attacks were a successful assault on the imagination, and they were (I believe), it was sublime.

But isn't it obscene to consider such an event sublime? Can the horrible even as it is unfolding be experienced as art? In 1757, Edmund Burke tackled this question in his treatise *On the Sublime and the Beautiful*. I will not discuss this work in detail but will quote only one of Burke's salient, if disturbing, observations:

Choose a day on which to represent the most sublime and affecting tragedy we have; appoint the most favourite actors; spare no cost upon the scenes and decorations, unite the greatest efforts of poetry, painting, and music; and when you have collected your audience, just at the moment when their minds are erect with expectation, let it be reported that a state criminal of high rank is on the point of being executed in the adjoining square; in a moment the emptiness of the theatre would demonstrate the comparative weakness of the imitative arts, and proclaim the triumph of the real sympathy. I believe that this notion of our having a simple pain in the reality, yet a delight in the representation, arises from hence, that we do not sufficiently distinguish what we would by no means choose to do, from what we should be eager enough to see if it was once done. The delight in seeing things, which, so far from doing, our heartiest wishes would be to see redressed.

(1909–1914)

In this vein, Vernon Hyde Minor discusses 9/11, Burke, Kant, and the sublime:

In the realm of the sublime, life and art collapse into one another; fear and danger – so long as our impulse to self-preservation isn't threatened – feed the soul. The sublime causes astonishment, a state in which everything in one's horror-filled mind remains in suspension. The sublime is not formed by reason, although it may anticipate or produce reason. [...] One of the less recognized aspects of the aesthetics of the sublime [...] is the acknowl-edgement that we are drawn to disasters not because of some perverse pleasure in others' pain, but because we cannot be of a caring disposition unless we find something agreeable in astonishment, something satisfying about the horrible. Or to put it differently, we are quite naturally aesthe-tized – rather than anesthetized – by horrific events of great historic sig-nificance. Then there is that paradoxical and bewildering experience of the sublime that Kant wrote about. The vast, powerful, terrifying forces unleashed by ill-used human technology overwhelms our cognitive faculties, revealing to us in gut-wrenching terms our inability to grasp, comprehend, or – and this is particularly challenging for an artist – to accomplish anything of such magnitude.

(2001: 91–96)

"Aesthetized – rather than anesthetized – by horrific events of great historic significance" is a deep insight of the process (many) people undergo in assim-ilating otherwise hard-to-swallow events. Aesthetization is not the only response to these kind of horrific-yet-fascinating-and-"attractive" events, but it is one strategy. Making art about them – in protest, awe, and sometimes support – is another response. And, of course, political and military action is still another. Far from wanting to eliminate one response in favor of another, I prefer to hold them all in consciousness with regard to the 9/11 attack on the World Trade Center.

But even if the 9/11 attack is art, is it "good" or "bad" from an ethical-moral-political point of view? Most of what we today call "art" carries an ideological or religious message. In the West, before the Renaissance and the advent of capitalism, there was no category of art as such. Notions of "art for art's sake" were not theorized in the West until the seventeenth and eighteenth centuries. At present, most art remains bound to forces outside itself and is not independent or disinterested. Most art is "good" or "bad" in an ethical-moral-political way in terms of values operating beyond or despite the "work itself." To cite two well-known examples of "great bad/evil art" according to today's value system: D. W. Griffith's *The Birth of a Nation* and Leni Riefenstahl's *Triumph of the Will*.[14] What is both obvious and troubling is that determining what's good and what's bad is dependent on the beliefs of whomever is making the judgment. In other words, there may be some agreement "universally" about what is art and what is not art, what is sublime and what is not sublime. But there is no universal agreement, nor can I foresee a time when there will be such an agreement, about what is ethically-morally-politically good or bad. As already noted, Osama bin Laden and those in sympathy with Al-Qaeda and the jihadist program celebrated when informed of the 9/11 attack.

According to American standards, the 9/11 attack was evil. Thus, it is understandable why Stockhausen's remarks were met with outrage. But why did Fo's even more harsh opinion regarding the USA and the victims of 9/11 hardly caused a ripple? Because Fo was not talking about art. He situated 9/11 within the sphere of politics, ideology, and war. Stockhausen placed 9/11 within the art world. And art is not as serious as politics: art is play; art is secondary, a representation. However, from the perspective of performance studies, the attack on the WTC was a "performance": planned, rehearsed, staged, and intended both to wound the USA materially and to affect and infect the imagination. The destruction of two iconic buildings, and the murder of so many people in one fell swoop, was intended to deliver a very specific message about the boldness of the jihad and the vulnerability of the USA.

A performance, surely, but art? I believe that the attack can be understood as the actualization of key ideas and impulses driving the avant-garde. Thierry de Duve writes:

> It is as if the history of the avant-gardes were a dialectical history cast off by the contradictions of art and non-art, the history of a prohibition and of its transgression. A slogan could sum it up: it is forbidden to do whatever, let's do it. [...] This is a duty and not a right. [...] What could anyone do once it is mandatory that everything be permitted or, as the rebelling students said in May '68, once it is forbidden to forbid?
> (1996: 332–333, 340)

Seen this way, the 9/11 attack was in direct succession to futurist, anarchist, and other avant-garde manifestos and actions; destructive as with the Vienna Aktionists; massive and spectacular as with Christo and Jeanne-Claude's drapings of buildings and the landscapes.[15] To those opposing Al-Qaeda, 9/11 was "bad art" in the ethical and moral sense. It was "illegal art" from the point of view of international law because it targeted civilians. But it was avant-garde art from the point of view of the tradition I am discussing. Is this kind of analysis perverse, not only doing dishonor to the dead and injured but also soiling what art is or ought to be? Does such a designation grant the jihadists much more than they deserve? And does it help us understand better the world we are living in?

Stockhausen was actually envious of the jihadists. "I couldn't do that. By comparison, we composers are nothing." He desired the most extreme place for art. "Artists, too, sometimes try to go beyond the limits of what is feasible and conceivable, so that we wake up, so that we open ourselves to another world." He was claiming an importance for art in the "real world." Not the artlike art that hangs in museums or is heard in concert halls and theatres, but Kaprow's lifelike art. Duve wrote before 9/11, while Frank Lentricchia and Jody McAuliffe wrote after, locating Stockhausen's opinion among a long tradition of artistic fanatics:

> The desire beneath many romantic literary visions is for a terrifying awakening that would undo the West's economic and cultural order [...] As any avant-garde artist might, Stockhausen sees the devotion of high artistic seriousness [...] in the complete commitment of the terrorists [...] Like terrorists, serious artists are always fanatics; unlike terrorists, serious artists have not yet achieved the "greatest" level of art.
>
> (2003: 100)

A single attack has changed world history. What (other) art act has done that? Having just written this, I confess that I am very uncomfortable. I have reasoned my way into a position that I ethically reject.

One way out is to assert that art requires artists who consciously choose to make art and spectators who willingly observe art. This is the modern humanist tradition – a local idea culturally speaking, bounded by both historical period and geography. There are rituals where participation is not voluntary; these rituals include dances, visual images, objects, and theatrical role-playing that can be studied "as art." The category "art" is not universal. Many objects and performances in Europe that today exist under the aegis of art – are displayed in art museums (themselves a relatively recent phenomenon) – were not conceived of nor made as art. Take, for example, the great cathedrals of the Middle Ages, including their architecture, stained-glass windows, altarpieces, chalices and plates, and so on. Surely today these are "priceless works of art." But this estimation is retrospective. The buttresses, vaults, spires, windows, sculptings, paintings, and objects were made for many reasons including use in worship, adherence to church hierarchy, honor to God, Jesus, saints, priests, and patrons. Or the funerary architecture and objects of ancient Egypt, from the pyramids to the treasures of the Valley of the Kings. These, and the many more examples across a wide range of cultures and times that can be given, were not "art" as modernists understand the term. Art in the modern sense can only exist where objects and processes can be marked off, framed actually or conceptually, marking objects and processes so that they can be assigned a money value (including that apotheosis of money, "priceless"). This money value does not necessarily replace whatever other functions these objects and processes may have. In brief, art in the modern sense arises alongside the individualism of the Renaissance and the commodity value system of capitalism. But this kind of art is not even today the only kind. Similar to pre-Renaissance churches, etc., there are ritual performances, objects, and architectures in all of the world's cultures which are extremely powerful in terms of performance, narrative, structure, color, rhythm, costume, and so on, that require and enforce participation and witnessing – but which are not "art" in the modern sense. From this point of view, 9/11 may be art in a nonmodern sense.

As for art being the product of artists freely choosing to make art, many things we today consider as art are not the products of free will. Or are artists only the planners and overlords and not the workers or victims? For example, the pyramids of Egypt and Mexico are generally regarded as architectural masterpieces. The Egyptian pyramids were constructed by slaves, and the Mexican pyramids were sites of human sacrifice. Time washes away the sweat of slaves and the blood of victims, leaving the magnificent (if silent) stones intact, receptive to our astonished, admiring gazing. 9/11 is too recent, too drenched in blood and destruction, too much a part of unfinished historical business. We reject the possibility that 9/11 may be art because so many of our own people were killed and wounded, and because our national and cultural psyche was violated. From our humanist perspective, the attack was ethically horrific: "innocent people" died. In quotation marks because, to the jihadists, those who died were not innocent. Their very presence on the planes and in the Twin Towers marked them as participating in hated Western culture. To this way of thinking, there are no "neutrals," no bystanders.

Still, neither Mohammed Atta nor the other hijackers thought of themselves as artists. They would absolutely reject the label "art" in relation to their actions. And most of those who write about 9/11 do not place it in the domain of art. If there is art in 9/11, it is in the reception and aftermath: what Stockhausen imagined when he saw the media representations of the attack. In the unfolding event, visual artists, performance artists, writers, artists of any kind can "do" just about anything with what happened. There is nothing new in that: Goya and Picasso – not to mention Homer, Aeschylus, Vyasa, Shakespeare, Tolstoy, Hemingway, and many more – have made masterpieces from the horrors of war. But all these works are reflective. They came after raw, unmediated events. 9/11 is different because 9/11 was mediated from the outset, and intended to be so – the intention of its authors was not to conquer or occupy territory, or slaughter an army or even as many civilians as possible. 9/11 was a stunning media event, a photo op, and a real-life show. As such, it exists in both the propagandistic and aesthetic realms – and existed as such while it was happening. This nowness is fundamental. It does not cancel out representations after the fact: the documentaries, dramas, films, writings, first-hand accounts, and memorials that came later, on September 12 and after. But all of these were supplemental to the attack itself, which was already mediatized as it happened. It is this primary event that paradoxically is "9/11 itself" and "9/11 the media event."

What was liminal were the hundreds if not thousands of impromptu "Have You Seen?" notices and photographs posted around and sometimes far from Ground Zero or put out on the internet. These were not accounts of what happened; nor were they ongoingly part of the attack. They were "collateral theatre" (parallel to collateral damage in a military operation). Even while the Twin Towers were burning, loved ones sought information about missing people. The media picked up on these notices, which, individually, were simply pieces of paper but collectively were walls of anxiety and grief. Each notice carried its own hope against hopelessness. No one knows exactly how many people found each other through this means. Soon enough, the notices were joined by flowers, a sure sign of condolence. If the 9/11 fireballs and astonishing tidal wave of dust and debris as first the towers collapsed were terrifying, gigantic, and sublime, the walls of notices seeking the missing were pitiful individual atoms of human yearning. These notices collectively were part of the spectacle even as they provided a human-scale entry into experiencing what was happening. People who didn't know anyone in the World Trade Center gazed at the notices as a way of empathizing with those who had lost someone. The walls of "Have You Seen?" tied the enormity of the collective catastrophe to thousands of smaller expressions of individual need.

Lentricchia and McAuliffe do not stop by situating the 9/11 attacks within a tradition of transgressive art. They go on to discuss 9/11 in relation to popular culture – how soon after 9/11 the New York site of the attack became "Groundzeroland," a "Mecca" (how's that for irony) for tourists, and a site for nationalist myth-making in the Wagnerian tradition:

> On December 30, 2001, Mayor [Rudolf] Giuliani opened a viewing platform for the folk over the mystic gulf that is Ground Zero, a stage to which he urged Americans, and everybody, to come and experience "all kinds of feelings of sorrow and then tremendous feelings of patriotism." [...] The platform's purpose is to connect tourists to their history at a site that perfectly conjoins terrorism, patriotism, and tourism.
>
> (Lentricchia and McAuliffe 2003: 103)

By now the platform is gone, replaced by the National September 11 Memorial and Museum whose mission is to:

> Remember and honor the thousands of innocent men, women, and children murdered by terrorists in the horrific attacks of February 26, 1993 and September 11, 2001.

Respect this place made sacred through tragic loss.

Recognize the endurance of those who survived, the courage of those who risked their lives to save others, and the compassion of all who supported us in our darkest hours.

May the lives remembered, the deeds recognized, and the spirit reawakened be eternal beacons, which reaffirm respect for life, strengthen our resolve to preserve freedom, and inspire an end to hatred, ignorance and intolerance.

(http://www.911memorial.org/mission-statements-0)

Of course, visitors to the site or the web page can also buy tickets or donate. The Twin Towers have been replaced by the 1,776-foot Freedom Tower, the tallest building in the Western Hemisphere.

I wish I had a neat conclusion to my ruminations. I don't. I cannot settle in my own mind the question of whether 9/11 in itself is art or can be more fully understood under the rubric of art. From the morning of 9/11 onward, I've been troubled by this question. The terrace of my apartment has a clear view of lower Manhattan. That morning, I was watching television when I heard shouts from workmen constructing an NYU building on La Guardia Place. I went onto my terrace, looked south, and about one mile away I saw the blazing north tower. I thought it was a horrible accident but wondered how such an accident could happen on a day when the sky was blue and clear. Moments later, I saw a plane flying low make a sharp turn from west to south. "Oh, my!" I said or thought. Something banal and full of shock. Then I saw the plane slice into the south tower as smoothly as a hot knife into butter. Not a sound. A silent movie in full color. A great ball of orange flame and black smoke. It was terrifying; it was sublime; it was horrible; it was beautiful. After that, except for about forty-five minutes when my wife and I fetched our daughter from school, I stood on my terrace with some neighbors who had come over because they knew of the view. We watched as the towers came down. What did I do? I offered people something to drink and eat, told them where the bathroom was. From the terrace we watched and talked, amazed, horrified, excited, scared, fascinated. We used binoculars. We saw some people flinging themselves from the towers. I wish I could report that I had only the "correct" reactions – I wish I could write that it so horrified me that I turned away daring not to look or that I was overcome with Aristotle's pity and fear. But it was a lot more complicated than that. I had seen high-wire acts in circuses. I had watched a lot of violence on television. What was happening was all in silence. I couldn't stop what was happening. I was not personally responsible for it. So in my own way I witnessed it in more of a spectatorial than a "this terrible thing is happening to me" kind of way. I cannot speak for my neighbors – professors and good people all – except to note that our conversation indicated that their response at this point in the unfolding story was akin to mine. People walked back and forth between the terrace and the television room. There was sympathy and anxiety, but nothing approaching a full-blown "pity and fear" tragic catharsis. That reaction, for me, came later, when I recollected the events and played them over in the theatre of my mind's eye. When new people arrived, they brought rumors and information. We took in what passed for analysis by media pundits. But, most importantly, everyone was very aware that from the terrace looking south we were watching the thing itself. What we saw heard on TV were explanations and rationalizations both describing and shaping reactions, reporting events and instructing how "we" the receivers were to react. The coverage and talking heads gave us both a wider horizon with which to comprehend what we were witnessing and closeups of events at and near Ground Zero. As I watched both in person and on television, I knew that whatever else it was, I was experiencing a spectacle, a "live movie," "real history happening," etc. Being the academic that I am, I referenced Debord's "society of the spectacle" (1967). And I knew that the jihadists intended it to be thus. 9/11 was no stealth attack, noticed only by its devastating effects, like anthrax through the mail or poison in the water. It was a "show" and a "showing." And I, and my neighbors, were among its designated intended spectators – as were supporters of the jihad. Globally speaking, we were a divided audience.

I am exploring these possibilities not to validate terrorist actions or to insult the memory of the dead and wounded but to point out that terrorism, at the scale of 9/11, works like art more on states of mind and feeling than on physical destruction. Or, if you will, the destruction is the means toward the end of creating terror, which is a state of mind.

9/11 is an example of what Burke and Kant called the sublime, arousing in spectators the Aristotelian tragic emotions of pity and fear. Or at least from the Western side. Al-Qaeda and its adherents saw in the attack the very wrath of God. Looked at in these ways – as event, shock, avant-garde art, tragedy, and/or vengeance – 9/11 performs Artaud's uncanny assertion from his 1938 essay "No More Masterpieces": "We are not free. And the sky can still fall on our heads. And the theatre has been created to teach us that first of all."

Notes

1 According to How Stuff Works, "[i]n 1967, the Federal Communications Commission met with AT&T to establish [...] an emergency number [...] that was short and easy to remember. More importantly, they needed a unique number, and since 911 had never been designated for an office code, area code or service code, that was the number they chose. Soon after, the U.S. Congress [...] passed legislation making 911 the exclusive number for any emergency calling service." See http://people.how stuffworks.com/question664.htm (accessed June 12, 2014).

2 See http://news.bbc.co.uk/2/hi/south_asia/1585636.stm (accessed June 12, 2014). This chapter was written while bin Laden was alive. I generally maintain that perspective discussing his activities, even as I have revised some passages in light of what's happened since he was killed in Pakistan on May 2, 2011, by US Navy SEALs, his body disposed of at sea.

3 According to the National September 11 Memorial & Museum website: "The 9/11 Memorial is located at the site of the former World Trade Center complex and occupies approximately half of the 16-acre site. The Memorial features two enormous waterfalls and reflecting pools, each about an acre in size, set within the footprints of the original Twin Towers. The Memorial Plaza is one of the most eco-friendly plazas ever constructed. More than 400 trees surround the reflecting pools. Its design conveys a spirit of hope and renewal, and creates a contemplative space separate from the usual sights and sounds of a bustling metropolis. Swamp white oak trees create a rustling canopy of leaves over the plaza. This grove of trees bring green rebirth in the spring, provide cooling shade in the summer and show seasonal color in fall. A small clearing in the grove, known as the Memorial Glade, designates a space for gatherings and special ceremonies." See http://www.911memorial. org/design-overview (accessed June 27, 2014).

4 See Kant's *Critique of Judgment* (1790) and especially therein his "Analytic of the Sublime." See also Edmund Burke, *A Philosophical Enquiry into the Origin of our Ideas of the Sublime and Beautiful* (1757). Burke writes: "The passion caused by the great and sublime in nature [...] is Astonishment; and astonishment is that state of the soul, in which all its motions are suspended, with some degree of horror. In this case the mind is so entirely filled with its object, that it cannot entertain any other."

5 According to the National Defense University's website, "The National Defense University is the premier center for Joint Professional Military Education (JPME) and is under the direction of the Chairman, Joint Chiefs of Staff" (http://www.ndu. edu/About.aspx [accessed June 12, 2014]).

6 From Bang on a Can's mission statement. See http://www.bangonacan.org/abo ut_us (accessed June 12, 2014). The World Financial Center is located in lower Manhattan just to the west of the World Trade Center memorial site. See http:// www.nytimes.com/2008/05/03/nyregion/03composer.html?_r=2&ref=nyregion&oref =slogin& (accessed June 12, 2014).

7 See http://georgewbush-whitehouse.archives.gov/news/releases/2001/09/20010915-4. html (accessed July 7, 2014).

8 According to 2012 US census updates, African Americans make up 13.1 percent of the US population; in the 2000 census, they were 12.9 percent. "In 2002, blacks made up about 22 percent of the enlisted personnel in the armed forces (20 percent of men and 34 percent of women) while blacks made up 13 percent of civilians ages 18–44. In 2002, the black component ranged from 28 percent in the army and 21 percent in the navy to 18 percent in the airforce and 15 percent in the marine corps" (http://www.prb.org/source/acf1396.pdf [accessed June 12, 2014]). Hispanics are about 14 percent of the civilian population, aged between 18 and 44, but only 10 percent of the non-officer military. Both African Americans and Hispanics are underrepresented in the officer ranks in all the military services.

9 On October 21, 2001, Osama bin Laden spoke of the economic consequences: "And if the fall of the twin towers was a huge event, then consider the events that followed it – let us talk about the economic effects which are still continuing. According to their own admission the share of the losses on the Wall Street Market reached 16 percent. [...] a collapse of this scale has never happened before [...] it reaches $640 billion of losses from stocks. [...] The daily income of the American nation is $20 billion. The first week they didn't work at all as a result of the psychological shock of the attack, and even today some still don't work because of it. So if you multiply $20 billion by 1 week, it comes to $140 billion – and the actual amount is even bigger than this. If you add it to the $640 billion, we've reached how much? [...] American studies and analysis have mentioned that 70 per cent of the American people are still suffering from depression and psychological trauma. [...]

These repercussions cannot be calculated by anyone, due to their very large – and increasing – scale, multitude, and complexity, so watch as the amount reaches no less than $1 trillion [...]." (bin Laden 2005: 111–112).

10 According to Thierry du Duve (1996: 430–431), Olinde Rodrigues, a follower of Henri de Saint-Simon, wrote in 1825: "It is we, artists, that will serve as your avant-garde; the power of the arts is indeed the most immediate and the fastest. [...] We address ourselves to the imagination and feelings of people: we are therefore supposed to achieve the most vivid and decisive kind of action."

11 See my "Self-Inflicted Wounds," chapter 6.

12 As narrated by *Time* magazine: "the dead man's next stop was the U.S.S. *Carl Vinson*, an aircraft carrier in the Arabian Sea. There, his body was washed and wrapped in a white sheet, then dropped overboard. There would be no grave for his admirers to venerate. The face that haunted the Western world, the eyes that looked on the blazing towers with pride of authorship, sank sightless beneath the waves." Operation Neptune Spear was thought out, rehearsed, and put into play as if it were a melodrama. Which it was. See http://content.time.com/time/magazine/article/0,9171,2069571,00.html (accessed June 12, 2014).

13 For more on the relationship between terrorism and television, see Dayan (2006) and Brady (2012).

14 Typical evaluations of these films are as follows. *Birth of a Nation*: "The 1915 film introduced many new conventions that would soon come to define American cinema, while it also drew large numbers of middle-class patrons to moviegoing for the first time. Though the film was a landmark aesthetic work, it was also a spectacle of unfettered racism, with a storyline that would inspire both bigotry and distrust" (Stokes 2007); "*Triumph of the Will* [...] is more than first-class propaganda. It is also a work of art. A work of creative imagination, stylistically and formally innovative, its every detail contributes to its central vision and overall effect. The film is also very, very beautiful" (Devereaux 2001: 240).

15 See http://www.christojeanneclaude.net (accessed June 12, 2014).

References

bin Laden, Osama (2005) *Messages to the World: The Statements of Osama Bin Laden*, ed. Bruce Lawrence, trans. James Howarth (London and New York: Verso).

Boal, Ian, T. J. Clark, Joseph Matthews, and Michael Watts (2005) *Afflicted Powers: Capital and Spectacle in a New Age of War* (London and New York: Verso).

Borger, Julian (2006) "Iraq a 'Work of Art in Progress' Says US General after 49 Die," *The Guardian*, available online at http://www.guardian.co.uk/world/2006/nov/03/usa.iraq (accessed June 12, 2014).

Brady, Sara (2012) *Performance, Politics, and the War on Terror: 'Whatever It Takes'* (Basingstoke: Palgrave Macmillan).

Burke, Edmund (1909–1914), *A Philosophical Inquiry into the Origin of Our Ideas of the Sublime and Beautiful with Several Other Additions*, The Harvard Classics, vol. XXIV, Part 2, ed. Charles W. Eliot (New York: P. F. Collier & Son). Available online at www.bartleby.com/24/2 (accessed June 12, 2014). First published 1756–1757.

Dayan, Daniel (2002) "Media, the Intifada and the Aftermath of September 11," *European Judaism*, 35 (1): 70–84.

——(2006) *La Terreur Spectacle* (Paris: DeBoeck University).

Debord, Guy (1990) *The Society of the Spectacle* (London and New York: Verso). First published 1967.

Devereaux, Mary (2001) "Beauty and Evil: The Case of Leni Riefenstahl's *Triumph of the Will*," in Jerrold Levinson (ed.), *Aesthetics and Ethics* (Cambridge: Cambridge University Press), pp. 227–256.

Duve, Thierry de (1996) *Kant after Duchamp* (Cambridge, Mass.: MIT Press).

Hessler, Peter (2007) *Oracle Bones* (New York: HarperCollins).

Kant, Immanuel (1999) "Critique of Judgment" in *Philosophical Writings*, ed. Ernst Behler (New York: Continuum). First published in 1790.

Kaprow, Allan (2003) "The Real Experiment" (1983), in *Essays on the Blurring of Art and Life* (Berkeley, Calif.: University of California Press), pp. 201–218.

Lentricchia, Frank and Jody McAuliffe (2003) *Crimes of Art + Terror* (Chicago, Ill.: University of Chicago Press).

Minor, Vernon Hyde (2001) "What Kind of Tears? 9/11 and the Sublime," *Journal of American Studies of Turkey*, 14: 91–96.

Sell, Mike (2011) *The Avant-Garde: Race Religion War* (Kolkata [Calcutta]: Seagull Books).

Shumway, Loren (1980) "The Intelligibility of the Avant-Garde Manifesto," in *Manifestoes and Movements* (Columbia, SC: University of South Carolina), pp. 54–62.

Stockhausen, Karlheinz (2001) "Documentation of Stockhausen's Comments Re: 9/11," available online at http://www.osborne-conant.org/documentation_stockhausen.htm (accessed June 12, 2014).

Stokes, Melvyn (2007) *D. W. Griffith's The Birth of a Nation: A History of "The Most Controversial Motion Picture of All Time"* (Oxford: Oxford University Press).

Chapter 5

Performed Imaginaries

The Ramlila of Ramnagar and the Maya-Lila Cosmos

A city may be regarded as a container of people, their residences, and the structures – both architectural and conceptual – that satisfy, or attempt to satisfy, the expressed and predictable needs and desires of the population. Traditionally, in India at least, a city has had definite boundaries, both physical and conceptual. One could even theorize that a city becomes dysfunctional, stops being a city, when it is no longer possible to define its material and conceptual boundaries. Such a breakdown can be either infrastructural (roads, buildings, sewer system, electrification, etc.), in terms of services (police, fire, sanitation, schooling, health care, etc.), or – what's most interesting – conceptual: the population and its leaders no longer know, or agree on, or can imagine what the city is.

Humans have a special facility for materializing dreams, desires, projections, imagos (identifying with the collective unconscious), and all kinds of not-yet-real or not-real-now projects. It is an aspect of this ability: the enactment of an imaginary space, an entire city materialized out of the imagination, that is my subject. The city I am referring to is Kashi, and its strangely placed satellite, Ramnagar, facing each other across the Ganga River (Ganges) in Uttar Pradesh, India.[1] The performed imaginary is Ramlila, a thirty-one-day cycle play staged under the tutelage of the maharaja of Banaras during the lunar months of Bhadrapada and Ashvina (September/October).[2] Thousands of Ramlilas are performed annually across the Hindi-speaking region of north India, but Ramnagar's is preeminent both from the religious and the theatrical standpoints. India is suffused with the notion of maya-lila, the playful manifestation of the divine, an ongoing enactment of the convergence of theatre and religion. In Kashi, theatre and religion are mutually supportive and not in opposition to each other as in the Protestant West.

Ramlila tells the story of Vishnu's seventh avatar, Rama (often spoken "Ram" in Hindi and its dialects), his birth, education, marriage, fourteen-year exile to the forest and beyond, and his war against Ravana (often spoken "Ravan") the ten-headed, twenty-armed rakshasa (demon) king of Lanka, who abducts Ram's wife, Sita. The story ends with Ram's coronation and restoration to the throne of Kosala in Ram's capital, Ayodhya. In Ramlila, Ram's story is told by chanting and acting out Tulsidas's *Ramcharitmanas*, a retelling of Valmiki's ancient Sanskrit *Ramayana*.[3] Not only is Tulsidas's text heard in its entirety, it is also "translated" into samvads, dialogues spoken by the characters of the Ramlila. The samvads were assembled and composed in the 1870s–1880s when the Ramnagar Ramlila took the shape that is to a large degree continued today. The samvads were revised in the 1920s. I write "assembled" because the samvads consist of poems and songs combined with new writing to form a drama closely reflecting Tulsidas's *Manas*. The *Manas* is chanted in its entirety during the Ramlila by twelve Hindu brahmin males, the Ramayanis. The samvads are the outcome of a collaboration between Maharaja Ishwari Prasad Narain Singh (ruled 1835–1889) and the Hindu cultural nationalist-playwright-poet-journalist Bharatendu Harishchandra (1850–1885), often called the father of both modern Indian theatre and modern Hindi literature. Harishchandra passionately advocated – and helped shape – Hindi as a national language. His motto "Hindi-Hindu-Hindustan" meant that if India's Hindus spoke Hindi they would inevitably cohere into the nation of Hindustan. The Ramlila samvads were meant to demonstrate that Ram – the ideal warrior king of an imagined unified powerful India – was a devout Hindu who spoke the national language. Ram spoke Hindi as Harishchandra and Maharaja Ishwari Prasad shaped it from a plethora of dialects. Of course, Indian patriots were not alone in advocating language nationalism; similar calls were made, and are still heard, in Europe and elsewhere.

For the month of its enactment, Ramlila takes over Ramnagar (literally, Ramtown). During the decades of the nineteenth century when Ramlila was becoming what it is today, Ramnagar was much less populated and built-up. The current royal family traces its lineage back to the mid-eighteenth century. In 1730, Mansaram Singh, a bhumihar brahmin zamindar (tax and rent collector) and his son Balwant Singh were installed as co-rajas by the then Muslim rulers of the region. After his father's death in 1738, Balwant ruled on his own until 1770. Members of this family – sometimes direct descendants, sometimes distant relations adopted when no male heir was available – have occupied the gaddi (throne) until today. The title of "maharaja" was conferred by the ascendant British power upon Ishwari Prasad Narain Singh in 1835 because of his steadfast support of the colonial rulers. In 1859, after Ishwari stood with the British during the First War of Independence/Mutiny of 1857, his status was further elevated to that of "Maharaja Bahadur" (brave great king). All of these titles, powers, and privileges were fundamentally reconfigured, if not revoked, after Indian independence in 1947. Maharajadoms were abolished, and, by 1949, all the princely states were integrated into the nation; privy purses were decreased until they ended in the 1970s. Thus, Vibhuti Narain Singh, who ascended to the gaddi in 1938, straddled two epochs: colonial India with its maharajas, nawabs, and such, and post-independence secular democracy India. Of course, "secular democracy" is a term that has its own meaning within the framework of India's highly charged religious allegiances which definitely affect politics. Vibhuti's son Anant Narain Singh became maharaja in 2000 upon the death of his father. Anant, however, is in political fact an "honorary maharaja," a king of ceremonies, rituals, cultural obligations, properties, and private social privileges without any official governing authority. Anant's authority, such as it is, in fact, depends largely on his sponsorship and management of the Ramlila, Varanasi's largest, longest, and most impressive religious-theatrical event.

To understand Ramlila as environmental theatre and as religious devotion, one must comprehend the physical shape of Ramnagar – why it is where it is, how it is dominated architecturally by its qila (fort, in Urdu), and how the Ramlila is deployed throughout the town. Ramnagar, across the Ganga river from Varanasi, is technically part of the city. But Ramnagar's history is not comparable to Kashi's. From the perspective of the holy city, Ramnagar is triply on the outside: It is outside the sacred Panchakroshi Road; it is on the wrong, or polluted, side of the Ganga; it is a Hindu king's palace on what was for centuries Muslim turf. The Qila, Ramnagar's most impressive structure (Fig. 5.1), was erected in 1850 by Raja Balwant Singh, who selected a strategic bluff overlooking river traffic coming down from Delhi and Allahabad toward Varanasi on its way toward Patna and Kolkata. Also, by being physically away from Varanasi, the maharaja was somewhat insulated from intrigues and insurrections. The question of pollution, or "wrong side of the river," did not

Figure 5.1 Ramnagar Qila (Fort), 1978, seen from the Ganga river (photo: Richard Schechner).

seem to concern him. The Qila is the place from which the maharaja emerges each day to confer his presence on the Ramlila.[4] From its inception in the early nineteenth century, the maharaja has been Ramlila's patron, most important single spectator, and theatrical producer.

Kashi, Varanasi, Banaras, Ramnagar

Cities are, of course, centers of commerce, sociability, politics, art, industry, residences, and, decisively, traffic. Traffic is essential to the idea of a city: getting here from there, mixing up people and goods in a melee of structured anarchy, the surrender to or struggle against all the jams, jumbles, crushes, and crowds. There are other qualities to urban life, such as neighborhoods and districts with their own peculiarities, architectures, delights, and offerings; opportunities commercial, cultural, religious, gustatory, and erotic not available in such profusion of choice elsewhere. A panoply, sometimes even a surplus, of entertainments, persons, eateries, temples, stores, vendors, animals, beggars, crooks, jobs, and experiences. People seek cities usually in hope of gain and pleasure. But once thrown into the urban excess, people in modern or Westernized cities at least take time out by respiting themselves in parks, simulated bucolic turfs cut from the traffic, the brick-steel-and-stone, and the ambivalent enjoyment-cum-anxiety of too many choices.

The festival – either as burlesque carnival (in Bakhtin's sense) or as hyperorderly civic celebration, and these two are often combined in tremulous dialectical (im)balance – as played out in the city is another kind of respite, a time-and-place-out, where the city's daily multiple life is pushed aside or suspended in favor of a more singular and focused activity that suddenly organizes a portion of the urban into that which it is usually not. On the fringes of or sometimes in the midst of this focus, carnivalesque activity seasons the day, and more often the night, with inversions, role-reversals, and the mockery of established hierarchies. Most people are aware of the way in which parades and other street fairs displace traffic, installing instead either the movement of official displays or the well-regulated ambling of pedestrians through temporary flea markets and/or festival spaces. In larger cities, these festivals are usually partial, taking up a relatively small portion of the civic space. Even major events such as New York's Macy's Thanksgiving Parade or the great tickertape welcomes and celebrations lower Manhattan is famous for are channeled down 5th Avenue or through the canyons of the financial district. New York's Halloween Parade, centered on 6th Avenue (Avenue of the Americas), spills into adjoining neighborhoods but does not come close to taking over the whole city. Some celebrations, such as Mardi Gras in New Orleans, combine well-regulated parading and formal balls with street parties, masking, cross-dressing, carousing, and social and sexual promiscuity typical of carnival. But the public melee of Mardi Gras is tightly policed into the French Quarter towards which the great floats of the parades amble. Trinidad Carnival does engage much of Port of Spain, but only for a day or two.

Ramnagar Ramlila is different than other similar events in that Ramlila takes place in multiple locations – almost each day a different place – widely dispersed throughout Ramnagar. Ramlila is also, in its own way, a carnival, or, in the Hindi word, a mela, or fair. People attend Ramlila not only to take darshan[5] of the five boys who become the gods Ram, Sita, Bharat, Lakshman, and Shatrugh – and the many other less numinous but still exciting characters from myth and religious texts, but also to enjoy the mela, taste the snacks, and get squeezed among the crowds. These crowds follow Ram and the other Ramlila personages from one place to another extending over most of the area of Ramnagar. From the Qila to the main crossroads at the center of town; from the banks of the Ganga to many fields, hills, waterways, gardens, streets, and buildings carefully placed throughout Ramnagar from its center to its outskirts. Some of these Ramlila environments are temporary, constructed and dismantled each year such as Chitrakut, where Ram, Sita, and Lakshman set up home early in the exile (Fig. 5.2). Others are permanent buildings, gardens, or grounds used only during Ramlila but known all year by their Ramlila names such as Ayodhya, Ram's birthplace and capital (Figs. 5.3 and 5.4) and Janakpur (the capital of Videha), Sita's home (Fig. 5.5).[6] Still others – fields, streets, temples (Fig. 5.6), and temple ponds (kunds) (Fig. 5.7) – are temporarily transformed from their eleven-months-a-year existence into Ramlila places. These uses and transformations are not comparable to stage settings or even commemorative lands and monuments familiar in many parts of the

Figure 5.2 Chitrakut, 2013 (photo: Richard Schechner).

Figure 5.3 Ayodhya empty, 2013 (photo: Richard Schechner).

Figure 5.4 Ayodhya full, 1978 (photo: Richard Schechner).

Figure 5.5 Janakpur, winter 2014. Vyas Lakshmi Narayan is living there, note laundry hanging out to dry (photo: Richard Schechner).

Figure 5.6 Rameshwaram temple, 2013 (photo: Richard Schechner).

Figure 5.7 Kund (pond) used as the Kshir Sagar (Ocean of Milk upon which Vishnu sleeps before incarnating himself as Ram), 1978. In the background, Durga Temple, one of Ramnagar's oldest structures (photo: Richard Schechner).

world. Throughout India, but in Kashi more intensely, places have multiple meanings, layered associations and significances, one or several or many of which can be summoned to action by the performance of a ritual, the arrival of a certain date on the calendar, the presence of a particular person or group.

In India, the names of places, and through these names the historical, mythical, and sacred geographies-geophanies they incarnate and express, are of utmost importance. Banaras aka Kashi aka Varanasi is a major and anciently settled, richly historicized city whose multiple names signify the layered and simultaneous experiences taking place within the sacred circle of the Panchakroshi Road (to be explained later). The city is also named Avimukta (never-abandoned), Anandavana (forest of bliss), Rudravasa (Rudra's, that is, Shiva's, place), Mahashmashana (great cremation ground). Each name suffuses its own different yet overlapping signification. Over time, the names Kashi, Varanasi, and Banaras have accumulated precedence. The suffusions of signification are not abstract; they are experienced, tasted, smelled, and pilgrimed. These experiences are not distributed evenly, as the year's ritual calendar emphasizes first one and then another of the city's offerings through a myriad of celebrations, some of an all-north-India kind (Durga Puja, Navaratra, Holi, Divali, Ramlila) and some local to this or that neighborhood, sect, or language community.

Kashi is the city of light (one of the word Kashi's meanings in Sanskrit), the capital of a kingdom known nearly 3,000 years ago and well established by the sixth century BCE when Siddhartha Gautama, the Buddha, came there to offer his world-changing teachings. Banaras is the Moghul and English pronunciation of the Pali Baranasi, a version of Varanasi, a name found in Buddhist literature and in the *Mahabharata*, and thus almost as ancient as Kashi. According to popular etymology, Varanasi demarks the settlement close to the Ganga between the Varana (north end) and the Asi (south end) rivers, waters said to stream from the body of the first person, Purusha, at the beginning of time. The land between these rivers is, according to the *Vamana Purana*, the "best place of pilgrimage in the three worlds, potent enough to destroy all sins" (Gupta 1972: 26–29). During its long history, Varanasi has been sacked, its temples razed (some replaced by mosques, others rebuilt), but from early times the place has kept its predominantly Hindu character and significance.

But what does "Hindu" mean? Hinduism is not a religion obedient to a single hierarchy but rather a conglomeration of contending beliefs and practices organized around a molten core. Today's Varanasi, with its population of 1,435,000 (according to India's 2011 census), is home to many Hindus and Muslims, some Jains, Buddhists, and Sikhs, and a few Christians and Jews. Varanasi pulses with all manner of commerce, offering a rich menu of city life. The dominant strain of Hinduism in Kashi is the worship of Shiva. Kashi, a city Shiva created, is his permanent home. He keeps it safe from the cosmic cycles of creation–destruction by elevating the city above it all on his trident. That Kashi should be Shiva's city is surprising because all around Varanasi the people of the Gangetic plain of Uttar Pradesh, India's most populous and densely populated state, are devotees of Ram, an incarnation of Vishnu, another of Hinduism's supreme deities. People say that Varanasi is an island of Shiva in a sea of Ram. There is a special, tangible interdependence between the city and the god who founded it and protects it. This special relationship is played out by the maharaja of Banaras who is greeted with shouts of "Hara! Hara! Mahadev!" – words signifying Shiva – whenever he appears in public because the maharaja is believed to be the representative of Shiva, if not his incarnation. In Ramlila, there is a particularly powerful confluence of religious intensity as Shiva himself, or his human agent, witnesses Ram's story enacted by Ram himself.

Before going forward with these connections, more needs to be said about Kashi. Kashi both contains and exceeds Varanasi, materially and religiously. The word "Kashi" most probably derives from the Sanskrit "kash," to shine, to be full of light and beauty. Or the city may take its name from the legendary King Kasha, founder of a lineage who ruled in Kashi. Or the name may be cognate to "kasha," a tall, flowering grass that grows wild along the Ganga's banks, also called "kusha," the name of one of Ram's and Sita's twin boys. In the *Kashi Khanda*, a collection of tales about Kashi, it is said that the city shines with Shiva himself who is the brightness of enlightenment. As an earthly territory, Kashi is bounded by the Panchakroshi Road (five krosha road), much traveled by pilgrims. The Panchakroshi Road begins where the

Varana empties into the Ganga in the north, sculpts a westward semicircular path enclosing all of Varanasi and more, and ends in the south where the Asi (a dry bed for much of the year) meets the Ganga. Even though Kashi is relatively large – a krosha is about two miles – its ritual centers, the Shiva Vishwanath and Madhyameshwara temples, the Hanuman Sankat Mochan temple, and the many Ganga ghats, are packed close together near or at the sacred river.

To Kashi come many Hindus to die – the crematory fires on Manikarnika ghat burn all day and all night, as they have for hundreds if not thousands of years. To die in Kashi is to achieve moksha, liberation from the cycle of birth-death-rebirth, from the flux and suffering of samsara, and to be absorbed into the absolute and unchanging Brahman. This is why many of the devout call the city "moksha-prakashika Kashi," "the liberating light of illumination, Kashi." Diana L. Eck, author of a comprehensive study of the place, writes:

> Kashi is the whole world, they [Hindus] say. Everything on earth that is powerful and auspicious is here, in this microcosm. All of the sacred places of India and all other sacred waters are here. All of the gods reside here, attracted by the brilliance of the City of Light. All of the eight directions of the compass originated here, receiving jurisdiction over the sectors of the universe. And all of time is here, they say, for the lords of the heavenly bodies which govern time are grounded in Kashi and have received their jurisdiction over the days and months right here. Thus all the organizing forces of space and time begin here, and are present here, within the sacred boundaries of Kashi. And yet Kashi is not of this earth, they say. While it is in the world and at the very center of the world, it is not attached to the earth. It sits high above the earth on the top of the trident of its lord and protector, Shiva. [...] Kashi is Light, they say. The city illumines truth and reveals reality. It does not bring new wonders into the scope of vision, but enables one to see what is already there. People have called this Light the Eternal Shiva (Sada Shiva) or Brahman. Where this Light intersects the earth, it is known as Kashi.
>
> (1982: 23–24)

According to Eck, Kashi is both a cosmopolis, a city that draws into itself the whole world, and a microcosm, a model and replica of the cosmos.

> The India we see here [in Kashi] reflects the elaborate and ancient ritual tradition of Hinduism. It is a tradition of pilgrimage to sacred places, bathing in sacred waters, and honoring divine images. It is a tradition in which all of the senses are employed in the apprehension of the divine. Its shrines are heaped with fresh flowers and filled with the smell of incense, the chanting of prayers, and the ringing of bells. It is a tradition that has imagined and imaged God in a thousand ways, that has been adept in discovering the presence of the divine everywhere and in bringing every

aspect of human life into the religious arena. It is a religious tradition that understands life and death as an integrated whole. Here the smoke of the cremation pyres rises heavenward with the spires of a hundred temples and the ashes of the dead swirl through the waters of the Ganges, the river of life. [...] To linger in Banaras is to linger in another era, an era which one cannot quite date by century. It is very old, and yet it has continued to gather the cumulative Hindu tradition, right to the present.

(Eck 1982: 8–9)

Eck quotes the ancient *Skanda Purana* to show how living in Kashi has long been considered in itself a religious act:

Here [in Kashi] sleep is yoga, and going about town is sacrifice.
O Goddess, eating whatever one pleases is the great sanctified food-offering to the gods.
One's play, O Goddess, is a holy act of charity.
Everyday conversation is the repetition of God's name.
And lying upon one's bed is prostration.

(1982: 322)

Kashi-Varanasi-Banaras has been continuously settled for at least 3,000 years, its cultural and religious traditions evolving from its earliest times in an uninterrupted flow. This sets the city apart from other ancient settlements, many of which have been ruined and abandoned, or resettled, or, like Athens and Jerusalem, marked by discontinuous or deeply conflicted traditions. In Kashi-Varanasi-Banaras, despite a strong Muslim presence since the twelfth century, Hinduism in many varieties but especially as the worship of Shiva has flourished supreme and unbroken for millennia. Change, both architectural and religious, especially along the Ganga riverbank, the ghats, comes less swiftly to this city than to all others.

According to Puranic literature and tradition, Kashi is exempt from the cyclical creation-extinction of universes, the yugas and kalpas of Hindu time-space. The Hindu cosmology developed in Upanishadic times (roughly 500 BCE), still believed in by many today, divides eternity into four ages or yugas: the krita (perfect), treta (third), dvapara (second), and kali (conflict). Today we live in the kali yuga. These four yugas repeat themselves as "days" and "nights" of Brahma. Thus, the cosmos is perpetually in the process of an endlessly recurring creation-destruction. Robert Zaehner writes:

For Hindus the world was created not once for all nor is there any end to it: from all eternity it had been recreating itself and dissolving back into its unformed and "unmanifest" condition, and those periods of evolution and devolution were called days and nights of Brahma. Each day and each night of Brahma last one thousand years of the gods and a year of the gods corresponds to twelve thousand years of men. Each "year of the gods" is in turn divided into four periods or yugas of varying length. [...] This will go on for thousands and thousands of kalpas [cycles of brahma's days and nights].

(1966: 62)

Although the present age is the kali yuga, a time of strife and misunderstanding, Kashi is not part of it. Kashi exists in the first and most perfect krita yuga. Kashi is exempt because when the cycle of creation-destruction arrives at Brahma's night, the point of void, Shiva holds Kashi aloft on his trident, rescuing it from dissolution. Yet, as any visitor to Varanasi knows, the indices of human misery register as high or even higher here than in other Indian cities. Because Kashi promises moksha to all who die inside the Panchakroshi Road (even Muslims, Christians, Jews, and atheists; even rats and roaches), the city attracts more than its share of the sick, poor, and desperate. Likewise, Varanasi is a thriving commercial center with all the attendant bustle, crime, shady deals, and emphasis on material gain. Furthermore, Varanasi has a reputation for the good life famous for its silks, sweets, bhang (a milkshake made from the juice of cannabis buds and leaves), poets, musicians, dancers, wrestlers, and skilled prostitutes (including some stunning cross-dressers). The point is: Kashi's life is multiple, contradictions coexist, inhabitants savor different aspects of the city's life at different times and according to varying tastes, religious inclinations, caste affiliations, class and economic status, and education. The same person, at different seasons, on different occasions, partakes of this or that of Kashi's options. Like so much else in India, what Kashi-Varanasi-Banaras is, just like what it is called, is a palimpsest that doesn't so much erase and replace associations as add to them, crowding in, overwriting, yet always leaving room for multiple interpretations, readings, and actions.

I will discuss this palimpsest, these options and contradictions, as rasa (an aesthetics based on taste, on flavor, on savoring) and as maya-lila (a theory of play and performance). I will attempt to understand the Ramnagar Ramlila as part of, and apart from, Kashi. Finally, I will theorize about the relationship between the city as a site of multiple opportunities and the city as a focused mytho-poetic-religious entity, what St. Augustine, in a different but appropriate context, was bold enough to call the City of God.

Ramnagar Ramlila

Kashi's greatest performance-performative event, Ramlila, takes place, ironically, not in the city itself but in Ramnagar. Near Varanasi the river swerves northward so that its southern bank is actually to the east. In Kashi the sun rises over the river – facing east and looking south, you can see Ramnagar's Qila. When crossing the Ganga to Ramnagar, a person is moving from north to south (as the river generally flows from west to east) and west to east (as the river flows from south to north at Varanasi). This conflation of directions is significant. Kashi, the Luminous City, arose at the place where pilgrims crossing the river and returning would move in all four cardinal directions. Directionality, defined spaces, and movements have been decisive qualities of Vishnu (whose avatar Ram is) from the earliest accounts of his acts. The Rig-Veda sings:

> I will now proclaim the manly powers of Vishnu
> Who measured out earth's broad expanses,
> Propped up the highest place of meeting:
> Three steps he paced, the widely striding!

$$(1, 154)$$

Vishnu means "Expander," the god who, by stepping through space, establishes his lawful authority. Following in Vishnu's steps, the Veda says, is to step in honey. Ram, Vishnu's seventh avatar, is known for his goings or journeys. The yana of Ramayana means travelling, following a path, tracing the movement of the sun across the sky: Ram is king of the Solar Dynasty, a Raghu descendant of Surya (the sun god). Measurement is a paradigm of order and proportion, while movement toward or within the sacred is pilgrimage. Following Ram is a physical as well as conceptual act: where Ram steps, order is; following in Ram's steps is not only pilgrimage but bringing order to a mixed-up world.

Ramlilas everywhere, but especially Ramnagar's, are celebratory performances tracing Ram's footsteps from before his birth in Ayodhya, through his childhood, his training as a warrior, the contest to win Sita, adopted daughter of King Janak of Videha-Mithila (Janakpur in today's Nepal), palace crisis followed by exile, moving for thirteen years in the forest, kidnapping of Sita by Ravan, about a year to gather his army of monkeys and bears and invade Lanka, the brief but decisive war against Ravan, victory, return to Ayodhya, coronation, and teachings inaugurating the golden age of Ram's rule, Ramraj.

Ram's story, as retold by Tulsidas in the *Ramcharitmanas*, is known by every Hindu and most Muslims living in Hindi-speaking north India. I have never met anyone in this region who was not versed in the deeds of Ram, his marriage to Sita, his alliance with the monkey god Hanuman (and other animals), and their war against Ravan. Many believe the events of the story are historical fact. This knowledge of and belief in the narrative is crucial because the ultimate text of Ramlila is that imagined by each partaker of the performance. This text is multiple, building from one or more of the official texts (*Ramayana*, *Ramcharitmanas*, samvads, teachings of one's guru, and so on), but elaborated by countless interpretations, favorite passages, and disputes. Not everyone agrees with what Ram does, especially how he treats Sita. Not everyone considers Ravan a villain: he is a favorite among the farmers in the district where the family who has portrayed Ravan for four generations live and in south India and beyond.[7]

In Ramnagar during one Ramlila scene or another, a person can visit sacred and historical places and participate in the actions of beings divine, human, and demonic of powerfully imagined and thereby strongly realized mytho-poetic-religious India: heaven, earth, underworld, forest, city, river, mountain, ocean, homeland, foreign place, temple, garden, bedroom, throne room, sage, renouncer, courtesan, teacher, god, person, elephant, monkey, bear, bird, demon, woman, child, brother, man, sister, wife, son, daughter, king, commoner, outcaste, exile, untouchable, royal, uncle, aunt, servant, stranger, intimate, foot soldier, charioteer, general, and more. Most of the sites of Ramnagar Ramlila were laid out about 150 years ago when Ramlila was made into its present form. Sometimes Ramnagar is all India and Lanka; sometimes the kingdoms of Kosala and Videha, birthplaces of Ram and Sita. During the closing days of Ramlila, Ramnagar is Ayodhya, Ram's capital. Since 1992, actual events have to a degree superseded mytho-poetic enactment. In 1992, Hindu zealots destroyed the Babri Masjid (mosque) erected in 1527 by Emperor Babur, India's first Moghul ruler, at the presumed site of Ram's birth in the "real Ayodhya" 124 miles northwest of Varanasi. This signaled a refocusing of the site of Ram's authority from mythic Ramlila to actual Ayodhya marked by pitched battles, bloodshed, and legal actions pitting Hindus against Muslims.

This kind of violence is not part of Ramnagar Ramlila. In Ramlila the reality is poetic-theatrical-devotional. The shifts in locale and scale occur organically during the course of Ramlila's thirty-one days. The various locations are not represented by temporary theatrical sets but by sites that are part of Ramnagar's townscape. When not in use they are still called by their Ramlila names. Some sites are physical structures or walled-in enclosures, such as Rambag, Ram's pleasure garden, with its once marble, now concrete, gazebo (Fig. 5.8).[8] Others, such as Lanka or Sita's garden in Janakpur, where she first meets Ram, are fields (Fig. 5.9). Still others, such as the Kshir Sagar (Ocean of Milk) or the rivers Ganga and Jamuna, are ponds or streams. For some time the real Ganga was used, but the great river's floods during Ramlila season are unpredictable, so a makeshift Ganga stands in for the real thing. Some locations, such as the small field that serves as Nishad's ashram or the street where Ram parks the pushpaka, the flying vehicle captured from Ravan that once conveyed Sita to Lanka and later brings victorious Ram, Sita, Lakshman, and their allies from Lanka back to Ayodhya after the war, are known locations with no special qualities except that during Ramlila they are part of the story.

Sometimes a major Ramnagar landmark is drawn into the story. Ramnagar's main crossroads at the very center of town is where the exiled Ram, Sita, and Lakshman are reunited with Ram's two other brothers, Bharat and Shatrugh; the Qila is the setting for the triumphant welcome the maharaja of Banaras gives to Ram and his royal party. Some places bring powers of their own into Ramlila, as do a sacred well near Chitrakut (where Ram and his party first go into exile) that is the focus of a ritual circumambulation and the 300-year-old Durga temple in front of which Ram meets the fire god, Agni. As important as

Figure 5.8 Rambag gazebo, 2013 (photo: Richard Schechner).

Figure 5.9 Sita's garden, 1978. Visiting Janakpur, Ram and Lakshman meet Sita. The figure in white in the foreground is a vyas. The live deer provides both beauty and irony. Later in the Ramlila, Sita will be kidnapped by Ravana, who uses the ruse of a golden deer which, when shot by Ram, utters a cry of pain in Ram's voice. Lakshman comes to the aid of his apparently wounded brother, giving Ravan the chance to take Sita (photo: Richard Schechner).

the fixed sites are the roads and pathways connecting focal points. Many lilas end at a moment in the story just prior to some move. Just after the next day's lila begins, everyone is off to some new location. Movement, pilgrimage, is consciously built into Ramnagar Ramlila. Ramlila's narrative map is a web of nodal sites and linking paths. In earlier times, a map was the official program listing both events and locations.

Moving from site to site is characteristic of Ramnagar Ramlila. This activity is the dramaturgical, processual, and ritual way of living out Vishnu-Ram's experiences in the human world. When Ram, Sita, and Lakshman go into exile, they renounce the material world. When drawn on a map of India, Ram's movements first cross from east to west and then descend from northwest to southeast across India and into (Sri) Lanka (Fig. 5.10). When Ramlila spectators follow Ram-Sita-Lakshman to the places made real by the swarups' presence, the spectators are undertaking a pilgrimage. Ramlila spectators know they are going on a pilgrimage. Without having to spend a lot of money or travel hundreds of miles, they can enjoy the benefits of pilgrimage: this transformation of space into place is a key benefit of living in Kashi. The very first movement of Ram's exile from Ayodhya is a procession into the forest accompanied by several thousand spectator-participants, many of them weeping, although they know full well how the story will turn out (Fig. 5.11). The theatrical environment furthest from the Qila is Lanka, where the great battle scenes are enacted. Lanka is a vast field on the southeastern outskirts of Ramnagar (Fig. 5.12), just as the island of Sri Lanka is off the southeast coast of India.

Even at the very end of Ramlila, after his coronation, durbar, and public sermon, Ram and his entourage are on the move, mounting two of the maharaja's richly adorned elephants for the short trip from Ayodhya to the Qila and back, a ceremonial visit that takes place in no other Ramlila than Ramnagar's. The maharaja also journeys every day during the Ramlila. Banaras's king is conveyed by elephant, horse-drawn carriage, or automobile. In these vehicles he sits attentively, flanked by a single, elderly companion, never conversing. I asked Maharaja Vibhuti Narain Singh about it. "He is on my household staff. I bring him because he looks dignified. He has no official importance." The current maharaja continues the practice of his father. Often the maharaja is preceded by an honor-guard of soldiers and a military band playing British-style marches. Only once does he move in the street on foot. After Ram's coronation, and a night of joyous celebration and sad leave-taking, thousands of exhausted spectators strew the street facing the Qila. At dawn, the maharaja and his entourage walk from the Qila to Ayodhya to witness the arati – a waving of a camphor flame, as in temple worship – that concludes Ramlila's only overnight performance.

The whole Ramlila apparatus shifts locales several times during the thirty-one days. When the scenes are at Ayodhya or in the Qila, the swarups live and rehearse at a dharamsala (pilgrimage residence) near the northern wall of the

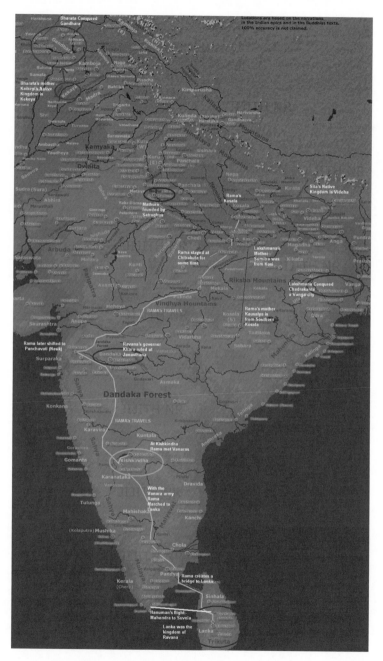

Figure 5.10 Ram's journey across India to Lanka.

Figure 5.11 Spectator-worshippers follow Ram, Sita, and Lakshman into exile, 1978 (photo: Richard Schechner).

Figure 5.12 Lanka with Ravan's blue effigy, 2006 (photo: Richard Schechner).

Qila. When the scenes are at Chitrakut or Rambag, they live at Rambag. When the scenes are at Lanka, they live just behind the garden of ashoka trees where Sita is confined. Rehearsals for Ramlila begin in July and from that time until the end of the cycle more than three months later, the swarups are away from home and school. In recent years this has caused problems because of conflicts between the demands of school and family and the needs of the Ramlila. In earlier times, most boys did not attend high school; the pay for Ramlila had more buying power than it does today;[9] and the desire to be in this sacred drama was more intense and widespread. To be a swarup, a boy must be from an observant brahmin family, have an strong yet pre-puberty voice, and be auditioned by the maharaja himself. In a period when secularism is confronted by fundamentalism, such boys are not easy to find. Often a boy will be Shatrugh or Bharat one year and Ram or Lakshman the next. Finding Sita is more difficult than finding the other swarups because what is required is a boy of delicate beauty with a strong yet light high-pitched voice (Fig. 5.13).

The maharaja attends all the lilas but does not see three of the thirty-one in their entirety. He leaves early before Queen Kaikeyi insists to King Dasharatha that Ram be sent into exile – the sadness of one king is too distressing for another king to witness. The maharaja leaves early before Ravan kidnaps Sita because seeing a demon lay hands on a goddess is unseemly. On Dussehra, the day Ram slays Ravan, the maharaja parades through the Lanka battlefield but does not watch the act which, arguably, is the narrative climax of the Ramlila.

Figure 5.13 Sita, her face sparking with jewels, 2006 (photo: Richard Schechner).

I asked Maharaja Vibhuti Narain Singh about his absences. "It is not proper for one king to witness the death of another." He went on to explain that it was not always this way. "My father [actually his uncle] started this practice [of absenting himself] and I have continued it." Regarding the maharaja not seeing Ravan take Sita, his absence is problematic because the real Sita is not touched by the demon. Knowing what is to happen, and wanting to protect Sita from defilement, Ram creates a "chaya" (shadow) Sita who undergoes the ordeals of kidnapping and imprisonment. He does this by sending Sita behind a barrier and having her immediately emerge, as the chaya Sita. Once Ravan is slain and the chaya Sita liberated, the real Sita is brought out of a circle of fire to rejoin Ram. Both real and chaya Sita are enacted by the same brahmin boy. From the audience's perspective nothing separates chaya from real but Ram's power to create maya (illusion).

One lila, the Bharat Milap, the meeting of the four brothers ending the Ram's exile, the maharaja sees twice. First, late in the afternoon, he goes to Nat Imli in "downtown" Varanasi, where the most famous scene of the city's oldest Ramlila, dating back 467 years (as of 2013) attracts a multitude of more than 100,000 packed into an urban square and peering from windows, balconies, and rooftops.[10] Then, at about 10 P.M. the next night, the maharaja watches the same scene in Ramnagar (Fig. 5.14).

Texts and Social Values

Ramlila enacts both literary and performance texts. Valmiki's *Ramayana* is never uttered but provides the fiber of Ram's story. Tulsidas's *Ramcharitmanas* is sung by twelve ramayanis, the maharaja's household priests augmented by a few invited persons. The ramayanis always sit close to the maharaja, making him the principal auditor of the *Manas*. Throughout the performance, the chanting of the ramayanis alternates with the samvads. The samvads are not spoken realistically as in modern Indian theatre but shouted out singsong and slowly so that the assembled thousands can catch every word. Microphones are not used. When Ram speaks, the crowd roars back, "Bol! Raja Ramchandra ki jai!" (Speak! King Ram, Victory!). At emotional or highly dramatic moments, the crowds, led by sadhus, holy beggars who attend Ramnagar Ramlila in the hundreds (the maharaja provides them food and lodging), break into kirtans, songs whose only text is a passionately chanted "Sitaram, Sitaram, Sitaram Jai!, Sitaram" (Sita Ram, Sita Ram, Sita Ram Victory! Sita Ram). Each lila ends with arati, a moment when the swarups hold very still as if they are temple statues. During arati, their faces are suffused first by the light of red flares and then etched brilliantly into the night sky by white flares. The great crowds press close and in silence to get darshan of the swarups who are gods. The flares, as with all the fireworks, effigy-making, and elephant tending, are jobs traditionally done by Muslims.

Figure 5.14 Bharat Milap, 2006. After fourteen years of exile, Ram, Sita, and Lakshman are reunited with Bharat and Shatrughna (photo: Richard Schechner).

But Ramlila is more than the chanting and proclamation of texts, movement through mytho-poeticized spaces, spectacle, and dynamic audience participation. Ramnagar Ramlila is a carefully crafted enactment of a narrative that transmits information and values of a particular north Indian devout Hindu view of the world, social practice, and values. To a large degree these characterize and radiate from Kashi-Varanasi. In Ramlila, they embody and sustain a hier-archical, male-superior, kshatriya (warrior) and brahmin (priest) ethos. And although the vast crowds of lower-caste people suggest general support for such a worldview, this is not always the case. In the 1970s, Linda Hess (my co-researcher) asked a number of women and men about a line from the *Manas*: "A drum, a peasant, a shudra [low caste], an animal, a woman – all these need to be beaten" (5.59.6). Some people simply accepted the instruction. But, Hess noted:

> more often th̄ answers were much less clear. [...] [T]he vast majority of speakers defended Tulsidas against the charge of condoning wife beating. Of these, nearly all focused on the verb "tarana," whose most common definition is "to hit" or "to beat." Many explained that here it means something like education or discipline. [...] The Maharaja [...] was clear on this point:

> MAHARAJA VIBHUTI NARAIN SINGH: The famous line about the drum and so on. It is only a problem of translation. The controversy is only on beating, tarana.
> LH: No, there is more controversy than just on beating. The juxtaposition of drum, peasant, shudra, animal, woman –
> MR: No, I tell you, it is only on tarana. I've looked at all the dictionaries. Tarana has ten meanings. Not only beating. Touching is tarana. Thumping is tarana. [...] The sense of this word is to bring out the best. So these – animal, shudra, woman – to get the best of them you must "beat" them, but not with a stick. You can't beat a woman with a stick and get the best out of her. An animal also, you can't go on beating it the way they beat bullocks here, you can't get the best out of it that way.
> LH: Do you think people might misunderstand, just hearing the line?
> MR: No, it is a foreign mind that would misunderstand.

> [...] As I tried to point out to the Maharaja, the very juxtaposition of these five terms – drum, peasant, shudra, animal, woman – implies the degradation of the human items on the list.
>
> (1988: 250–251)

Other spectators were more direct in rejecting the *Manas* on this point. "I don't believe that," said a member of the Yadav (milkman) community, a shudra by caste. But, by and large, the *Manas*, the samvads, the spectacle, the narrative, and the devotional aspects of the Ramlila support a hierarchical and conservative (but not fundamentalist/Hindutva) construction of society. Not surprising, given who and what the maharaja is and is imagined to be.

Ramlila's Theatrical Environments

Ramnagar Ramlila is played out in a unified space made sacred by the performance. The playspace contains ten main stations: Rambag, Ayodhya, Janakpur (Mithila in the *Ramcharitmanas*), Chitrakut, Panchavati, Kishkindha, Rameshwaram, Lanka, Bharat Milap, and the Qila. These are linked by paved roads, unpaved paths, ponds, and streams. The overall pattern of movement among these stations is a gyre. The action during the days before Ram's exile rotates slowly around a tight axis from Rambag to Ayodhya to Janakpur and back to Ayodhya. When Ram goes into exile, the action opens eastward from Ayodhya, then south from Chitrakut to Panchavati and Kishkindha, and then finally to Lanka, Ramlila's largest space. Once Ram defeats Ravan, the demon's giant corpse consumed by crematorial flames (Fig. 5.15), the gyre is wide open. All of Ramnagar becomes Ram's Kosala over which he rules during the treta yuga's perfect kingship, Ramraj. Even the maharaja plays his role as a subject when on Ramlila's final night he welcomes King Ram, Queen Sita, Ram's brothers, and Hanuman to the Qila as "official" honored guests who are gods. The swarups are fed, wreathed, and worshipped. The maharaja gives one silver rupee to each swarup as "dakshina," a ritual donation. Once the swarups leave the Qila, they return to Ayodhya, where the formality of the previous month is tossed aside. The vyases stand below the throne room gazing up at the swarups; people go up the steps for darshan of the swarups – but in a more relaxed way than on other nights; characters such as Jambavan and Sugriva, out of costume and just plain citizens of – Ayodhya? Ramnagar? – chat among themselves near to the throne room; the Ramayanis, having finished chanting the *Manas*, sit in an uneven circle ready to offer the music for Ramlila's final arati, the camphor flame waved by Kaushalya, Ram's mother. The whole feeling in Ayodhya for this last hour or two of the Ramlila is of celebration, relief, accomplishment, joy, and easiness. The maharaja is absent, I think, because if all Ramnagar is now Ram's Ayodhya, the maharaja's place is in his own home as a subject of Ram – his presence is no longer royal, no longer needed because Ramraj is in force: Kosala has only one king.

The experience of spectators during those final four days is one of ecstatic spinning through the multiple time-spaces of Lanka-Ayodhya-Rambag-Qila-Ramnagar-Kashi-Kosala-India-Cosmos. The scenes move from the outermost theatrical environments at Lanka and Rambag to the inner courtyards of the Qila. And the characters shift identity from swarups to subjects to kings to courtiers to commoners.

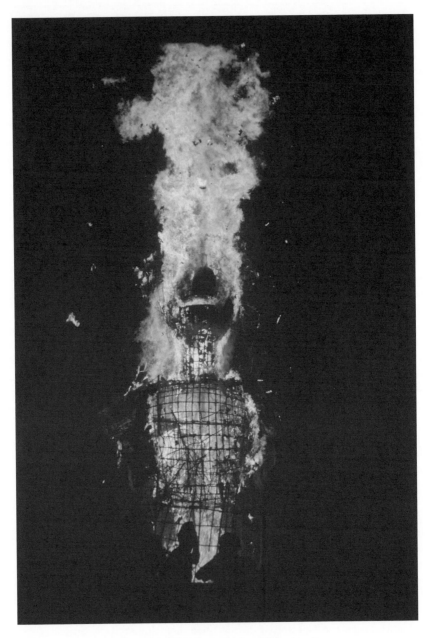

Figure 5.15 Ravan is cremated, 1978 (photo: Richard Schechner).

Here's how it happens. After Ram is crowned in lila 30, he and Sita sit on their throne in Ayodhya, Ram's brothers to each side, Hanuman behind. One by one, Ram's allies – now acting as both characters and performers because the Ramlila is coming to its end for one year – bid the swarups farewell. These figures are leaving Ram's kingdom to continue serving him as vassals in the far-flung territories of India and Lanka that Ram, Sita, and Lakshman have traversed and either conquered or drawn into binding alliances. Those bidding farewell – Sugriva, Vibhishan, Jambavan, Nala and Nila, Angad, and Nishad – are not only leaving Ayodhya, they are also leaving the stage and the narrative. Then, thousands of people of Ramnagar, Kashi, and the surrounding areas, crowd up the stairs for close darshan of Ram, Sita, Lakshman, Bharat, and Shatrugh, with Hanuman standing behind them. People press the swarups' feet, accept tulsi leaves and marigold malas from their hands. The people are worshipping and adoring, coming face to face with the numinous, the theatrical, the royal, and boys of their own place and kind. So hard are Ram's and Sita's feet grasped that by the middle of the night they are bruised and swollen. At about 2 A.M., the swarups are removed to a room on the upper level of Ayodhya, where they sleep for a brief three hours, tended to by the vyases and others who make sure the gods lay still, faces up, straight on their backs. Just before first light, the swarups are reinstalled on the throne. At dawn, the maharaja's honor-guards force their way through the crowd, and the maharaja witnesses Ramlila's only early-morning arati. Finally, the exhausted swarups are hoisted on the shoulders of Hanuman and an assistant to the vyases and carried off to the dharamsala for a day of rest before the Ramlila's ultimate scenes at Rambag, the Qila, and Ayodhya. These scenes feature Ram's teachings delivered in the gazebo at Rambag's center, the maharaja's welcoming of the swarups to the Qila for supper, worship, and the Kot Vidai (farewell) (Fig. 5.16), followed by the Ramlila's final arati at Ayodhya, an arati sans maharaja, the "people's arati."

After the people's arati, the swarups are carried to their dharamsala, where the ones who are not Ram prostrate themselves to him (Fig. 5.17). The next day – the thirty-second day, the day after Ramlila – the boys who were swarups return to the Qila as the maharaja's subjects and employees. All the major players except Ravan attend. After the rakshasa's death, the player who enacts Ravan returns to his village. "The Ramlila is over for me," he told me in 1997. At the Qila, the maharaja thanks the swarups and the role players for fulfilling their ritual duty. He pays them for their hard work. Then, the ex-swarups and the characters go to Janakpur for an after-Ramlila party. The swarups sit in a place of honor (Fig. 5.18). They are no longer gods, but they are not yet "just boys." And so, step by step, the normative social order is reinscribed.

The deployment of place is so important that, as noted earlier, at least in 1946 a map served as a program detailing the where as well as the what of Ramlila (Fig. 5.19). Comparing this program map with a scale map of the Ramlila as it was in 1978 discloses some differences. The discrepancies signal

Figure 5.16 At Kot Vidai (farewell), 2013. In the inner courtyard of the Qila, the maharaja washes the feet of the swarups, then feeds them a supper of sweets and gives each of them – and other important participants in Ram-lila – a silver rupee. Members of the royal family join in honoring the swarups (photo: Richard Schechner).

Figure 5.17 After the drama is over, the other swarups, one at a time, prostate themselves to Ram, 1978 (photo: Richard Schechner).

Figure 5.18 The day after Ramlila, all the participants except the maharaja gather in Janakpur for a celebration, 2006 (photo: Richard Schechner).

either changes over the thirty-two-year gap between maps (a development other evidence makes doubtful) or the difference between the Ramlila as it is and as its authors imagine it to be. The 1946 program map conflates the distances separating Ayodhya, Janakpur, and Rambag; Panchavati (where Sita is kidnapped, a very inauspicious place) is pushed to the east away from Ayodhya and nearer to Lanka. It gives the overall impression of Ramlila's action neatly conforming to the directionality of the narrative as told in the *Manas*. The 1978 scale map shows less of a correspondence between narrative and space. Chitrakut and Rambag are in the northeast, Janakpur in the northwest, the Fort and Ayodhya in the west, Bharat Milap at the center, and Panchavati, Kishkindha (where Ram meets Hanuman), Rameshwaram, and Lanka to the south and southeast. Or, looking at the 1978 map another way, the Qila, Ayodhya, and Bharat Milap form a central axis; Ram's boyhood adventures, courtship, and first days of exile are to the northeast; Sita's kidnapping and the war against Ravan are to the southeast. At the end of the Ramlila, after Ram's coronation, the central and northern sectors are in use as Ram moves among Rambag, Ayodhya, and the Qila. The bad or foreign south is left out – the south that was not fully Sanskritized at the time of Valmiki's *Ramayana* and is not now Hindi-speaking or Manas-loving.[11]

The theatrical environment with the most scenes and the most breadth of lila time is in and around Rambag (Ram's garden), a 515 × 340 foot walled-in park

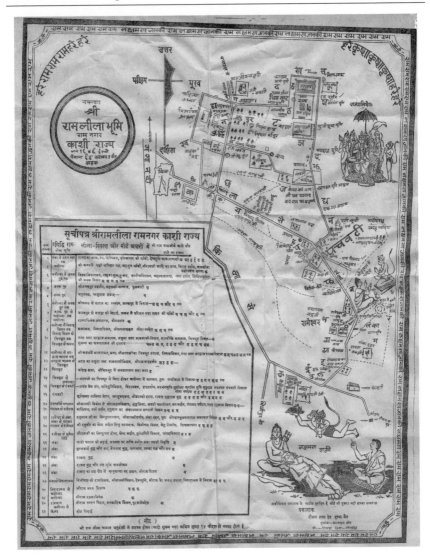

Figure 5.19 Program-map, 1946 (photo: Richard Schechner).

built for Ramlila in the mid-nineteenth century. Rambag contains several buildings, including the gazebo where Ram delivers his teachings on Ramlila's last day. Rambag also contains a large storage building and scene shop for making effigies and props, a small rehearsal room, and living quarters for the swarups from lilas 9 to 19. Ramlila's first episode takes place just outside Rambag's front gate where Ravan acquires the powers he immediately abuses. Standing within Rambag's auspicious northwest tower, Vishnu (with Lakshmi by his side) hears the pleadings of the oppressed. "For your sake," he proclaims, "I will take on the form of a human and rid the earth of its burden." That night, the scene shifts to the 550-foot-square kund fronting the Durga temple just north of Rambag. Brimming with water because late summer is the rainy season, Vishnu dozes on Sesha, the 1,000-headed king of serpents, floating on the kshir sagar, the endless ocean of milk. Ram awaits his own birth, his legs stroked by his wife-to-be, Sita. But, and this is typical of Ramlila and the time loops of Kashi, it is not definite who is resting under the hoods and on the belly of serpent drifting across the temple kund (Kshir Sagar): Vishnu, Ram, Lakshmi, Sita, swarups, boy actors …

Rambag may have been built where it is because of the female power associated with the Durga temple, which dates from around 1700, about 150 years before Ramnagar Ramlila took its present form. Just how strongly Rambag anchors Ramlila's gyratic spatial harmony is shown by an anecdote told to me in 1978 by the maharaja's younger brother, C. P. Narain Singh.

> Some years back, but during my lifetime, the wall of Rambag collapsed so that the first day's lila could not be enacted there. Everything was transferred to Retinbag near to Lanka where there also was a tank and a garden, but in miniature scale. For ten or twelve years, the Ramlila began in Retinbag. […] When Rambag was repaired, a controversy arose. Some people said, "Why not utilize Retinbag? There is a logical justification for continuing there [near Lanka], why bring it back?" But other people argued the Ramlila should start just outside Rambag. The middle of the cycle, the days at Chitrakut, are also at Rambag, and the end of the Ramlila is inside Rambag. The cycle begins outside of Rambag in chaos and ends inside Rambag with perfect harmony. So to many people it was less important to have the real Lanka than to experience this rhythmic harmony. So the first lila was brought back from Retinbag.

Need I note that the "real Lanka" is a Ramlila environment?

At 900 × 600 feet, Lanka is, or was, larger than Rambag and the Durga temple pool combined. Since 2011, the size of Lanka has been reduced by a large stone-making facility installed there with the maharaja's permission (and profit) (Fig. 5.20).[12] Although some distances covered during some lilas-journeys are three miles or more, no single Ramlila stage is vaster than Lanka. Ravan's kingdom is Lanka's great open space. Within it is Ravan's large earthen Qila on top of which he will be cremated, and next to it his smaller throne room (Fig. 5.21). The demon's Qila faces Ram's camp some 650 feet away on Suvel Hill (Fig. 5.22). In between the demon's gigantic fortress and the god's rustic battle camp stands a relatively small, slightly raised rectangular battlefield. There Ram dismembers Ravan's monstrous brother, Kumbhakarna; there, Hanuman struggles against but cannot defeat Ravan; there, Lakshman is critically wounded by Ravan's son Meghnad; and there, ultimately, Ram slays Ravan.

Figure 5.20 A factory in Lanka, crushing stones for highway construction, 2013 (photo: Richard Schechner).

Figure 5.21 Ravan's qila in Lanka with with his son Meghnad guarding a gate, 2006. Workers are preparing to arm Meghnad with the shakti weapon that will badly wound Lakshman (photo: Richard Schechner).

Figure 5.22 Ram's camp on Suvel Hill, 2013 (photo: Richard Schechner).

On the west side of Lanka is a 15-foot-high wall holding back a large embankment with a small cupola and, behind that, a building where the swar-ups live and rehearse during the days Ramlila is in Lanka. Under the cupola, roughly halfway between Suvel Hill and Ravan's Qila, Sita sits calmly accept-ing her captivity. Surrounding the mother of the universe, the faithful, mostly women, attend and worship her. On the outskirts of Lanka, on the road leading from Lanka back to the center of Ramnagar, Ramlila's largest mela is set up. Sweets, hot snacks, games, tea, soft drinks, herbs, colors, cloths, toys – and all manner of items – are for sale. People attending Ramlila come for darshan but they also attend for the mela. In 2013, I noticed that the mela had invaded the northwestern corner of Lanka, extending outwards almost to Suvel, blocking the direct line between Ravan's Qila and Ram's camp. This, I felt, was wrong.

During some of the battle scenes in Lanka, and especially the day of Ravan's defeat, between 60,000 and 75,000 spectators gather (Fig. 5.23). But if the weather is terrible, as it was in 2013, even Dussehra Lanka will be void of spectators (Fig. 5.24). It was not always that way. In 1978, the weather was very rainy during the first lilas, but thousands of the devoted turned out anyway to stand under umbrellas and in the mud of Ayodhya, including the "150-year-old sadhu" who never protected himself from the weather (Fig. 5.25). One would think that the physical and metaphysical immensity of Lanka would swallow you. But the experience for ordinary people is of closeness and intimacy, a chance to elbow up to the divine and the demonic, and during sandhya puja break, to mingle and snack. The farmers and shopkeepers, clerks, students, wives, children, and sadhus who make up most of Ramlila's

Figure 5.23 Lanka, Dussehra 2006. A huge crowd surrounding the Ramayanis as they chant the Ramcharitmanas (photo: Richard Schechner).

Figure 5.24 Lanka, Dussehra, 2013. Bad weather kept the crowds away, but not the maharaja, who made his required trek across the battleground before returning to the Qila (photo: Richard Schechner).

attendees, crowd in close to Ram and the other swarups who are vulnerable boys, delighting in these children whom they also worship. The monkeys and bears are familiar. Ram is not terrifying, awesome, strange, and contradictory like Shiva. Often framed by small-scale temple architecture, or in his modest camp on Suvel Hill, Ram radiates intensity, not grandeur. His adversaries are

Figure 5.25 Rainy, muddy Ayodhya, 1978. The "150-year-old sadhu" rejects shelter (photo: Richard Schechner).

Figure 5.26 Ravan, 1950s. Note the vyas holding the samvad book (photo: Archive of the Maharaja of Banaras).

beings who, having distorted the world, take on monstrous if magnificent shapes. The very bigness and super-bright colors of the demon effigies embody the scope and boldness of their evil. Yet, paradoxically, these outsized figures are also comedic: bamboo and papier-mâché giants destined for dismemberment and incineration. Ravan in his human form is different. His impressive mask, costume, and weapons inspire both fear and respect (Fig. 5.26).

Studying old drawings and photographs, one published in 1830 (Fig. 5.27) and some from the 1920s, it is clear that in recent years the battles are not as

Figure 5.27 Dussehra, 1829. Note the number and size of the demons and the number of royal elephants (photo: Richard Schechner of engraving by James Prinsep).

grand as they were. The number of elephants and effigies is fewer, due to reduced budgets, if not changing tastes. In the early 1980s, a small road was built across Lanka. A major highway is under construction close by. "Think what that would mean," Maharaja Vibhuti Narain Singh told me. "During some of the most delicate scenes, Ram grieving for wounded Lakshman, Sita's lament as she sits in the ashoka garden, we would hear the roar of trucks, smell the benzene." Vibhuti died in 2000; his fears are actualized. Pressures build for further development. Maharaja Anant Narain Singh insists he needs the money that leasing or selling land would bring. Eyeing Lanka's expanse in 2006, a young farmer asked me, "Why should so much land just lie unused most of the year, when we poor farmers have nothing on which to grow our crops?" When the land is sold, it will not be to farmers.

Why Is Ramnagar Ramlila So Big?

All other Ramlilas are more modest in both space and time than Ramnagar's. Mansa Ram, founder of the current royal line in the early eighteenth century, rose from being a rent collector for the Mughals. His lineage gained power and respectability through allying itself with the faltering Mughal power at Awadh (Lucknow) and then later with the British. Raja Balwant Singh (ruled 1738–1770) established his residence in Ramnagar and built the rudiment of what was to become the Qila. Raja Chait Singh (ruled 1770–1781) built the Durga Temple and Rambag. Raja Mahip Singh (ruled 1781–1796) added to the

Qila. As with many such fort-palaces, structures were added, modified, or rebuilt over time by a succession of rulers.

Legend has it that in the early nineteenth century, Raja Udit Narain Singh (ruled 1795–1835), prevented from crossing the Ganga to attend a Ramlila in Varanasi, first attended and then decided to upgrade the Ramlila of Chota Mirzapur, a village about ten miles south of Ramnagar. In any event, by the end of the second decade of the nineteenth century, an elaborate Ramlila spectacle was taking place in Ramnagar. In 1828, Reginald Heber, Lord Bishop of Calcutta, and in 1830, James Prinsep, founding editor of the *Journal of the Asiatic Society of Bengal*, published accounts of Ramlila – Heber's probably of a Ramlila in Varanasi, Prinsep's certainly of Ramnagar's Ramlila.

> I received a visit from the Raja of Benares [Udit Narain Singh], a middle aged man, very corpulent, with more approach to colour in his cheeks than is usually seen in Asiatics, and a countenance and appearance not unlike an English farmer. [...] I regretted to learn, after he was gone, that he resided at some distance from the city on the other side of the river. [...] At Benares, I am told, the show [Ramlila] is on such occasions really splendid. The Raja attends in state with all the principal inhabitants of the place, he lends his finest elephants and jewels to the performers, who are children of the most eminent families, and trained up by long previous education.
>
> (Heber 1828: 448)

> Five or six different spots in the town [Banaras] become, annually, at this season the scene of a Ram Leela. In most of them the exhibition is cur-tailed and imperfect: in some, it is little better than a bonfire of Rawun's gigantic image on the day of Dusera. [...] But the Rajah of Benares, on his estate at Ramnugur, conducts the performance in a very complete manner; nearly the whole of the *Ramayana* is read through in the course of twenty or thirty days, and whatever incidents are capable of being acted, or displayed, are simultaneously exhibited.
>
> The whole of the acting is, necessarily, in dumb show; and the dramatis personae are so numerous, and in general so unskilled in their duty, that the leaders, who may be said to act the part of stage-managers, have great difficulty in making the performance keep pace with the oral declamation of the choir, or band of priests, who chant the sacred legend. The scenery is, as far as it can be, real; for instance wherever the Ganges or the sea is required, the scene is shifted to the bank of some Tulao; such incidents as are adapted to the night are performed by torch-light: separate gardens receive the designations of Ayodhya, Junukpoor, Citrakot, and Kishkindha, which are the principal localities of the poem.
>
> For Lunka, Rawun's capital, an artificial fort is constructed of earth and paper, painted yellow to imitate gold, and in the centre of it a huge

figure of Rawun is erected, 60 or 70 feet high which is filled with fireworks and combustibles. The chief dramatic action of the piece is carried on within an arena enclosed with bamboo rails, in the middle of an extensive plain, which is crowded, especially towards the conclusion of the Leela, with an immense assemblage of all classes of Hindoos.

The last battle, in which Rawun is killed, occurs on Dusera, or the tenth day. This is, at Ramnugur, the principal day of the spectacle, and is represented in the accompanying plate [see Fig. 5.27 again].

In the evening, the Raja of Benares, in full procession, issues from his palace gate, under a discharge of artillery; his state elephants are preceded by banners, music, equipages, and soldiery, extending as far as the eye can reach. On the way, the Raja stops to make the customary offerings of flowers, rice and a cocoanut to a sacred Sumee tree (Mimosa suma), for prosperity during the approaching season. When this splendid train arrives on the plain, the elephants seem to be swimming in an ocean of heads, and their rich caparisons aid greatly to the brilliance of the scene.

(Prinsep 1830: 84–85, 88)

Tradition has it that the Ramlila took on its current shape under the tutelage of Maharaja Ishwari Prasad Narain Singh, who reigned for more than a half century, from 1835 to 1889. But what Prinsep describes – and I have quoted only a few of his six pages – dates from at least five years before Ishwari's reign began; Prinsep is a reliable witness to an event close to how the Ramlila is performed even today in Ramnagar, including its grandeur and its appeal to "an immense assemblage of all classes of Hindoos." The major differences are that when Prinsep saw Ramlila, there were no samvads, and the number of elephants, effigies, and stage effects was far greater than now.

Ishwari was kept on the throne by the British, who valued his loyalty; they promoted him from raja to maharaja when he stuck with the colonialists during the rebellion of 1857. Ishwari oversaw the building of many lila structures still in use today. He worked with Harishchandra and other writers and scholars in the composition of the samvads. This was a big change, making Ramnagar Ramlila a drama as well as a spectacle and a recitation (of the *Manas*). It was during Ishwari's reign, and the almost-as-long reign of his successor, Prabhu Narain Singh (1889–1931), that the make-believe/make-belief qualities of the participation by the maharaja came into full play. Even as the king's actual political and economic power evaporated under the British Raj, his influence and authority over aesthetic and religious matters increased.

In 1910–1911, the colonial power created the new princely state of Banaras with the maharaja as its monarch, yet keeping in British hands direct rule over Varanasi itself. In other words, the king was a toy politically, militarily, and economically.[13] By this time, largely through various forms of pageantry and ritual, and especially the Ramlila, the maharaja was fully identified with both Shiva, Kashi's own deity, and with Ram, the chief deity of the surrounding region. The British understood how useful it was to have a devout Hindu maharaja ruling his princely state as a counterbalance to increasingly active Indian nationalists, both Hindu and Muslim, and some of whom were communists. Divide and rule had long been the British colonial strategy globally. But perhaps as a surprise to the British, Ramlila fed into nationalist desires by actualizing the imagined-for Ramraj. The British didn't understand how powerful and compelling the performed imaginary was in India and in Kashi especially. From the 1920s on, Gandhi seized the revolutionary possibility of Ram as a culture hero; the Great Soul enlisted the masses devoted to Ram in the struggle to free India from both Mughal and British rule.

Haunting Ramnagar Ramlila is Hindu India's national dream of Ramraj: the whole subcontinent as one free, united, and strong nation. To actualize this India – merging the mythic past with the political present – demanded not only a big field of play but play that was more than play in the trivial sense. It demanded "maya-lila," an alternative imagined reality. Ramlila is all about participating with Ram, the great Hindu solar king, walking in his footsteps as his army and his devotees. Ramlila powerfully fuses religious devotion to nationalist fervor. Evidence of this could be heard in the 1970s–1990s aboard many of the boats leaving the Ramnagar ghat for the row back to Varanasi across the swollen, tumbling Ganga (Ramlila occurs at the end of the flood season).[14] On board, people sang (in Hindi):

> King Ram, leader of the Raghu dynasty,
> Born from Shankara's [Shiva's] drum,
> Born from the waves of the Ganga,
> Husband of pure Sita!

This is very close to Gandhi's rallying song, sung to the same tune:

> King Ram, leader of the Raghu dynasty,
> Husband of pure Sita:
> May we worship this Sita-Ram!
> He is known as Ishwara or Allah.
> May this God bestow good sense on everyone!

Even without the hymn-singing while crossing the river, the idea of a Hindu state still undergirds Ramlila. This desire is exploited by adherents to Hindutva – radical Hindu nationalism combined with anti-Muslim activism – who champion Ram as their culture hero. Gandhi's all-embracing Ram who used to animate the Ramlila morphed into the more militant for-Hindus-only Ram of post-1992.

The maharajas, who, in the eighteenth and nineteenth centuries, built and enlarged their Qila on the bad side of the Ganga, wanted both to appease and to separate themselves from their Mughal lords in Awadh. The Qila extended Hindu influence into the predominantly Muslim hinterland even as it blocked further encroachment by the Mughals, whose power was failing anyway. Then, as the British came in, the maharajas aligned themselves with the new power, even as Ramlila celebrated – if only for one month a year and only as play (lila) – dreams of Hindu hegemony. The maharajas of independent India continued to enjoy the benefits of piping this double tune. No matter that they were stripped of their princely states. With regard to the maharaja of Banaras, the Uttar Pradesh government supplies him with money to help pay for Ramlila; his Kashiraj Trust also gives him money; and the people of Varanasi honor him as their king, the incarnation of Shiva. Everyone seems to benefit by this performed imaginary.

The assertive military aspect of Ramlila is forcefully demonstrated on Dussehra, also known as Vijayadashami (the victorious tenth), the tenth day of the month of Ashvin when Ram kills Ravan.[15] Before the final battle in Lanka between Ram and Ravan, the maharaja, in the presence of a few invited guests, performs a special ceremony, his hathiyar puja (weapons worship). On Vijayadashami, people worship the tools of their trade: weapons, paintbrushes, books, whatever. The maharaja worships swords, long-barreled rifles, daggers, etc., implements from bygone days laid out for viewing. He is asking the gods to bless Ram in his final battle against Ravan. Ironic, of course, because why would Ram, a god, need help from a mortal, even a king? The ritual is doubly ironic as these archaic actions testify both to the royal line's imagined past glories and present-day (military) irrelevance. Furthermore, this royal line barely fought a battle.[16] Nor does the maharaja have any martial role to play today, even symbolically. The weapons puja seems to say, "If Rama is a warrior-king, so are we; and here is our proof, these old weapons." Performed with solemnity, the weapons puja approaches Gilbert and Sullivan parody.

After the hathiyar puja, the maharaja leads Ramnagar Ramlila's largest and most opulent procession – even the elephants have their heads painted and their bodies adorned with silver and silks. The king and his retinue, huge kettledrums booming, issue from the Qila and proceed down Ramnagar's main street, surrounded by cheering crowds (Fig. 5.28), past where Bharat Milap will happen, and out to Lanka where, if the weather is good, up to 80,000 people fill the demon's vast domain. Not stopping at all, the maharaja marches across the battleground, abruptly turns, and leaves Lanka the way he came. His presence in Lanka lasts less than ten minutes. He misses the day's lila entirely, the narrative climax of Ramlila, the reason Vishnu took human form. The maharaja does not witness Ram's ultimate triumph. Thus, one king-in-imagination, in order to preserve his royal etiquette, avoids watching another boy-become-king-god shoot toy arrows in the direction of a farmer-become-demon-king.

What is the meaning of this strange procession where for the only time in the Ramlila the maharaja violates the performing space? Usually the maharaja remains firmly anchored behind other spectators, marking the far end of the playing area. The hathiyar puja is a restored behavior of a warring traditional

Figure 5.28 Dussehra procession, 2001, as seen from front gate of the Qila (photo: Richard Schechner).

show of royal might. On Dussehra, a day of military victories, a king marched his army to the border of his domain, displaying his ability to make war. After briefly confronting an opposing number across the line, everyone went home. This performance of the king is modeled on the Vedic ashvamedha yaaga (horse sacrifice), which King Dasharatha performs in both the *Ramayana* and the *Manas*. Maharaja Vibhuti Narain Singh confirmed this. He told me that, in earlier times, the reigning raja would, on Dussehra, march an armed force to the borders of Banaras state near Mirzapur, about thirty miles east of Ramnagar. It was a show back then and now it is a show of a show.

How Much Has Ramlila Changed Over Time?

The Lanka environment has suffered encroachment. Is this a trend? What other changes are taking place? After studying writings, drawings, lithographs, and photographs, as well as interviewing many people, the evidence shows the Ramnagar Ramlila is surprisingly stable in terms of its physical environments and staging over the past half-century. But we know next to nothing about the Ramlila's first century – from about 1820 to 1920. Beginning in the 1920s, there are photographs which show that the mise-en-scène is more or less the same over the past seventy-five years, except that, as previously noted, there are fewer effigies and elephants. This reduction is confirmed by long-time spectators, including a farmer, who by 1978 had attended for fifty-five years. He said:

> The difference is that the maharaja's glory was far greater 30 years ago [1948]. He came with 100 horses, 30 or 35 elephants, bullock carts – so much finery that all the people in this field [of Lanka] could not carry it all. But there's no difference in the lila itself. Absolutely none. Everything is done exactly as it is written in the *Manas*.

That is essential. The devoted attendee, a "nemi" (from the Hindi "niyami," someone who follows something closely), checks the Ramlila against the *Manas*. The core of the actualization is how closely the world disclosed in the performance conforms to the world imagined by Tulsidas.

Still, the Ramlila is changing, because India has radically changed over the past 150 years. Values are different; the authority of the maharaja is reduced if not entirely eliminated; the nation is independent; large parts of the whole have been partitioned into Pakistan and Bangladesh; and the population has quintupled since 1850 to more than 1.24 billion in 2013. Spatially speaking, Ramlila has shrunk relative to the surrounding areas. The journey from the Ayodhya/city to Chitrakut/countryside, then to Panchavati/deep forest and on to "wild" Lanka no longer discloses much of a change. Processions that in the nineteenth and early-twentieth centuries moved from city to field to forest and from avenue to road to path today move on paved streets next to houses, factories, and farms. Bhardwaj's ashram and Nishad's forest kingdom, both narratologically in the forest and probably once actually in a forest, are today enclaves wedged into well-settled areas. No place is hard to get to via automobile or auto-rickshaw. There are houses and paved roads everywhere, fewer fields, and no forests.

Yet, for all this, the actual walking from one locale to another, the participation in the pilgrimage-movement from near the Qila across several miles of differing if not forest landscapes, gives to Ramlila its sense of adventure, exile, and danger, followed by war, victory, and the triumphant return home. The Ramlila's narrative is so strong and deeply believed in, so clearly enunciated by the *Manas* and the samvads, so played out in such detail, inscribed in the theatrical environments, the paths connecting them, the unhurried acting, even the weather – stormy when Ramlila begins, calm and crystalline by its final full-moon nights – that nemis testify to their experience of living for a month inside Ram's world. As Linda Hess noted of the performance in 1978:

> In tonight's Lila [day 3], the sage Vishvamitra takes Ram and Lakshman on a foray to kill demons in the woods. The use of the world as a stage set goes beyond anything the West might call "verisimilitude." We move from the main street to narrow lanes, a troop of horsemen in front, the Maharaja with his elephants behind, the golden gods in the middle gliding along at shoulder level [borne by devotees drawn from the spectators] – the swarups' feet never touch the ground [except when part of the drama]. Shopkeepers and laborers stop to watch the gods go by, saluting them with joined palms. The setting becomes steadily more rural. Roads change from pavement to cobblestone to dirt, houses from plaster to brick to mud, on varying levels, with glittering algae-covered ponds, fields of leafy vegetables and corn, moist greenness everywhere. People are at the doorways, in the yards, on the roofs [Fig. 5.29]. If Ram really did go to the forest with Vishvamitra, would it not have been through lanes like this, past houses, from town to village, while the local people stopped to watch? The sky is brilliant salmon and mauve in the luminous moments before sunset.
>
> (2006: 121–122)

What happened to Hess, and to many others too, is that they are drawn into an imaginary-yet-real experience that is Kashi's genius, a doubling of time and space, a multiplication of realities.

Audience Experiences

Kashi is the luminous city, a place of many simultaneous and sometimes contradictory realities: a release for the dying, a pilgrimage destination, a city of the good life, a typical north Indian urban center where Muslims and Hindus live cheek by jowl, a commercial hub, a vehicular traffic-bicycle-autorickshaw-

Figure 5.29 People watching Ram, Sita, and Lakshman go by, 1978 (photo: Richard Schechner).

animal-pedestrian mess. The Ganga river is holy and polluted, the very liquid of life and a muddy stinky cesspool. Ramnagar Ramlila swallows its participants, maharaja and scholar, sadhu and swarup, farmer and shopkeeper, believer and mocker, as it is meant to do. Vishnu's expanding creates the cosmos, Vamana the dwarf whose two incalculable steps recuperate the world;[17] Ram's goings mark and animate India. For the days of Ramnagar Ramlila is transformed into mytho-poetic epic India. The extended space and time of Ramlila draw people inside the action. One can't "watch" Ramlila because, in Ramnagar, Ramlila is everywhere – in the lilas themselves, in the mela, in the environments active either today or yesterday or tomorrow, in the small shrines where after the day's lila is over people gather to sing kirtans, in the dominating presence of the Qila, whose immensity reminds everyone of the maharaja's family's journey from obscurity near Lucknow to royalty in Banaras and residence in the Ramnagar outpost/extension. Ramlila's efficacity is heightened by how time is experienced. One does not go to Ramlila as to a theatre or a temple. Ramlila is not a destination: it is an immersive experience. Attending Ramlila on a regular basis throughout a whole month is a full-time job. The mind and body are loaded, even overloaded, with Ramlila; there is no respite. Yet, for the several hundred nemis, this total immersion invigorates rather than exhausts. Of course, as the numbers attending varies daily from about 1,500 to nearly 100 times that many, clearly relatively few attend all the lilas. A sizeable number see ten or more.

Again and again, those at the Ramlila told me, "God dwells here for a month," revealing their experience of the actualizing power of Ramlila. Going to the

Ramlila is an act of bhakti, usually translated as devotion but literally meaning participation. Gazing at the swarups is a participation in darshan, an intense looking at or envisioning the divine. People go to the lila or they wait for the lila to come to them watching from doorways and rooftops. The food eaten at Ramlila, even the deep-fried junk food or inexpensive sweets sold by mela merchants, is considered prasad (grace), analogous to the temple offerings made to gods and returned to worshippers to be eaten for spiritual benefit. Many go barefoot throughout Ramlila, as if the whole town were a temple. As Hess comments:

> People of Ramnagar recite poems of praise from the rooftops on coronation day, and actors stop in their tracks to listen. This reflects Tulsidas's description of how people recited poetry on joyous occasions like Ram's birth and coronation. Again and again the audience and citizens of Ramnagar act out what Tulsidas narrates. They drop their work and rush to gaze at the gods as they pass through town or village. They move with processions or climb on roofs to see. They illumine triumphant fireworks from their balconies as Ram's chariot returns slowly from exile. Some climb onto the chariot to make offerings. Others decorate their homes and shops as the citizens of Ayodhya are said to have decorated theirs.
>
> (2006: 119)

"Yes, yes, God is in the temple too," a woman told Hess (who conducted her interviews in the local Hindi dialect), "Oho! God is in a stone, a tree, in you, in me, everywhere. But here it is a walking, talking God" (2006: 129). A seventy-nine-year-old man who attended Ramlila since he was nine, interrupted Hess as she was questioning him about his experiences.

> "Enough, enough, enough. What can I say to you? Yesterday I experienced this: I am sitting in Ramji's court, and today is the Lord's coronation. Today it is also my experience. I am sitting in the Lord's court. In the whole world there is nothing else. There is only the Lord. [...] At the time of arati the Lord himself is present. Whenever and from whatever angle you look, the Lord himself is present. The Lord himself creates this experience, face-to-face, before these very eyes. Whoever wants to experience it, let him experience it."
>
> (2006: 134)

And when Hess asked a sadhu in a tea-stall to explain why different persons' experiences varied so much, from deep belief to mockery:

> "Look, this is milk. Do you see anything in the milk? But if you heat it, the cream comes up. It's the same with God: until we heat it up here [points to chest], we can't know. Just as there is butter mixed with milk,

so God is hidden in the world. We must heat this body, we must churn it, to find out. Otherwise we just look and see milk."

(2006: 132)

To go to Ramlila from Varanasi as a nemi takes all day. Preparations begin with an early-morning bath in the Ganga, memories of last night's lila still alive in the mind and body. Routine activities must be completed by noon. Coming from Varanasi means leaving for Ramnagar between 2 and 3 in the afternoon. One can cross the river by bus at both the north and south ends of Varanasi where there are bridges or join with friends and hire a motor boat.[18] Until about 2005, hundreds pushed aboard an always-overcrowded public ferry – called the steamer – that left from Samne Ghat; or they rowed across. These conveyances are no more, and I miss them. Once in Ramnagar, a person easily falls into the stream of pedestrians, cyclists, rickshaws, and motorcycles. A festive atmosphere takes over. There are snacks and tea and familiar faces. Even the tragic lilas are fun; and the ultimate outcome is assured. Everyone looks forward to the day's story, the further already known adventures of beings who are also already known. Familiarity breeds love. The performance begins at 4:30 and breaks at about 6 when the maharaja leaves to perform sandhya puja (twilight prayers). After socializing, more snacking, and maybe a few prayers for some, the lila starts again at 7:30. By 9:30 or 10, it's over. Five lilas run late: lila 5, the contest for Sita's hand which Ram wins by lifting and breaking Shiva's enormous bow; lila 27, Dussehra ending with Ravan's cremation; lila 29, Bharat Milap; lila 30, Ram's coronation which ends at dawn; and lila 31, the final lila, Ram's teaching, Kot Vidai, and the "people's arati." After each day's lila, most people go directly home. A few stop to sing kirtans or listen to others singing; or they buy some paan (betel leaves, areca nuts, and tobacco) to chew or tea to drink. Mixing devotion, socializing, meditation, and celebration is what Ramlila is all about, and typical of pilgrimage behavior all over India (and not very different from what Chaucer described in *The Canterbury Tales*). A happy time out is what Kashi specializes in, part religious obligation, part vacation, part vocation. In the old days, because the steamer no longer ran after dark, thousands returned to Kashi via the rowboats. Now only a few climb aboard motorboats. Most return by bus, auto-rickshaw, or car. Although the total number of people attending remains huge, fewer come from Varanasi, more from the Ramnagar side of the river. By the time a person gets to sleep it's well past midnight, the next day's lila isn't far off.

Many private practices blend in with Ramlila, in keeping with Kashi's pre-eminence as a pilgrim's destination. Ramlila places become the places they represent just as surely as the swarups become the deities. For example, near Ramlila's Rameshwaram is a small Shiva temple and pool. On day 19, before the regular lila begins, a group of men gather at the temple. They perform a puja to the lingam in the temple; they celebrate by enacting Ram's preparations for crossing into Lanka. Because some of the men are high on bhang, the crowd is rowdy. When the lila begins, Ram and Lakshman worship the same linga in the same temple. Very few spectators can see into the small shrine, but the crowd is deliriously satisfied that honor has been done to Shiva, twice. What Ram and his brother are doing is what Ram did on the coast of India, establish a Shiva linga before building the bridge to Lanka for his army of monkeys and bears. Over the years, the gathering of the men before the lila has knit itself into the more public performance later in the afternoon.

Other even more private gestures and practices have found their way into Ramlila. I am certain that some of these will fade away and others will take their place. For example, a Banaras businessman makes malas (flower necklaces) with his own hands and wreathes the swarups with them daily. The man who played Hanuman for many years but grew too old for the physically demanding role, attends the swarups offstage, bringing them yogurt and sweets, washing them, and seeing to their ordinary needs. For many years until his death in the late 1980s, an old vyas, no longer able to coach the actors, was given the task of shouting Chupraho! Savdhan! (Keep quiet! Pay attention!) to the crowd before each utterance of Ram. The practice continues, performed by another older vyas.

Until his death in the early 1980s, a Ramlila regular was a man called the 150-year-old sadhu. He wore only a palm-leaf groin cloth, even on the wettest, coldest days; and he delighted doing things the "wrong" way. Other sadhus begged for money, he gave money away; others huddled under cover when the rains came, with nothing to protect him from the weather, he squatted in the mud puddles (see Fig. 5.25 again). For Ram's wedding, the maharaja installed this sadhu on the dais next to his royal self. Everyone knew the 150-year-old sadhu was mad for Ram. In the 1970s and 1980s, a corpulent and aggressive police sergeant was both feared and admired by the crowds he threatened with his stout bamboo. Years later, retired from service, this "fat sergeant" (as he was known) became a nemi.

The swarups can play their roles only for a few years, at most, until their voices change and hair begins to grow on their cheeks. In speaking to some ex-swarups, I learned how important being a god was for them. "This was the best time of my life," a man in his thirties told me. His father beamed as he told me that his grandfather, father, himself, and his son had all been Ram.

Many non-swarup characters are held for life and passed down along family lines. The current Ravan's father played the role for fifty-eight years, sharing it with his son when he got too feeble to do the more strenuous scenes. The man playing Brahma, now deceased, was ninety-six when I interviewed him in 1978; he had played the god longer than he could remember. Sometimes playing a Ramlila role changes a person's life. The man who played the sage Narad from 1948 into the 1980s, and whom everybody called Narad-muni (not Omkar Das), used his Ramlila fame and respect to become a temple mahant (owner or chief priest). He joined the Ramnagar Ramlila as a performer in 1948 but had attended Ram for the whole month since 1929. His role in the

Ramlila, his strong stage presence and powerful yet haunting singing voice, earned him his reputation and his work in the temple.

For ordinary people too, Ramnagar Ramlila is special. It is a tirth, or pilgrimage destination – not only Ramlila as a whole, but the places actualized within Ramlila. As noted earlier, Ramnagar Ramlila is a geophany, the making real and present of many of India's sacred places. Everywhere Ram goes is transformed into itself by his presence. Through the agency of the Ramlila environments, spectators visit powerful tirths such as Ayodhya, Chitrakut, Panchavati, and Rameshwaram. Crowds cross the real Ganga to watch Ram and Sita cross the pond that is the Ramlila Ganga: but this Ganga is, to them, as real as the one flowing half a mile away. Surveying the 1979 Ramlila crowd with special attention paid to the question of pilgrimage, William S. Sax found that 80 percent consider Ramlila a pilgrimage destination.

SADHU: This is certainly a pilgrimage [site, a tirth]. It is the biggest Ramlila in all of India. Everywhere that Ram went on his wanderings is now regarded as a place of pilgrimage: Ayodhya, Janakpur, Chitrakut ... all of them [...]
SAX: Is the Ramnagar Ramlila a pilgrimage place?
SADHU: Of course it is. See how many sadhus there are? No less than two thousand! [...] Wherever so many sadhus are gathered, that place is certainly a pilgrimage [destination]. [...] Look over there ... do you see all those people reading the *Ramayana* [*Manas*]? If you experience the entire Ramlila with them from start to finish, walk, read the *Ramayana* and enjoy the lila with them, you have a total pilgrimage experience. Those people really do go to Ayodhya, Chitrakut, and so on.
ANOTHER SADHU: It's true. [...] That temple over there is Rameshwaram temple and none other.

(1990: 139, 149–150)

The World Opened Up

The maharaja and Ram are mirrors of each other, twin foci of Ramlila. The maharaja is as much a mythic figure as Ram. He has no legal political power as king, the title is honorary. Even during the British Raj, the king of Banaras ruled at the pleasure of the colonial power. But this dismissal is too simple: in Kashi the imagination rules, and to the populace of the place the maharaja is king and more, the chief living representative of Shiva, their deity of choice. Residents of Kashi and Ramnagar know the maharaja is not Ram of Ramraj, a divinely just sovereign with absolute powers; often, and with some affection, they called Vibhuti Narain Singh "poor maharaja," meaning both the fact that his purse had been deflated considerably over the years and that his job of maintaining the lila, the play of appearances, was not easy. Vibhuti's son, Maharaja Anant Narain Singh, born in 1963, does not have the same purchase as his father. Yet Anant is admired when he is proudly atop his elephant or in

Figure 5.30 Maharaja Anant Narain Singh, 2006 (photo: Richard Schechner).

his carriage (Fig. 5.30). I have watched him over the years grow into his role.[19] Throughout Ramlila, the maharaja's maharajaness is displayed more completely and more often than at any other time. The maharaja appears on his elephant, raised far above the masses; or he rides in his open horse-drawn carriage; or in his automobile (once a 1928 Cadillac, now an Indian-made Ambassador with the license UP1111). From his perch, the maharaja sometimes nods recognition of an individual or gives a quiet pranam (prayer salute) to the crowd. At Ramlila the maharaja appears in different costumes and different guises: for the wedding of the swarups he is dressed in full turban and glorious silks; for Dussehra he is similarly dressed but with some royal details added; on other days he may wear plainer clothes but always traditional north Indian garb. For arati on coronation dawn, he wears a white jacket and a Nehru cap.

Furthermore, during Ramlila, the maharaja shows his royal self as gracious host. Important guests are accommodated in the Qila; known scholars and holy persons sit next to the maharaja when the king enters the drama as he does when he is a guest at swarups' wedding. At Kot Vidai, his family joins him in welcoming their mythic, actual, royal, divine guests. The maharaja washes the swarups' feet; from his own hands, and from the hands of the royal family, the swarups are wreathed and fed. As they eat, the maharaja hands a silver rupee to a servant who gives the money to one of the performers; one by one, each is given dakshina. The payment is ceremonial; real money will be distributed later. During Kot Vidai, the status of the maharaja with regard to the swarups and the other Ramlila participants, shift back and

forth from the maharaja being king and patron to his being subject and wor-
shipper. Near the end of Kot Vidai, the maharaja himself waves the camphor
flame as arati is performed. Then the swarups mount their elephants, and,
amidst bursting flares and billowing smoke, they pass through the Qila's gates
and back to Ayodhya for the Ramlila's final hours and concluding arati.

In Kashi, the maharaja's identification with Shiva is celebrated. Everywhere
he goes, the maharaja is hailed with the rolling roars of "Hara! Hara! Mahadev!"
(Destroyer! Destroyer! Great God!), announcing one of Shiva's contradictory
selves.[20] Maharaja Vibhuti Narain Singh, whose very name "Vibhuti" means
Shiva's three ash lines drawn across the forehead, recognized his family's
identification with Shiva:

RICHARD SCHECHNER: The people call you "Mahadev."

MAHARAJA VIBHUTI NARAIN SINGH: It's not personally for me. It is for my whole
family. My ancestor who started the dynasty also began a renaissance of
Hinduism.

RS: The Ramlila is part of the renaissance?

MR: The Ramlila was started by Tulsidas. My family gave it a push.

RS: For the people, the eternal realm of Ram is mirrored in the role of your
family?

MR: Not quite.

RS: But Ramlila is the only drama I know of that can't begin until a certain
spectator arrives. What happens if you are sick?

MR: Some member of my family must represent me.

RS: That means?

MR: It is really an administrative aspect. Someone must be in control. From
the audience point of view, my presence does give some prestige. Someone
has to take the lead. It is also spiritual: in the Ramayan, Shiva tells the story
to Parvati. So the representative of Shiva must be there.

This last is revealing. Kashi was Shiva's city long before the bhumihar brahmin
Singh family bought into its karma. The maharaja's family benefits from their
association with Shiva just as the Ramlila benefits from the maharaja's
patronage. It is a relationship of mutual benefit. If the maharaja is Shiva, then
the Ramlila is the story he is telling to … whom? The rani (queen) is not
allowed to appear in public, so there is no first listener.[21] But there are thousands of others who pay close attention to the story. They constitute a kind of
collective Parvati, soaking up the narrative. For them, the maharaja is not
apart from the spectacle; he is a big part of it.

The maharaja, on or in his vehicle, forms one of the spatial limits of the
scene with Ram forming the other. Both Ram and the maharaja are elevated,
though usually the King of Banaras is higher than the King of Kosala. The
audience was more gender-segregated in the 1970s when I first attended Ramlila
than it is in the second decade of the twenty-first century. Still, women tend to

cluster with younger children sticking close to their mothers or other female relations. At Ayodhya, the males are on the ground level and the females above on the surrounding walls. The gods watch many scenes – after all, Ram's embodiment as a human is for their benefit. The god's presence is represented by effigies atop very tall bamboo poles. Though far from the action, the maharaja is aware of the gestures necessary to sustain his role.

RICHARD SCHECHNER: Sitting so far away on your elephant, you can't see the scene very clearly, or hear [the samvads].
MAHARAJA VIBHUTI NARAIN SINGH: My father used to use opera glasses. I don't. There is a practical reason for my sitting at the back. My presence establishes control. The crowd is in front of me.
RS: What do people think when you sleep during the performance?
MR: I don't know what they think. But I am aware of the way I watch. I keep a serenity, a dignity. I don't talk.

Every scene, both processional and fixed, features the maharaja as strongly as Ram. There are scenes when Ram is not present, but the maharaja is almost always watching. There is a regular rhythm to most lilas. Ramlila begins late in the afternoon, breaks for sandhya puja, resumes after dark, and ends at around 10 P.M. The timing is approximate, inclement weather (and there always is some), means certain scenes have to be rushed, delayed, or even rescheduled. The long break for sandhya puja is a time when the drama of Ramlila relaxes into a mela. While the maharaja prays, the people play. Sadhus celebrate their love for Sita and Ram wildly, dancing and singing, sometimes even, especially at Chitrakut where a special stage is set up, going onto the stage. Performers in costume mingle with spectators. Once I took tea with Hanuman, a clerk by trade, and chatted with him about his performance; another day with Sugriva. Families picnic, food stalls and people selling toys and cosmetics do a brisk business. At the mela there is a festive feeling very different from the focused devotional attention to the lila itself. During the sandhya puja break, everyone relaxes but the swarups. Their crowns are off, they are not regarded as divine during this time, but their demeanor remains serious. Often spectators approach them to get a close look or to touch their feet. A person will snack and gossip, and then change mood to approach the swarups for darshan.

The open structure of sandhya puja is best actualized on Dussehra. Before the break, Ram slew Ravan. A great sixty-foot-high bamboo and papier-mâché effigy of the demon king sits atop his Qila (see Fig. 5.12 again). A huge crowd is present. The maharaja has come and gone. At this climax, the story opens a time-space where the many themes of the Ramlila are in suspension: good v evil, the ever-present v the evanescent, gods v demons, people v superhumans and animals, commoners v rulers, caste v we-are-all-equal, the outer circle of the mela v the inner circle of the lila. For a few hours, as it grows dark, all is suspended, the great struggles neutralized, the principles of the cosmos open for all to experience. Ravan, who represents an evil, insatiable appetite, is dead but not cremated; Ram and Lakshman, who are absolute good in "lila," in play, sit on their temporary thrones; Sita, who is mother of the world and a wife beyond reproach, waits patiently under her tree, her humiliating fire ordeal still one day off. The lila-goers who represent the population of the whole world circulate among and between these great figures triangulating Lanka. Of the gods, the lila-goers take darshan, but they also peer up at Ravan's monstrous effigy, horrific and comic simultaneously. The great figures are immobile, but spectators and lesser performers in costume drink tea and chat: a demon next to a monkey next to a sadhu next to a businessman next to a beggar next to Schechner next to a one-armed vendor selling roasted peanuts next to a crying child next to a blind man next to an English tourist next to an itinerant singer next to a student next to a mother nursing her infant next to three men on camels. "Where do you come from?" I ask them, imagining a very long, dusty journey from Rajasthan. "We are the men who come on camels," one answers. "Each year we come, this day only." Nearby, sadhus dance so energetically that sweat soaks clear through one man's saffron shirt from shoulder to hip (Fig. 5.31). Their drumming and singing pierce the evening air. In no other theatre does the audience as such emerge so clearly and effortlessly as part of the performance. Nowhere else have I seen spectators given such a large time and space to fully play out their roles. At Ramlila, people watch, drop out, say their prayers, eat, join small bands singing bhajans, sleep, pressing close for scenes of high drama. Dussehra night at Lanka in 1978 was a great scene with no single center yet full of harmony, thousands of people organized by their interdependent activities. And above them, overlooking it all, the three poles of the Ramlila world on the last night of their conflict and captivity.

Geophany

The map of India drawn by Ramlila captures ancient references to rivers and river junctions, hilltops, forests, cities, temples, caves, trees, wells, and paths. Every Indian knows the story of the *Ramayana*, which has been retold in countless variations in many languages. Ram's adventures are the subject not only of Ramlila but of many other media ranging from the immensely popular 1987–1988 TV serial broadcast nationally to folk and classical dance, theatre, movies, books, and comic books. In the *Manas*, Ram's domain stretches from Mount Kailash in the Himalayas (Shiva's other abode) to Mithila (Janakpur) in Nepal, from Ayodhya northwest of Varanasi and Prayag (Allahabad) on the Gangetic plain southward across the Ganga, Jamuna, and Godavari rivers to the Dandaka forest of central India, and from there to the Deccan plateau of peninsular India and on to Rameshwaram and Lanka. Ram's sovereignty over this vast territory is renewed each year by the thousands of Ramlilas performed all over north India. Each of these marks out by means of theatrical

Figure 5.31 Sweat-drenched sadhu dancing, 1978 (photo: Richard Schechner).

environments and scripted movements a concrete model of the Indian sub-continent as Hindus might imagine it. Ramlila conflates and reshapes historical events that underlie the story, turning these into the mythic field of Ram's appearance (at the center), marriage (a bride from the north), exile and adventures (to the west, south, and east), return (to the center), and rule (universal in space and time).[22] The creation of India and Pakistan in 1947 (and Bangladesh in 1971) fractured both Ram's and Gandhi's vision of one India coexistent with the subcontinent.

Seen this way, the geophany of Ramlila operates between two poles. Ayod-hya = home = Ram = Ramnagar = the Qila = the maharaja = Kashi = Shiva = rightful authority both political and religious versus Lanka = away = beyond the city = untamed mela = Ravan = rebellion-disorder. But of course it's not so simple. Ram has willingly surrendered – or at least postponed for fourteen years – his right to home. He is always on the move. Ravan's king-dom is both outside and within; it is part of the *Manas*. A brahmin, Ravan acquires his powers through severe austerities. As is so often the case in Indian tales, the worst ruler is the good one turned bad through pride. Ravan is a model of such a king. In between Ram's and Ravan's places are the liminal lands and cultures of the monkeys and bears eager to join Ram and Lakshman in their war of recovery. Between the just order of Ayodhya = the Qila and the upside-down helter-skelter of Lanka = mela (where the rich eat chaat, poor people's snacks, and the poor save up for a taste of those famous Banarsi sweets) is an adventurous no-man's land of mountains, rivers, and jungles populated by India's folk villains and heroes – rakshasas, rishis, tribals, mon-keys, bears. The swarups, characters, and spectators experience a range of possibilities by means of Ramlila. There are places to visit (Janakpur and Chitrakut), to explore (from Nishad's to Chitrakut, from Chitrakut to Pampasar), to face crisis (from Panchavati to Kishkindha), to gather all one's strength (Rameshwaram), and to conquer (Lanka). Remarkably, this geophanic, highly dramatic and active map has remained more or less constant from the time of the Valmiki Ramayana to the present. This map writ large on the subcontinent and as a living model in Ramlila continues to shape the beliefs, thoughts, pilgrimages, and political actions of hundreds of millions of India's Hindus.

Rasa, Maya, Lila

The consistency of the theatrical-religious-geophanic experience in Kashi and its temporary extension into Ramnagar is special. Other cities in India (Delhi, Mumbai, Bangalore, Kolkata, Chennai, for example) were founded, formed, or transformed by the Mughals and/or the British. Kashi, though certainly showing the marks of Islam and Europe, has kept its own Hindu character. This character is not changeless by any means, but it follows historical patterns different than those operating in many other Indian cities. Perhaps Varanasi and even Banaras are modernizing rapidly, but not Kashi. Kashi occupies the same turf as the other cities but transcends them in Shiva's residency and in Ram's lila. Kashi often gyres back on itself, recapitulating, restoring, replaying ancient themes. That is not in any way to deny the politics of Ramnagar Ramlila or Ramlila's impact on all of India through the enacted embodied desire to accomplish Ramraj.[23] But powering these politics are old, perdurable belief-systems of experience, reincarnation, recycling of soul-stuff, theophany, and the immediacy of the presence of the swarups-gods. Also, the belief that the contained can contain the container, that the Ramlila grounds and month of play are vast enough to swallow all its participants even as such a tiny time-space can stride as Vamana did to encompass in its mythic and historical time the subcontinent.

Indian theories of rasa and maya-lila can help explain these belief systems.[24] A full exposition of these complex matters is not my intention. So, briefly: The first and hugely influential Sanskrit text on performance is Bharatamuni's *Natyasastra*, second century BCE–second century CE, roughly the date of Valmiki's *Ramayana*.[25] The *Natyasastra* gives a mythic explanation of the origins of theatre. Then it details a theory of emotional expression, the use of face and body gestures to express emotions, the types of dramatic plots, theatre architecture, music, and many other components of what must have been a dynamic dance-music-theatre tradition. The *Natyasastra* insists that theatre is not just for the rich or the poor, the brahmin or the shudra; theatre "belongs to all the colour groups [varna]" (people of all castes) (*Natyasastra*, 1.107). The *Natyasastra* insists that theatre is "a representation of the way things are in the three worlds. Sometimes there is duty, sometimes games, sometimes money, sometimes peace, sometimes laughter is found in it, sometimes fighting, sometimes love-making, and sometimes killing" (*Natyasastra* 1.106–107).

This kind of large-scale, didactic, devotional performance, designed for an audience of all castes and classes, is Ramlila.

> The way such a performance works on its audiences is by means of rasa: literally taste, flavor, savor.
>
> It is said that as taste results from a combination of various spices, vegetable, and other articles [...] so the sthayibhava [durable psychological states] when they come together with various psychological states attain the quality of a rasa. Now one asks, "What is the meaning of the word rasa? [...] How is rasa tasted?" It is said that just as well-disposed persons while eating food cooked with many kinds of spice enjoy its tastes and attain pleasure and satisfaction, so the cultured people taste the durable psychological states while they see them represented by an expression of [...] words and gestures.
>
> (*Natyasastra* 6.32)

Experience is privileged over "objectivity." Ramlila is a total theatre of inclusion and immersion, theatre where the event swallows the participant. One does not regard Ramlila from a critical distance. The most intense scenes of "looking" in Ramlila is the darshan of the gods at arati. Darshan is an ecstatic participatory gazing that dissolves difference, eliminates distance, and fuses the viewer with the viewed.

Rasa is consistent with the Sanskrit-Indian maya-lila theory of reality. As Wendy O'Flaherty explains:

> [Maya originally] meant *only* what was real; through its basis in the verbal root *mā* ("to make"), it expressed "the sense of 'realizing in the phenomenal world'["] [...] to "measure out" the universe was to create it, to divide it into its constituent parts, to *find* it by bringing it out of chaos. [...] Magicians do this; artists do it; gods do it. But according to certain Indian philosophies, everyone one of us does it every minute of our lives.
>
> This concept of *māyā* as a kind of artistic power led gradually to its later connotation of magic, illusion, and deceit [...] Thus *māyā* first meant making something that was not there before; then it came to mean making something that was there into something that was not really there. The first describes the universe in the Vedic world-view; the second, the universe in the Vedāntic world-view. The first is *samsāric* [cycle of birth-death-rebirth]; the second *mokṣic* [release from the cycle]. In both cases, *māyā* can often best be translated as "transformation."
>
> (1984: 117–118)

Lila is a more ordinary word, meaning play, sport, or drama. Gods in their lila create the maya of human existence. Vishnu's lila is the maya of his taking human form as Ram – thus the very name "Ramlila." Ram's lila is the maya of his appearing in Ramnagar in the form of the swarups. The same lila is performed in thousands of Ramlilas in India and beyond throughout the Indian diaspora. Just as Krishna multiplies himself to satisfy each and every Gopi, not just Radha, so Vishnu multiplies his Rams for each and every Ramlila. At the same time, there is no denying the specialness of Ramnagar Ramlila. But this specialness is at the level of human performance, not at the level of maya-lila. Except that Ramnagar Ramlila – along with the many other Ramlilas of Varanasi – partakes in the power of Kashi. Or does it? There is a paradox because Ramnagar is outside the Panchakroshi Road – and yet Ramnagar's Ramlila is the most fully realized of them all. Whether or not Ramlila is more real or less real than daily existence depends on the attitude one brings to such experiences. For some, the Ramlila is nothing out of the ordinary. As Ramesh Chandra De, for years the personal secretary to Maharaja Vibhuti Narain Singh, told me in 1978: "My views on Ramlila have not changed. It is all playacting. Can you take street urchins and make them gods?"

Why not?

Notes

1 Ramnagar is actually part of Varanasi, but because it is on the "wrong" side of the Ganga (Ganges) river and, even with two bridges and a third under construction, not easy to get to from the Varanasi side, Ramnagar is treated as a separate entity.

2 There is a rich literature on Ramnagar Ramlila. See Hess (1988, 1993, 2006); Schechner and Hess (1977); Schechner (1985); Sax (1990); Kapur (1990); Lutgendorf (1991); Parkhill (1993); and Rani (2011).

3 Tulsidas composed the *Manas* from 1574 to 1577. No exact date has been established for the Valmiki *Ramayana*. The earliest manuscript is from the eleventh century CE. However, most scholars date the epic between the fifth and the second centuries BCE. It probably was a sung poem, comparable to Homer's epics with which there are significant narratological similarities: a great war fought by an expeditionary force led by two brothers to recover the stolen/eloped wife of one of them. To wage this war the brothers gather a conglomeration of allies who travel a long distance and cross the sea to battle against a well-fortified citadel defended by a ruling family of warriors.

4 Except for parts of three lilas, the maharaja witnesses them all in their entirety. He leaves early when Queen Kaikeyi behaves "improperly" to King Dasharatha by asking her husband to send Ram into exile; the maharaja leaves just before Ravan kidnaps Sita; and the maharaja enters Lanka, parades through the battleground, and leaves before Ram kills Ravan. "It is not proper for one king to witness the death of another," Maharaja Vibhuti Narain Singh told me. Nor, I suppose, is it right for the maharaja to witness a demon laying hands on a goddess. This last is somewhat ironic because in order to protect Sita from just such defilement, Ram creates a "shadow Sita" who undergoes the ordeals of kidnapping and imprisonment. The "real Sita" is restored soon after the shadow Sita is liberated. Both real and shadow are enacted by the same pre-adolescent brahmin boy. From the audience's perspective there is nothing distinguishing shadow from real but Ram saying that he is creating the shadow as the boy who is Sita takes a few steps and then returns. Such is the power of theatre.

5 "Darshan" means to look at, to see in the religious sense of glimpsing the numinous, the divine. Hindus go to temples to take darshan of the murtis, the icons/idols of the gods which are presumed to actually be the gods. In Ramlila, living boys are murtis.

6 In Valmiki's *Ramayana* and Tulsidas's *Ramcharitmanas*, Sita was not born but adopted by King Janak after he found her in a furrow as he ploughed his field. There are other versions of Sita's origins, including that she is Ravan's daughter.

7 Especially in the south of India and in Sri Lanka, Ravana is often considered a great king, warrior, and innovator. There are many books, films, and internet sites celebrating Ravana. For a recent one see Obeyesekere, *Ravana, King of Lanka* (2013). The blurb reads, "Ravana may not have lost the war to Lord Rama but for the 'betrayal' by his wife Mandodari and half brother Vibhishana 'who gave away war secrets to the enemies.' The 174-page book on Ramayana's villain is based on extensive research by a Sri Lankan, Mirando Obeyesekere, based on archaeological evidence as well as palm leaf writings from a bygone era."

8 In 2012, Maharaja Anant Narain Singh sold the delicately carved marble gazebo and replaced it with a concrete edifice lacking grace and fragility. The maharaja told me that the marble gazebo was being vandalized and damaged by weather. Knowing the structure since 1978, I had not noticed. At present the marble gazebo is in the bar at Varanasi's Taj Hotel.

9 The pay for being a swarup – "dakshina," religious offering, rather than a salary – has gone up from 500 rupees in the 1990s and before to 2,500 rupees as of 2013.

Other participants also receive dakshina. Under current economic circumstances, being in Ramlila is a service to the god, the community, and the maharaja, not a job.

10 The Nati Imli Ramlila is said to have begun in 1546 by Megha Bhagat, a contemporary of Tulsidas.

11 On the subcontinent, the *Ramayana* is told and retold in Sanskrit, Hindi, Nepali, Bengali, Telugu, Tamil, and Malayalam (at least). The story is widespread throughout Southeast Asia where it, and the narratives of the *Mahabharata*, are mother lodes for literature and the performing arts, even in Islamic nations such as Malaysia and Indonesia.

12 The maharaja assured me that this industrial intrusion was temporary. "They are making stones for the roads. Once the highways for the new bridge across the river are complete, we will take away that factory." But in India (if not everywhere), this kind of temporary has a way of becoming permanent. Especially if a rent is being paid, an income earned.

13 With regard to actual power, the maharaja was no different than his counterpart in London: like the British monarch, the maharaja of Banaras's authority is embedded and exercised in pomp, ceremony, rituals, the arts, and other expressions of culture and religion; he owns much property and is admired by his subjects. The royal family was and is the object of gossip and curiosity.

14 With the opening of new bridges and the exponential growth of vehicular traffic, increasingly people attending Ramnagar Ramlila no longer use boats. And the boats are motor-driven, the roaring of the engines making singing impossible. In 2013, the experience of crossing of the river to and from Ramlila was very different than it had been twenty years earlier.

15 Also the day that Durga slays the demon Mahishasura, making Vijayadashami special to Shaivites as well as Vaishnavites.

16 At the start of the line in 1770, the raja was a vassal of the Moghul Nawab of Avadh. Authority soon passed to the British led by Warren Hastings, India's first governor-general. In 1781, Raja Chait Singh rebelled, was defeated, and fled into exile where he remained until his death in 1810. In 1781, the British installed Chait Singh's nephew Mahip Narain Singh as raja. In 1828, the British confiscated the last of the royal lands. These were not returned to the rajas until the long rule of Maharaja Ishwari Prasad Narain Singh (1835–1889). Ishwari was a stalwart supporter of the British, who rewarded him for his loyalty. However, he never had autonomous military power. Nor did any of the maharajas coming after him. Thus, the weapons puja pays homage to a fiction.

17 The story goes that Brahma granted to King Bali, an ascetic who ruled his people with complete justice, sovereignty over the three worlds. Fearing their days were numbered, the gods entreated Vishnu to intervene. Vishnu's fifth incarnation was the brahmin dwarf, Vamana. Praising Bali's generosity, Vamana requested a boon. Bali, whose dharma included honoring brahmins, asked the dwarf what he wanted. "I desire only as much space as I can cover in three steps," Vamana replied. Laughing, King Bali said, "Take as much ground for your kingdom as you can cover in three steps." Vamana swelled to immeasurable size. His first step covered the earth, his second the sky. He refrained from taking a third step: that would have deprived the good King Bali of all his kingdom, and Patala was left for him to rule.

18 In 2012, construction began on a third trans-Ganga bridge. This new bridge replaces a pontoon bridge temporarily laid across the river each year during the dry season. The new bridge runs from just south of Samne Ghat to the embankment less than 500 feet north of the Qila. As of 2013, the bridge was less than one-tenth completed; there were no access roads on either side of the river. Once (or if) completed, this bridge will profoundly affect the traffic in Ramnagar, and, probably, the Ramlila.

Of the bridge, which he supports, Maharaja Anant Narain Singh complained, "It blocks my view of city." So why didn't he insist on placing it a few thousand feet further north, or to the south of the Qila? Possibly the maharaja no longer has the power to enforce such requests.

19 In person and out of his ceremonial and/or Ramlila role, Anant Narain Singh wears a simple sports shirt, absorbed into the business of being a maharaja – hotels, properties, boards of directors, family disputes. He is more shy than his father, less assured: after all, Anant Narain Singh was never an actual king. But he is growing into his role, and he is also training his eldest son, Aniruddh Narain Singh, (b. 2005), who is next to him for many lilas, to fit the part he is destined to play.

20 Shiva is a god of contradictions: destroyer-creator of the universe, dancer, ascetic, lover, Raudra-rageful, inhabitor of cremation grounds, plunderer, yogin, the linga–phallus, the feminine–masculine, swallower of venom, possessor of the third eye of wisdom and of the fire that turns everything to ashes. For all these, and more, Shiva is worshipped, loved, feared, needed, distrusted, honored.

21 See Hess (1993) for an analysis of the frames or loops of the narrational strategies of the *Manas*. See also O'Flaherty (1984) and Lutgendorf (1991).

22 See Sankalia (1973) for a consideration of the historicity of the *Ramayana*. Many scholars have commented on the subtext of Sanskritization: the treatment of the inhabitants of lower India as animals, bears, and monkeys; the implication that the dark-skinned rakshasas, or demons, represent the peoples of India whom the Aryan invaders from the northwest met and subjugated, not so much eliminating indigenous religions but fusing them into their Aryan cosmic order. This is certainly true of Vishnu and Shiva, whose presence in the subcontinent before the advent of the Aryans cannot be doubted, and whose skin color is dark. Ram is described as being dark like the underbelly of a thundercloud; his arms reach to his knees, simian-like; Krishna means "black." Shiva appears white because his dark complexion is covered with ashes.

23 See Schechner (2012).

24 See Schechner (1985, 1993) and O'Flaherty (1984).

25 There are several translations of the *Natyasastra*. I am using Manomohan Ghosh's (Bharata-Muni, 1951).

References

Bharata-Muni (1951) *Natyasastra*, ed. and trans. by Manomohan Ghosh (Calcutta: Asiatic Society of Bengal).

Eck, Diana L. (1982) *Banaras, City of Light* (Princeton, NJ: Princeton University Press).

Gupta, Anand Swarup (ed.) (1972) *Vamana Purana* (Varanasi: Motilal Banarsidas).

Heber, Reginald (1828) *Narrative of a Journey through the Upper Provinces of India from Calcutta to Bombay, 1824–25* (Philadelphia, Pa.: Carey, Lea, & Carey).

Hess, Linda (1988) "The Poet, the People, and the Western Scholar: The Influence of a Sacred Drama and Text on Social Values in North India," *Theatre Journal*, 40 (2): 238–255.

——(1993) "Staring at Frames Till They Turn into Loops: An Excursion through Some Worlds of Tulsidas," in Bradley R. Hertel and Cynthia Ann Humes (eds.), *Living Banaras: Hindu Religion in Cultural Context* (Albany, NY: State University of New York Press), pp. 73–102.

——(2006) "An Open-Air Ramayana: Ramlila: The Audience Experience," in John Stratton Hawley and Vasudha Narayanan (eds.), *The Life of Hinduism* (Berkeley, Calif.: University of California Press), pp. 115–139.

Kapur, Anuradha (1990) *Actors, Pilgrims, Kings and Gods: The Ramlila at Ramnagar* (Kolkata [Calcutta]: Seagull Books).

Lutgendorf, Philip (1991) *The Life of a Text: Performing the Ramcharitmanas of Tulsidas* (Berkeley, Calif.: University of California Press).

Obeyesekere, Mirando (2013) *Ravana, King of Lanka* (Colombo: Vijitha Yapa Publications).

O'Flaherty, Wendy Doniger (1984) *Dreams, Illusions, and Other Realities* (Chicago, Ill.: University of Chicago Press).

Parkhill, Thomas (1993) "What's Taking Place: Neighborhood Ramlilas in Banaras," in Bradley R. Hertel and Cynthia Ann Humes (eds.), *Living Banaras: Hindu Religion in Cultural Context* (Albany, NY: State University of New York Press), pp. 103–126.

Prinsep, James (2009) *Benares Illustrated in a Series of Drawings* (Kathmandu: Pilgrims Book House). First published in 1830.

Rani, Bhargav (2011) "The Axis of Sacred Beginnings: Plotting Spatial Sacralities in the Ramlila of Ramnagar," in C. S. Biju (ed.), *Approaches to South Asian Cultural Studies* (Chennai: Centre for Performance Research and Cultural Studies in South Asia), pp. 13–33.

Sankalia, H. D. (2009) *Ramayana: Myth or Reality?* (New Delhi: People's Publishing House). First publilshed in 1973.

Sax, William S. (1990) "The Ramnagar Ramlila: Text, Performance, Pilgrimage," *History of Religions*, 30 (2): 129–153.

Schechner, Richard (1985) *Between Theater and Anthropology* (Philadelphia, Pa.: University of Pennsylvania Press).

——(1993) *The Future of Ritual* (London and New York: Routledge).

——(2012) "Who Is Rama?" in Lance Gharavi (ed.), *Religion, Theatre, and Performance* (London and New York: Routledge), pp. 185–191.

Schechner, Richard and Linda Hess (1977) "The Ramlila of Ramnagar," *TDR*, 21 (3): 51–82.

Zaehner, Robert Charles (1966) *Hinduism* (Oxford: Oxford University Press).

Chapter 6

Self-Inflicted Wounds

Art, Ritual, Popular Culture

Why do people wound themselves? Are there advantages in parsing these practices as art, religion, politics, war, psycho-pathology, anthropology, and/ or sociology? Are the subincisions of Indigenous Australians more or less acceptable than the penis-cutting options offered on BMEzine.com (body modification) or events advertised on torturegarden.com? And "acceptable" or not for what reasons? How can one parse the categories and grammatize the practices, separating art from ritual from politics from mentation from sickness from popular culture? Why not accept overlapping practices and complex functions? Ought there to be ethical and/or legal limits to self-wounding? What is "self-wounding" anyway? Only wounds caused by the person herself? Or would voluntarily sought wounds performed by others such as tattooing, piercing, and cosmetic surgery count? What about "simple" suicide? Or the Buddhist monks who set themselves on fire to protest the Vietnam War? Or "martyrs" who suicide themselves as acts of terrorist war? Must an injury stop short of death to be called a wound? Indeed, what constitutes a "wound"? Tissue damage? Or should we also admit subjective experiences – imaginary wounds – within specific cultural contexts and practices? What chain reaction of art did Chris Burden's 1971 *Shoot* (more on that later) set off? Can all these different kinds of violence-against-the-self, some of desperation, some artworks, some religious ritual, some in the service of politics, some for beauty-fashion – what a range of "functions" – be accommodated by a single theory?[1]

Anthropologists teach us that subincision among some traditional communities in Australia is multivalently symbolic: life-giving as the blood soaks into the earth; gender-bending as the men become "as if" menstruating women; courageous because the operation is painful. By means of initiation, the boys leave the domain of "mother" and join the "community of men," who also bleed as women do. The bloodletting seen in Christian art depicting persecuted saints and willing martyrs is different, not self-inflicted in the immediate sense. It is self-inflicted insofar as the saints and martyrs do not resist or avoid what is done to them. Rather, they willingly imitate Christ, suffering his agony for the sake of humanity. Similarly, the self-whipping of Shi'a zealots commemorating the martyrdom of Husayn in the Muharram rituals are the means by which these believers punish themselves for what happened to Husayn; or, in another interpretation, these flagellants experience the pain Husayn felt when besieged and annihilated. But words such as "suffering," "agony," "punishment," and "pain" are not fair descriptives. Many who wound themselves or allow themselves to be wounded (or worse) achieve ecstasy – literally, the transportation of the "soul" outside the body. Being in ecstasy is to stand outside one's own body as it is burnt, scourged, pierced, boiled, and hacked. The martyrs and self-wounders are role players in a very special kind of theatre. Turning to popular culture, a perusal of even a few of the many "body modification" web sites – they number more than a million as of 2014 – uncovers functions equally complex.

Some cases are both compelling and peculiar. Such as the imaginary wounds of Catherine Benincasa (1347–1380), a lay affiliate of the Dominican order and later St. Catherine of Siena, who received the stigmata of Jesus in 1375 though the marks remained invisible until after her death. According to tradition, Catherine went into trance, levitated, drank the pus from infected plague sufferers, and met Jesus face to face. Mad woman or saint (or both), she had powers. She convinced the Pope to return the administration of the papacy to Rome from Avignon. Catherine was canonized in 1461, and in 1970 Pope Paul VI conferred on her the title "Doctor of the Church," along with St. Teresa of Avila, the first women to receive this honor. Catherine's wounds and self-punishment are legend:

> Catherine tortured her body in the belief that she could thereby help to expiate not only her own sins, but the sins of those whom she loved, and of all the world. The charity of her motive did not suffice to save her from the horrible reactions with which the body repays those who torture it. [...] It was while at Pisa, at Mid-Lent in 1375, in the Church of Santa Cristina, that Catherine [...] received the stigmata, marks as of the nails which pierced Christ's hands and feet on the cross. Her confessor, Fra Raimondo, who had given her the Holy Communion, watching her prostrate in one of her usual trances after receiving it, saw her little by little rise to her knees, her face radiant, her arms outstretched, and when she had stayed long in that position, suddenly fall back as if mortally wounded. Her friends thought that she was dying [...] Her ecstatic illusions [...] may be naturally explained as resulting from her treatment of her body.[2]

Must we moderns doubt the stigmata? Perhaps. But how can we doubt Catherine's experiencing in her own flesh what she believed was the suffering of Jesus?

More demonstrably real in ways that can be verified in accord with rules of evidence are the widespread self-administered whipping with chains and knife blades during the annual Ta'ziyeh performances of the Shi'a followers of the

Husayn ibn Ali, the Prophet's grandson. In 680 CE (61 in the Islamic calendar), Husayn and fewer than 100 followers and his family, including his infant son, were surrounded at Karbala (near Kufa, present-day Iraq) by the forces of Khalif Yazid who far outnumbered Husayn's group. For ten days in the desert heat and dryness, Husain's people were deprived of water and food, as one by one they were grievously wounded or killed by Yazid's troops – martyred, according to Shi'a doctrine. Ultimately, almost all the males, including Husayn and his son, were killed. A few surviving men and some women and children were taken prisoner and sent off to Damascus, where Yazid waited. These events (and there are various versions of what happened at Karbala) remain fresh to Shi'a Muslims especially. Each Muharram, the season of Husayn's martyrdom, both the battle at Karbala and, even more graphically, the suffering and blood of the defeated are re-enacted by thousands. Mary Elaine Hegland reports what she saw in Pakistan:

> Whenever the sound of clanging metal arose, people ran in the direction of the noise to see men striking their backs with chain flails ending in knives, for the few moments before others forced them to quit their bloody self-mortification. As men cut away at their backs, blood ran down, soaking their shalwars sometimes even to the ankles and showing up in striking red contrast against their pure, white cotton pants.
>
> (2010: 343)

Scenes such as these – though sometimes suppressed or sublimated into blood drives – are not uncommon where Shi'a celebrate Husayn's martyrdom. I write "celebrate," because, bloody and painful as these manifestations are, the actions are voluntary, people want to perform them, and there is pleasure in bodily identifying with the subject of one's veneration. If St. Catherine was pierced by Jesus' wounds, so do the flagellants of Muharram embody Husayn's martyrdom. The word "ecstasy," a standing outside, is an appropriate metaphor for this kind of experience. Outside of what? Of daily life, of low-key involvement. In ecstasy, one steps out of ordinary reality into another realm of being-in-doing. This is a quality of pain the great Sufi poet Rumi (1207–1273) celebrated:

> Pain renews old medicines and
> lops off the branch of every indifference.
> Pain is an alchemy that renovates –
> where is indifference when pain intervenes?
> Beware, do not sigh coldly in your indifference!
> Seek pain! Seek pain, pain, pain!
>
> (Rumi 1983: 208)

Did Rumi know that it is harder to fake pain than to fake pleasure? Rumi, who lived in the thirteenth century, would be fascinated, if not happy, watching television or cruising the internet in the twenty-first century. He would note how the media relishes displaying pain. He would empathize with the suffering so vividly shown and repeated, the amplification by means of camera close-ups of the pain that is part-and-parcel of violence. But what would Rumi think of the millions who "seek pain" only passively? Those who watch other human beings in pain? This viewing is not the self-inflicted suffering of Muharram. Wouldn't Rumi condemn how the most extreme human-against-human mayhem has become spectacle? Indeed, how do the world's "spectators" – the people who watch the violence happening – make sense of the mayhem? The pain is both local and global simultaneously. The violence takes place within specific communities, particular individual human beings are killed and wounded. The media shows grieving relatives. Often the perpetrator is a suicide-murderer whose act is both political and personal, dying for a cause or to call attention to injustice. Indeed, a violent act is labeled "senseless" when it cannot be tied to a specific agenda. The more outrageous and/or large-scale the act, the more instantly media translates the local into the global. With regard to spectacle, nothing in my lifetime surpassed the 9/11, 2001, attack on New York's World Trade Center.

What "delight" do people take in viewing such atrocities? Is it, "There but for the grace of God go I"? Or do people tremble in fear as if watching a for-real horror movie? Or is sado-masochism intrinsic to the human condition? Weirdly, one day a person may be a viewer of violence, the next its object, and then a day later back to watching again. Prior to the omnipresence of media, grand violence – akin to grand larceny – was commonly "represented" in the visual arts, theatre, film, and literature. Think *Medea*, the *Mahabharata*, Jacobean drama, kabuki, *Paths of Glory* ... Is what we see today unmediated or at least less mediated? Is it less artful? Is the paradox of "media" that it often presents actions as if they were really real, first-hand, without filters? We are sophisticated enough to know this isn't true, but we are also visceral enough to experience this stuff as really real, unedited. On the other hand, doesn't everyone know that the very process of transmitting events as they are happening is a way of transforming "real events" into representations? That's why the really juicy catastrophes are broadcast over and over. How many replays does it take for a catastrophe to lose its purchase? Is the physical co-presence of both enactors and spectators necessary for an event to be "really happening?" Is the camera a person? Is society creating selfies of its own worst moments?

If this sounds like an enormous tangle, you are right. I am in the process of wrestling with some muscular problems: presence versus mediation (can there be presence?); nonrepresentational art after Duchamp; the conflict between freedom of expression and censorship (internal and/or imposed); the paradox of the coexistence of globalization and niching – the Balkanization of artistic conventions and societal rules. This last is extremely interesting. For eons there have been widely divergent cultural values and practices. But before global media, these values and practices encountered each other mostly at the boundaries, or via relatively slow-moving trade, or by conquest and colonization. One system usually dominated others: people converted or died; they were absorbed or exterminated. But with global media there are fewer defined boundaries. Populations and cultures overlap and contradict each other everywhere, in the centers and not just on the borders. Massive migrations both sanctioned and illegal are reshaping populations. Contradictions are exposed and unresolved – unresolved even at the level of theory. Not only is there a breakdown of agreed-on norms but the very possibility of "one law for all" seems far-fetched. Which side are you on in the ongoing debate between cultural relativism and universal values? If there are no "universal human rights," then is any and every practice permissible within defined cultural circumstances? Slavery? Clitorectomy? The death penalty? Torture? Local genocide? And if there are universal rights, who should "enforce" them; or more placidly "argue for" them? Even before enforcing or arguing, which are the "universal human rights"? Those enunciated by the American and French revolutions? Isn't it begging the question to define "universal human rights"? And if these rights need to be "argued for," how to balance access to the instruments of information guaranteeing to the unpopular or even (to some) the abhorrent access? Or isn't this still another question begged – that "free speech" is a universal human right? And isn't it axiomatic that self-perpetuating neo-medieval corporations – already recognized by the US Supreme Court as "persons" – control the media and, therefore, sooner rather than later, will rule the world? Or do the Chinese and Islam assert otherwise?

Self-wounding is as good an arena as any to wrestle with these questions.

Because this is an essay and not a book, I will concentrate most of my remarks on the activities of several artists who bleed by cutting, piercing, or sewing themselves. I trace this line of work back both to Chris Burden's *Shoot* and to an attempt, both conscious and unconscious, to amalgamate art to religion. Not in terms of belief but in a complex weave of "seriousness" and consequentiality – efficacy – with a rejection of formal religion in favor of appropriating ritual actions for artistic expression. I will try to explain why these art practices should be considered in the same conceptual sphere as blood rituals and blood popular-culture practices.

Shoot was very undramatic, especially given what its title promised. There is a YouTube of *Shoot* including Burden's eight-second film of the performance, some preparatory audio, and Burden's comment on his piece.[3] In *Shoot*, Burden stands against a wall inside an empty warehouse, and, with about a dozen people watching, a friend shoots Burden in the arm with a .22-caliber rifle. In Burden's own words:

> Guns and American culture are intertwined in some perverse way. Being shot is as American as apple pie. It was during the Vietnam era and for the first time on news you would see people actually being shot. [...] I was

trying to wrestle with the question, "What is being shot?" And turning and facing this dragon that everybody tries to avoid. If you face the dragon head-on, what does it mean?

I had structured the performance in my mind's eye where the bullet would whiz by and scratch my arm and literally draw one drop of blood. [...] My worst fear was that he [Burden's friend] would miss entirely. [...] There were under a dozen people there, it was inside, in this warehouse space. The gunmen stood 12–15 feet from me, he had a rifle, a .22 caliber rifle, I stood facing him directly, he said, "Are you ready?" I said "Yes" and I stood still with my arm there [...] and he pulled the trigger. And the bullet went in my arm and out the other side, it just went through sort of fatty tissue, it didn't really do any damage. I had a hole in my arm, a smoking hole which was very disgusting and, uhh, it made me actually go into shock. It's not that it hurt, it's that it was such a violent act. People asked, "What did it feel like?" Well, I can only speak for myself, I'm sure being shot can be very painful. In this particular case, I compare it to standing on an expressway and having the corner of a giant truck hit you on the side of your arm as it whizzes by – so your arm just goes, basically, numb but when you look down at it you see a hole that is smoking out of both ends and it's very upsetting. [Interviewer: How did the audience react?] "Ooo! It went all the way through, a bad one. Mmmm." I staggered forward, I sat down, they put a tourniquet on my arm, and they took me to the hospital. The hospital put a drain in it, cleaned it out. [Interviewer: Did it scar?] Yes, it looks like two vaccination marks, there's an in and an out. I don't usually show it to people [...], it's not a tattoo, something that I try to flaunt, know what I'm saying? [...] I was trying to make art.[4]

Two years after *Shoot*, Burden had himself crucified to the back of a Volkswagen Beetle – nails driven through his hands. Although Burden remained impaled for only two minutes as the Beetle's engine raced, *Trans-Fixed* was surely more painful than *Shoot*. Art dealer Josh Baer, who curated a 2004 retrospective of Burden's work, had this to say about *Trans-Fixed*:

> In experiencing this type of pain and vulnerability first-hand, Burden is able to make it more familiar and, in turn, he demystifies the horror of such acts by making them knowable, both for himself and for the audience. As a result, the collective fears that society uses to keep people in order are exposed and the idea that the human body is governed by law is rendered impotent.[5]

There was hardly any blood in *Shoot*; and no reference to martyrdom, saints, or religion. In *Trans-Fixed*, the photos show Burden's bloody hands, his outstretched arms reference Jesus on the Cross. I think Baer reads too much into Burden's action, which, to me, is an ironic crucifixion, perhaps mocking Germany's post-Holocaust industrial resurgence on behalf of American consumerist "volk," the "folk" that the Nazis so celebrated.

Trans-Fixed has blood, and blood is the body's most ambiguous/ambivalent liquid. In the post HIV/AIDS world, blood can heal or kill. Blood is the synecdoche for lineage ("bloodline") and compulsion ("it's in my blood"). Blood is the battle cry of sports teams, gangs, clans, and armies ("out for blood," "The Bloods," "blood feud," "blood and glory," "blood and guts"). In Christianity, blood is the divine life itself; among the Aztecs the heart pumping blood was ripped from the sacrificed. The subincision traditional rituals of Indigenous Australians feature the slicing open of the underside of the penis so that blood flows onto the dry earth both to fertilize it and to imitate the flow of women's menstrual blood. The monthly blood of menstruation signals a woman's continued fertility. Menstruation affects only females, and only for a portion of their lives. In many cultures, menstrual blood is hidden from men. Women take steps to absorb and get rid of the blood. Except for menses, people want to keep human blood in its place, inside the skin and within the capillaries, veins, and arteries. Blood runs within and under the skin; it nourishes the organs, the brain, even the bones. Blood leaves the body when the skin is cut, ripped, pierced, shot, or battered. If a vein is cut, blood flows softly; arterial bleeding is eruptive, draining a person to death in a few minutes. In surgery, blood is sponged away as it appears as fresh blood is transfused into the patient. But in art, and in ritual, blood flows visibly, even triumphantly: making a spectacle of bleeding is the point.

The display of blood is related to public nakedness, both primary (all are born naked) and secondary (choosing to be naked in public). And, although I cannot examine the system here, I believe there is a continuum leading from nakedness as a natural occurrence to genital coverings, face and body painting, hair styling, through to various body modifications wrought by piercings and cuttings, ordinary surgery, and artistic surgical practices such as ORLAN's "defiguring" and "refiguring" (her terms) or Stelarc's bionic third hand, third ear, or robot arm. From the early 1970s through to 1988, Stelarc had hooks inserted into his flesh and suspended himself. Stelarc says he took the practice from India, but it is also known among Native Americans. In 2012, in Melbourne, Australia, Stelarc once again had himself suspended by sixteen shark hooks inserted into his back, arms, and legs, his body floating over a large sculpting of his own outstretched arm. For Stelarc, the body is in transit from the biological to the meta-biological:

> It is no longer meaningful to see the body as a site for the psyche or the social, but rather as a structure to be monitored and modified – the body not as a subject but as an object – NOT AN OBJECT OF DESIRE BUT AS AN OBJECT FOR DESIGNING.[6]

This "object for designing" needs to be worked on, intruded into, refashioned. In fact, body modification is wildly popular, at least on the internet. On February 16, 2014, I googled "body modification" (in quotation marks: a narrow search) and was offered more than 1,670,000 entries. The 2014 number was more than in 2010. Does this signal increasing interest in body modification or is it an artefact of the internet? The internet allows people to find like-minded others with a few strokes of the key. As never before, people who were in various closets are now virtually dancing in the streets. Stelarc's practice (and, clearly, not his alone) suggests a continuum from the gross interventions of false teeth, prosthetic limbs, and jewelry piercing the flesh to the more subtle and far-reaching processes of genetic engineering. Conceptually leading the way are design, fashion, and art – trivial from one perspective but a profound human self-made evolutionary process from another. The endpoint of an earring dangling from a pierced lobe is the remodeling of the human genome.

What is it that ORLAN, Stelarc, Franko B., Ron Athey, and Rocio Boliver do? Franko B. is a heavily tattooed man, several of whose performances consisted of his opening a vein in his arm and bleeding on the stage. He has done many such performances. Jennifer Doyle described Franko's 2003 *I Miss You* at London's Tate Modern:

> Naked, covered in white body paint, Franko walks down a long canvas aisle. He is lit up on either side from the floor by florescent tubes, and bleeds from calendulas in his arms that hold his veins open as he slowly and ceremoniously walks the length of the canvas towards a bank of photographers at its base. Blood pools at his feet at each end of the "cat-walk," where he stands before turning around and beginning his march again. The performance is structured to resemble a fashion show, and the blood splattered canvas Franko leaves in his wake is used to make unwearable, or at least, un-marketable haute-couture, to mummify household objects, and to make pocket-sized souvenir paintings.
>
> (Doyle 2013: 74–75)

A ordinary enough response. But then Doyle goes on, in a way very unexpected from a critic:

> It seemed to take forever for Franko to complete his walk down the aisle, and he repeated this back and forth march several times. As he walked past us, I was unsettled by the intimacy of the piece. Franko seemed honestly vulnerable, noble, and, somehow, very lonely. While, to be honest, I felt glamorous for having been invited to attend what was a sold-out marquee event, I also found myself feeling lonely, and helpless. As I watched, I realized that I was worried about Franko. Although always composed, he was, near the end, clearly straining with the effort to keep up his march. But I was also shamefully aware of the inappropriateness of my concern. He certainly knows what he's doing, and it isn't as though I have any claim on him, except as one friend among many.
>
> (74–75)

A friend's concern is one reaction. Another comes from Amelia Jones:

> When I stand, shifting from one foot to the other in the crowd-filled roaring silence of Tate Modern's turbine hall watching B's white body, in *I Miss You*, traverse an increasingly bloodied catwalk (his feet stick to the blood after the first traversal, making a strange snapping, sucking sound as he extricates them), I am both definitively separated from his "present," live body (which, after all, is staged like the objectified bodies in a fashion show, their agency evacuated by their production as fetishes "over there," rendering the models "absent" subjects), and absorbed into its inexorable, brute "thereness" (the suck of his feet on the bloodied canvas is my punctum, opening his body to me as receptacle for my desperate projections of my own status as alive).
>
> (2006: 19)

On July 3, 2014, Franko emailed me a personal statement in which he states, "In my early career I was best known for my blood based performances, but in 2006, I reached a turning point and decided to discontinue this line of work." Franko states:

> *Don't Leave Me This Way* (2006–2009) marked a challenge in my practice, formalising my departure from bleeding. While I remained seated on stage, a bank of bright lights flooded the audience to the point of averting their gaze. Carefully choreographed in collaboration with lighting designer Kamal Ackarie, we used lighting to mimic the visceral effects that my bleeding body had had on audience members in previous works, while also opening up a new range of emotional bodily responses. I was searching for a way to bleed without actually bleeding, to continue the sense of wounding and create a suggestive rhythmic cycle of visual pleasure, aversion, discomfort and seduction.

After 2009, Franko moved into installations and, most recently, in his words, "Hardcore, Post Punk" music.

Ron Athey's most notorious performance took place in 1994 at the Walker Art Center, Minneapolis. In *Four Scenes in a Harsh Life*, part of his "torture trilogy" (*Martyrs and Saints* and *Deliverance* are the other two), Athey made 2-inch-long incisions in the back of his co-performer Divinity Fudge, soaked the blood with paper towels, and then, as if hanging out laundry, sent the rectangles out over the audience. Spectators, knowing that Athey is HIV+, assumed that Fudge was too (he wasn't). A near riot was followed by a scandal. Earlier in *Four Scenes*, Athey intentionally mimicked St. Sebastian by inserting more than a dozen hypodermic needles in his right arm, drawing blood. After removing the needles from his arm, two assistants threaded them into Athey's bald skull, creating a crown of (not) thorns. As he bled, the assistants carefully mopped Athey's HIV+ skull and forehead. Later in the performance, Athey, in a singsong declamatory style, described his evangelical Christian childhood, his forced labor as a preacher-faith healer. Clearly, Athey was very aware of the religiosity of his performances and the masochistic cathartic power of blood. On his website, he writes (using the first, second, and third person to both tell his story and to distance himself from it):

> If the inside of your head gets pummelled with enough emotional force trauma to splinter the psyche, you develop ways to punish the body, that fleshy prison which houses pain. [...] The sight of your own blood, brought forth from your own hand, spells an almost immediate relief, a release to the pressure valve. It's a violation that you yourself now control, providing a temporarily [sic] satiation which stifles the nauseating screams and endless insinuations of a world turned inside out. [...] Ron Athey forces the body to transcend its confines. [...] by pushing the boundaries of endurance through artistic expression, he shakes his compassionate epiphany. We all need to break free from the shackles placed upon the individual by society, family, religion, and gender. And possibly through the catharsis of performance, and ritual, we might finally be able to lay to rest the demons who've sent us in search of the respite only a knife or needle could at one time provide.[7]

Ariel Glucklich, in a deep study of self-injury and pain across disciplines and cultures, notes:

> Given the enormous diversity [...] and variety of self-mutilators (though the single largest group seems to consist of young women in their teens and twenties), it would clearly be foolish to reduce self-injury to one or two causes. On the neurophysiological level, the injury seems to produce natural endogenous opiates known as beta-endorphins that can lead to temporary states of euphoria after the infliction of the injury. At an entirely different level of analysis, self-mutilation has been linked with post-traumatic stress syndrome, particularly following sexual abuse or rape, imprisonment, and war experiences. Naturally, none of these explanations has been universally recognized as a definitive and exclusive factor. [... T]he self-mutilation of some patients, regarded from the subjective point of view, may not be entirely different from the self-injury of mystics or saints. The heuristic concept of pathology, which differentiates the patient from the saint, might actually distort an important insight. Both types of violence appear to revolve around a sense of empowerment and a positive affirmation of some sort. [...] The mental life of individuals who injure themselves rarely matches either the traumatic shock that observers attach to injury or the reductive processes of neurological and psychological sciences. If anything, in its complexity and ambiguity, the inner world of

self-hurters more closely resembles that of mystics and other technicians of the sacred who acquire, or claim to acquire, "spiritual" power by austerities and discipline.

(2001: 80–81)

In fact, many have noted the ancient history of self-wounding and its practice as religious zealotry, initiation, shamanism, preparations for going into battle, and fashion-and-beauty. In recent years, self-wounding in the USA has been medicalized and linked with post-traumatic stress syndrome and other "disorders."[8] Adler and Adler comment on how these actions represent a theatre of the body:

Self-injurers' bodies represent the site of contested social control, the site of struggle between the realm of the symbolic (the self) and the realm of the physiological (the corporeal). People who practice this behavior semiotically and subjectively inscribe their inner selves onto their corporeal bodies, freeing themselves, yet in doing so they brand and objectify themselves with a mark that stigmatizes them in the gaze of others as belonging to a damaged, devalued caste. The skin can be viewed, thus, as the nexus where the self intersects with society, where ownership and judgment coincide and sometimes clash between competing domains.

(2011: 203–204)

Certainly, the Adlers' and Glucklich's observations apply to Mexican performance artist Rocio Boliver.

In 2003, as part of the Encuentro of the Hemispheric Institute for Performance and Politics meeting at New York University, I saw Boliver's *Cierra las Piernas* (Close Your Legs). Dressed as a nun, Boliver entered the classroom-cum-theatre where about fifty spectators sat facing a hospital bed at one end of the rectangular room. Nearby, a movie camera with a capped lens and a TV monitor, not yet turned on. On the bed, raised to about a 35-degree angle, Boliver spreads a white sheet. After taking out from plastic bags small boxes and medical supplies, which she places on tables to either side of the bed, Boliver lays on the bed and lifts her skirt so that everyone has a clear view of her clean-shaven pudendum. But just in case someone is too far away or has the wrong angle, the cameraperson removes the lens cap, turns the monitor on, and there appears a close-up of Boliver's vulva and vagina. There is no way of being in the room and avoiding this performance.

Out of a box, Boliver takes a 5-inch-long action figure Jesus, with bendable hands and legs, dressed in traditional crucifixion garb of white loincloth and crown of thorns. He is both an infant Jesus and a tiny man, a homunculus. Boliver forms a small bed from cardboard and placed Jesus on it. After setting up a small mirror in front of her so that she can see what's she's doing, Boliver rips open a package of clinical wipes, spreads her legs wide, and applies disinfectant to her pudendum and upper inner thighs as if prepping for surgery. The liquid stains her skin a mustard yellow. She opens a tube of petroleum jelly and squeezes a dab of it onto a dish. Then she opens a sterile package, and with her right hand takes out a large needle, dips it into the jelly, and passes the needle and thread through a small white cylinder about 3 inches long. Then, with her left hand, she stretches the skin of her right labium and pierces the flesh with the needle. On the monitor, a close-up of the piercing.

Among the spectators, murmurs of shock, sympathy, and disgust – as Boliver's face contorts into a grimace. No one moves to intervene: Boliver is doing this to herself under the aegis of art. It takes a big effort to force the needle through her flesh. Boliver draws the white cylinder through the flesh also, opening up a wide hole, like a pierced ear with a large gap. Then she slips the cylinder off and stretches the thick green thread along her hips. She repeats the procedure on her left labium.

Next, Boliver takes Jesus and wraps him in a red robe. Then she unwraps a condom, slips it over Jesus, covering his head but leaving his two feet sticking out. She anoints Him with lots of jelly. His arms extended, the crown of thorns stretching the condom, Boliver slowly and painfully inserts the Jesus-dildo into her vagina. Blood flows from her vagina. As she works inserting the Son of God, Boliver heaves with heavy "birthing breaths." A painful deflowering of Boliver-the-Virgin-Nun. Once Jesus is in as far as she can push Him, the artist takes the two threads, pulls her labia tightly together, and ties herself tightly shut, Jesus within. This effort gives Boliver a lot of pain.

Then Boliver takes off her nun's habit and shakes her red hair free. Naked, she reaches into a bag for a red bra, stockings, and garter belt. Carefully – because of the pain? because she did not want to rip her labia open and expel the Son of God? – she dresses. Boliver wears the bra below and not over her breasts. With difficulty she pulls on the stockings – even the slightest move of her lower body is painful. Finally she gets the stockings on. Then she reaches over and fetches a pair of very high-heeled red shoes standing by the side of the bed. She puts the shoes on and slowly stands up. The stockings are equipped with a zipper that fastens them to each other. Boliver zips her legs together. *Cierra las Piernas*. In putting on these clothes, Boliver abandons the nun persona and enacts the classic Virgin-Whore dyad. Ironically, this nun-turned-whore cannot spread her legs as whores do because her legs are zipped together locking between them inside her vagina, Jesus. A toy, action-figure Jesus. Painfully, Boliver totters to the side of the room, finds the wall, and leans there, not moving. Something in her body and face, a slight nod or relaxation of bodily tension signals, "end of performance." A smattering of applause – vigorous clapping seems out of place, as does silence. There is no "right" response; nothing to rescue those gathered in this room.

As I follow Boliver to the dressing room, I remember something she posted on her website (which I repeat here as Boliver updated it):

What better than to dive headlong into the forbidden, perverse, censored, singled-out topics to gird myself against the passing of time, which is leading to the destruction of my vitality, my charm, my lucidity, my beauty, my strength. [...] How far can you go when you're offered a space of complete freedom, how much are you prepared to go out on a limb?[9]

An assistant removes the green thread. Boliver and the assistant take Jesus out amidst plenty of blood. Discharging the Savior is painful: Boliver screams and moans. Is she giving birth or getting rid of what has raped her (culturally speaking)? Or both? Is this the afterbirth of a performance? Is the blood also a kind of menstruation? Soon Boliver and I are talking. I ask her if she has ever done this before. "No, and I won't do it again." Almost all her performances are one-time events. Before *Cierra las Piernes* she had no body piercings at all. She is very aware of the "Virgin-Whore" conjunction, as well as of the women saint-martyrs of medieval Christianity. But she is also aware of the parody, of pop culture, the action-figure Jesus, the condom as protection against STDs and as a shroud for Jesus. And the strong medical overlay, as in many of Franko B.'s blood performances.

Returning to Stelarc's notion of the body as an object for redesigning, performance artists who bleed are on the lower rungs of this evolutionary ladder. Franko B. displays his bleeding self on a mockery of the fashion-show runway, but his message, if there is any, is not Stelarc's. Franko, Athey, and Boliver are not modifying their bodies as much as they are performing its irreducible physicality.

ORLAN (all caps, birth name Mireille Porte), a French artist who changed her name into something like a synthetic fabric, is extremely self-conscious and theoretically sophisticated concerning the nine face-altering surgeries she had performed on her from 1990 to 1993, collectively titled *The Reincarnation of Sainte ORLAN*. ORLAN's progression from slow-motion walker to Sainte ORLAN to the theatre of surgery to visual and installation artist is hyper-documented; in fact, self-regarding is ORLAN's core performative action. Here I focus on her surgeries, "carnal art," as she calls it, during which, using an epidural pain-blocker, ORLAN directed the surgical team and supervised the documentation. The 1993 procedure in New York was live-streamed to France, Canada, and other locations globally. As the scalpel cut and the tweezers lifted her skin from her face, the artist began to read.

It was on reading a text by Eugenie Lemoine-Luccioni, a Lacanian psychoanalyst, that the idea of putting this into action came to me (a move from reading to the carrying out of the act). At the beginning of all my performance-operations, I read this excerpt from her book, *La Robe* [1983]: "Skin is deceiving ... in life, one only has one's skin ... there is a bad exchange in human relations because one never is what one has ... I have the skin of an angel, but I am a jackal ... the skin of a crocodile, but I am a puppy, the skin of a black person, but I am white, the skin of a woman, but I am a man; I never have the skin of what I am. There is no exception to the rule because I am never what I have."[10]

ORLAN is simultaneously the object and agent of these "operations," a word denoting both surgery and its surplus as artistic-military process. During the surgeries, ORLAN directed "revisions" of her nose, lips, and cheeks and the placing of implants under her skin. "Her eyes wide open, her powerful voice, her conscious operated-on body are connected to the interactive transmission networks, a combination of cybernetics and biology" (in Donger 2010: 31). Aware and theoretical, ORLAN writes:

> Each surgical operation performance was built on a text, philosophical, psychoanalytic or literary: Lemoine-Luccioni, Serres, Hindi Sanskrit texts, Allais, Artaud, Fiebig-Betuel, Kristeva. I read the texts for as long as possible during the surgery, even when my face was being operated on. As a result, in the last surgeries, this produced the image of a corpse during autopsy whose speech still continued, detached from the body. [...] This series of performances was created to put some face on my face. A work between the figurative, defigurative, and refigurative, in a body that is at times the subject and at other times the object, navigating between having a body and being a body, and playing between my presence and my representation in order to attempt at unwriting myself from the tradition; and while trying to unwrite myself to inscribe myself into the hollow and fake models that society designates and asks us to integrate, whether those are from art history or magazines or publicity – the woman one should be, the art one should make and what one should think.
>
> (in Donger 2010: 42–43)

From ORLAN's "Manifesto of Carnal Art":

> Carnal Art [...] It swings between defiguration and refiguration. Its inscription in the flesh is a function of our age. The body has become a "modified ready-made." [...] Carnal Art is not interested in the plastic-surgery result, but in the process of surgery, the spectacle and discourse of the modified body which has become the place of a public debate. [...] As distinct from "Body Art," Carnal Art does not conceive of pain as redemptive or as a source of purification. [...] Hurray for the morphine! Down with the pain ! [...] Carnal Art repudiates the tradition of suffering and martyrdom, replacing rather than removing, enhancing rather than diminishing – Carnal Art is not self-mutilation. [...] I can observe my own body cut open without suffering! [...] Carnal Art not only engages in aesthetic surgery, but also in developments in medicine and biology questioning the status of the body and posing ethical problems. [...] Carnal Art loves

parody and the baroque, the grotesque and the extreme. Carnal Art opposes the conventions that exercise constraint on the human body and the work of art. Carnal Art is anti-formalist and anti-conformist.[11]

Interestingly, the "Manifesto of Carnal Art" was first issued in 1989 – before ORLAN began her surgical performances. ORLAN has revised the manifesto only slightly since 1989. The manifesto serves as a script, a road map, a theory to be put into action. This is typical of ORLAN's highly conceptual approach, putting her in the same league as Burden and far from Boliver, Franko B., and Athey, whose works are experiential more than theoretical (the artists themselves do not theorize). Stelarc is in between. Boliver, Franko B., and Athey embrace, embody, and exemplify the martyr's suffering, ORLAN parodies it; they sink into or try to surpass their pain, she blocks it with an anesthesia that does not deprive her of consciousness. ORLAN observes herself in the midst of her performances embodying a Brechtian distancing from within. Burden, in *Shoot*, prefigures ORLAN; in *Trans-Fixed* he prefigures Athey, Franko B., and Boliver.

Ordinarily, what's inside the body issues forth as milk, sweat, spit, tears, vomit, urine, shit, semen, and menstrual blood. Making oneself bleed adds a uniquely personal and cultural possibility to the natural flow of things. It is a way of taking over, of empowerment.

> Jane [an adolescent girl] made a list of reasons for cutting herself in which she included more than thirty items. However, the word that recurred most frequently in that list was power. "I cut right into the fold of a finger ... It was so sharp and so smooth and so well hidden, and yet there was some sense of empowerment. If somebody else is hurting me or making me bleed, then I take the instrument away and I make me bleed. It says, 'You can't hurt me anymore. I'm in charge of that.'"
>
> (Glucklich 2001: 81)

Jane is not an artist, her self-wounding operates at a personal, private level. She takes the knife to herself secretly. But she does want an audience, she is sending a message. One can variously interpret the bleedings of Franko B., Athey, Boliver, and ORLAN – but, undeniably, they publicly display themselves. Whatever else they are, they are entertainers. They earn their livings by self-wounding.

This is not to denigrate the other functions of their performances. Like many artists from the Romantic period forward, the professional bleeders tell their own intimate stories. They frequently invoke and enact a neo-medieval religious iconography. They play with dying, but in a theatrical way, through allusion more than illusion: to bleed is to risk death. There is an erotics at work also, which medical opinion isolates as "masochism," a pathology, but which others see as necessary. As Georges Bataille noted in his *L'Erotisme*,

"If a taboo exists, it is a taboo on some elemental violence. This violence belongs to the flesh" (1986: 92–93).

And there is the question of pain. Rumi again. Franko B. appears to enjoy what he is doing, while Athey grimaces in pain and Boliver both grimaces and then cries out. ORLAN makes sure she feels no pain – or any sensation at all – by having her doctors inject her with an epidural analgesic. It was relatively easy to watch Franko, he seemed to take such delight in his performances, which he framed as an homage to blood. But it was very difficult to watch Boliver. Should this matter? Athey appeared to reach a certain calm after the immediate pain of the insertion of the syringes into his scalp passed. Perhaps his natural endorphins took over. Not so with Boliver, who suffered with every puncture of the needle and with the insertion and removal of Jesus. I have never seen ORLAN in surgery or Stelarc suspended.

Until the introduction of anesthesia in the nineteenth century and a wide range of analgesics in the twentieth century, pain was part of daily life. As Glucklich observes, "We have lost our capacity to understand why and how pain would be valuable for mystics, members of religious communities, and perhaps humanity as a whole. The role of pain, before it was displaced, was rich and nuanced, and ultimately situated persons within broader social and religious contexts" (2001: 201).

Seen in this perspective, these artists, ORLAN excepted, are throwbacks, archaic more than avant-garde, recuperating sacrificial violence and sacred terror. In performing their ordeals, they share with audiences something akin to initiation rites, mystical experiences, and sacrifice.

Is this kind of art acceptable in "civilized" society? If not, why not? Yes, I know I am overdoing it: many come to watch out of sheer curiosity and voyeurism; and many perform or wound themselves to show off. Maybe within the frame of contemporary psychiatric theory they are sick. But, even so, perhaps something more constructive is also operating. Isn't there in the art and in the orgasmic subincisions, bleedings, and piercings of popular culture a complex mix of pain and pleasure, a Goth-medievalism derived not from a careful study of history but from fantasy, mass media, comic books, and what's available on the internet?

At the level of performance theory, these acts test the limits of representation. They are nonmimetic. Real blood is really flowing, the performers are not pretending. Of course, even in orthodox theatre something is really happening. The actors are speaking, moving, breathing, etc. But these actions are subsumed into fictional roles enacted to advance a narrative. For the time of his performance, it is Hamlet not Richard Burton who is speaking – although it is Burton and not Hamlet who accepts the applause after rising from the slaughter that ends the play. In *Hamlet*, no one really dies or is even wounded. But in the kind of blood performances I am discussing (even though no artist has died in a performance), a Rubicon was crossed more than a half-century ago by the Vienna Actionists.[12] After the Actionists, it is not stage or animal blood that Athey and Franko B. shed; those aren't fake labia that Boliver is putting a thick needle through; that is ORLAN's face being opened surgically. This is part of what Carol Martin dubs "theatre of the real," though she means something more like performances made from real events, while I am writing about performances made of real here-and-now processes. Martin's "real" is a meeting of past and present (see Martin 2010 and 2012). The "real" of the artists – and the Muharram flagellants, the teenagers who cut themselves, and the Indigenous Australians (more examples can easily be marshaled) – is in the present. These acts may continue a tradition, cite art history, bewail martyred heroes, or be indexed in a book of mental disorders. But their doing leaves marks on the body; their testimony is irreducible activity.

Determining what kinds of reality can be staged is an important theoretical question with consequences for more than aesthetics. Up to now, the tendency among performance theorists, me included, has been to expand the purview of representation – to take literally the notion of "all the world's a stage" and its concomitant "performances in/of everyday life." After Duchamp, anything at all can be art. But blood art and body modification confronts theory with a dilemma. First, there is the matter of limits. Are there or ought there to be limits? Up to now, I have found limits politically and aesthetically unacceptable. Anything that people voluntarily enact and witness is OK. What people do for fame and money, or out of compulsion, or even in deference to tradition can be so extreme that … what? Be forbidden? By law? There are two slippery slopes, one slanting toward (voluntary) deadly gladiatorial games, – *Hunger Games* made actual – the other toward regulation and censorship – and we've certainly seen too much of that, from Plato through Stalin and beyond. Who's right, Leibniz or Pangloss?

When someone actually cuts, pierces, or sews herself, when real blood flows, when the performance persona is the person himself and not a fictional character, what is going on? We know that the Romans staged such events – thousands were slain in the Coliseum. In some dramas a condemned man took the place of an actor and actually was killed onstage. Have we arrived at an historical epoch analogous to imperial Rome? For now I am setting this question aside. I want instead to deal with the dilemma of representation.

Let me put it this way: Two competing interpretations lead to two very different theoretical outcomes. If reality can be framed as representation, then there are no limits on what can be enacted "as art." Doctrines of free speech will protect all representations. On the other hand, if artists are legally or conventionally prohibited or discouraged from performing these kinds of actions, we give to the "authorities" – legal or critical – the power to set limits. And here is the dilemma: art and ritual without limits yields some very abhorrent (to me) practices, such as female genital mutilation. If we say, as many do, that the determining factor is "free will" and "voluntarism" – if a person wants to sew up her labia, then let her – I can accept that, up to a point. The point being deciding when a person actually has the agency she is presumed to have, even the agency she claims she has. But if an artist's claim of having made an independent judgment is to be questioned, who has the wisdom or presumption to decide for or against the artist? Does one by purchasing a ticket or attending a performance endorse the acts performed? Also, what about cultures or situations where the basic social unit is not the individual but kin, the local community, or some other group? I cannot at present work myself out of this dilemma: I am on both sides of the question. And this is precisely where the arts, performance art especially, comes in. Earlier in this essay I ruminated about universal human rights v. cultural relativism v. the media under the aegis (note the irony) of the "corporate person." Which of these will decide for the artist? Where freest, art is most offensive, if not decadent; where guided, art is functional on behalf of a dominant ideology or religion; and where sponsored, art is a smart monkey on a leash.

Back to blood. In the 1980s, as AIDS was ravaging two overlapping communities, gays and artists, the meaning of blood changed radically. AIDS was a new disease, incurable, transforming the prime of life into a slow, wasting death. Living with HIV+ blood, as Ron Athey does, or dying of AIDS, as many I knew have, was something unexpected and "unfair." First responses to the disease were defiant anger, risk-taking, and terror of "bodily fluids." Semen, of course, but blood too, because blood, finally, was where AIDS came to kill. There was no cure; there was avoidance and protection. Soon artists noticed the paradox. They drew a line from Christ's all-saving blood to AIDS's killing blood. Drinking the wine-into-blood of Jesus signified eternal life; receiving even a tiny amount of the blood from one's lover might mean a long-suffering death.

Early in this writing I noted that I was enmeshed in a tangle. It's true – and I cannot untangle the mess and tie the loose ends together. In today's highly mediatized world, there is a very strong desire for "the real" (I, too, wish there were a better word for it). Artists, like ordinary people, want to "get real." Some wound themselves. Some non-artists get real by blowing themselves up – with the media in mind. Cutting and bleeding are ritualized actions, sometimes painful and always evocative. The ritualists seek transformation, the flagellants seek presence, the artists seek expression, the teenagers who cut themselves seek empowerment. Or maybe all these groups seek all these things. Franko B., Stelarc, Ron Athey, Rocio Boliver, and ORLAN are five artists among many who are simultaneously archaic, risky, dramatic, semiotic, and, in their own ways, beautiful.

Notes

1 I am not writing about forced bloodletting: Aztec priests ripping out the hearts of victims; Agamemnon sacrificing Iphigenia, etc. Often victims "agree," that is, they perform the rituals: walk to the place of execution, sit in the electric chair, ascend the scaffold, etc. Sometimes, they are celebrated and treated specially, as the Aztecs

did with high-ranking warrior victims. Isaac obeying his father Abraham and Jesus accepting crucifixion are in-between cases. Here I am concentrating on people who wound themselves or invite others to wound them.

2 See http://archive.org/stream/stcatherineofsie00polluoft/stcatherineofsie00polluoft_dj vu.txt (accessed July 3, 2014).

3 See http://www.youtube.com/watch?v=26R9KFdt5aY (accessed June 14, 2014).

4 From BBC's *Witness*, November 19, 2012, available online at http://www.bbc.co.uk/ programmes/p010d95z (accessed July 1, 2014).

5 See http://wtfarthistory.com/post/14868420227/crucified-on-a-volkswagen-beetle (accessed June 14, 2014).

6 See http://stelarc.org/?catID=20317 (accessed July 3, 2014).

7 See http://www.ronathey.com/bio.pdf (accessed June 14, 2014).

8 See Adler and Adler (2011) for both a review of the literature and case studies.

9 See http://www.rocioboliver.com/#!principios (accessed June 14, 2014).

10 See http://orlan.eu/adriensina/conference/extract2.html (accessed July 3, 2014).

11 See http://www.orlan.eu/texts (accessed July 3, 2014).

12 Vienna Actionist Rudolph Schwarzkogler staged a piece in which he seemed to slice off a colleague's penis piece by piece. Later, the story was that Schwarzkogler sliced his own organ and died as a result – not true. Schwarzkogler died in 1969, three years after the famous hoax. Several Actionist pieces were bloody, but the blood was that of animals.

References

Adler, Patricia A. and Peter Adler (2011) *The Tender Cut: Inside the Hidden World of Self-Injury* (New York: New York University Press).

Bataille, Georges (1986) *Eroticism, Death and Sensuality*, trans. Mary Dalwood (San Francisco, CA: City Lights Books). First published in 1957.

Donger, Simon with Simon Shephard and ORLAN (eds.) (2010) *ORLAN: A Hybrid Body of Artworks* (London and New York: Routledge).

Doyle, Jennifer (2013) *Hold It Against Me* (Durham, NC: Duke University Press).

Glucklich, Ariel (2001) *Sacred Pain* (Oxford: Oxford University Press).

Hegland, Mary Elaine (2010) "Flagellation and Fundamentalism Transforming Meaning, Identity, and Gender through Pakistani Women's Rituals of Mourning," in Peter J. Chelkowski (ed.), *Eternal Performance: Taziyah and Other Shiite Rituals* (Kolkata [Calcutta]: Seagull Books), pp. 334–379.

Jones, Amelia (2006) "Corporeal Malediction: Franko B's Body/Art and the Trace of Whiteness," in Dominic Johnson (ed.), *Franko B., Blinded by Love* (Milan: Galerie Pack), pp. 17–26.

Lemoine-Luccioni, Eugénie (1983) *La Robe* (Paris: Éditions du Seuil).

Martin, Carol (2012) *Theatre of the Real* (Basingstoke: Palgrave Macmillan).

Martin, Carol (ed.) (2010) *Dramaturgy of the Real on the World Stage* (Basingstoke: Palgrave Macmillan).

Rumi (1983) *The Sufi Path of Love*, trans. William C. Chittick (Albany, NY: SUNY Press).

Chapter 7

"Points of Contact" Revisited

In 1985, I published "Points of Contact between Anthropological and Theatrical Thought" as the first chapter of my pointedly titled *Between Theatre and Anthropology* (1985: 3–33). Not yet two years after Victor Turner's death, I used the word "between" – a stand-in for "liminal" – to announce my intention of further extending Turner's ideas into the then almost-brand-new field of performance studies, whose first academic department had come into existence at New York University in 1980. And not only Turner, but a whole gamut of North American social scientists who were taking the "performative turn." From Erving Goffman to Clifford Geertz, Richard Bauman to William Beeman, Barbara Myerhoff to Barbara Kirshenblatt-Gimblett ... and many more ... performance promised a dynamic way of understanding how people relate to each other both in everyday life and in a variety of special situations. "Performance" as I summarized it then (and still do today) is a "broad spectrum" of activities ranging from ritual and play (in all their perplexing and hard-to-define varieties) to popular entertainments, celebrations, activities of everyday life, business, medicine, and the aesthetic genres of theatre, dance, and music. It was not that everything about all these activities is performative but that they each had qualities that could be effectively analyzed and understood "as" performance. The reach of the theory was not limited. I argued that anything could be apprised and analyzed "as" performance while what "is" performance – a much more limited domain – could only be determined within specific cultural contexts located within specific points or ranges of time.

The six "points of contact" discussed in that essay were:

1. transformation of being and/or consciousness;
2. intensity of performance;
3. audience–performer interactions;
4. the whole performance sequence;
5. transmission of performance knowledge;
6. how are performances generated and evaluated?

After discussing each of these in turn, I wrote: "These six points of contact need to be broadened and deepened. Anthropological and theatrical methods are converging. An increasing number of people in both directions are crossing boundaries" (1985: 26). I then gave as examples of this boundary-crossing the directing work of Peter Brook, whose *The Ik* (1975) was based on Colin Turnbull's *The Mountain People*; Eugenio Barba's "International School of Theatre Anthropology," "performing ethnography" as theorized and practiced by Victor and Edith Turner, McKim Marriott's "game of Indian castes" at the University of Chicago, and Jerzy Grotowski's "objective drama" project. I concluded my chapter by observing:

> I turn to anthropology not as to a problem-solving science but because I sense a convergence of paradigms. Just as theatre is anthropologizing itself, so anthropology is being theatricalized. This convergence is the historical occasion for all kinds of exchanges. The convergence of anthropology and theatre is part of a larger intellectual movement where the understanding of human behavior is changing from quantifiable differences between cause and effect, past and present, form and content, et cetera (and the linear modes of analysis that explicate such a world view) to an emphasis on the deconstruction/reconstruction of actualities: the processes of framing, editing, and rehearsing.
>
> (1985: 33)

So where do I stand on these questions today? Are the older "points of contact" relevant? Are there new points of contact? Have some of the ones I discussed more than a quarter of a century ago faded away? Have the theatrical and anthropological paradigms converged even more or have they separated? Is human behavior more likely today to be analyzed in cultural or quantifiable terms? The older points of contact are still valid. But these were all about how ways of making and receiving performances ought to be examined with methodologies that would bring performance studies (just then in the early 1980s being formed) and anthropology closer together – a mutual methodological program, if you will.

Things have progressed a long way since then. The "performative turn" in anthropology came: especially keen in the works of Goffman, Singer, Turner, and Geertz, if one keeps to US anthropologists (where my knowledge is most secure). And in light of that, increased interest by both performance theorists and anthropologists in a broad range of topics from mirror neurons/neurobiology, the study of paleolithic performance centers: a refiguring of "cave art" not as visuality but as ceremonial venues; the application of Turner's pioneering "performed ethnography" particularly in the work of his wife, Edith Turner; the multiplication of "local knowledges" (to use Geertz's term) in relation to Theatre of the Oppressed and various "theatres for development" – liberatory actions or, more negatively, postcolonial neoliberal interventions. All these and more constitute a new galaxy of contacts between anthropological and theatrical thought.

These points of contact do not stand alone. They are interlaced with each other, reflecting and interacting with each other. However, they can to some degree be parsed into:

Embodiment. Experience as the basis of indigenous knowledge that is shared through performing. Indigenous epistemologies and practices which enact the unity of feeling, thinking, and doing. Some of this work follows from the "performed ethnographies" staged by Victor and Edith Turner in the 1980s. It critiques classical "objective" Western scholarship and respects indigenous theory-in/as-action.

The sources of human culture are performative. The question of what makes humans unique is frequently asked because we are a narcissistic species. Upright stance and locomotion, thumb and finger dexterity, tool-making, making/controlling fire, clothing, brain complexity, developed language that is both practical and poetic, arts creating beauty and depicting and enacting fantasy. Of course, all of these, and more, are absolutely unique but evolutionarily developed from qualities and behaviors seen in other animals. No single biological, behavioral, or cultural trait sets humans apart. It is the confluence of them all, the incredible complexity of the package that marks homo sapiens. What interests me here is "performativity": the ability of humans to behave reflexively, to play with behavior, to model behavior as "twice-behaved."[1] This is evidenced strongly in the paleolithic "cave art" of southwest Europe and somewhat later in south Africa; and perhaps elsewhere in yet to be discovered sites.

The brain as a performance site. Is the mind a muscle (after Yvonne Rainer's 1968 dance program, *The Mind Is a Muscle*)? Can the brain can be trained? What do trance performances, catharsis and empathy, mirror neurons, and emotional training techniques such as "rasaboxes" have in common? What does recent research indicating that some learned behavior can be coded into the genes and transmitted across generations say about traditional knowledges that rely on "brain tuning" by means of rhythm, music, dance, and song? Are we after two centuries rehabilitating the theory of the heritability of learned behavior proposed by Jean-Baptiste Lamarck (1744–1829)?

What undergirds these three (new) points of contact is Diana Taylor's idea, paraphrased by Virginie Magnat, that "performance constitutes a repertoire of embodied knowledge, a learning in and through the body, as well as a means of creating, preserving and transmitting knowledge" (2014: 35).

In my first essay, I spoke of "theatrical and anthropological" thought; I now speak of the embodied knowledge of anthropology and performance studies. This is not the venue to define performance studies; it has been thoroughly defined – maybe over-defined – by me and others.[2] But for those less familiar, let me say that performance is twice-behaved behavior, restored behavior. Performance is a broad spectrum of entertainments, arts, rituals, politics, economics, and person to-person interactions. Everything and anything can be studied "as" performance.

Let me now look in a little more detail at each of the new points of contact.

Embodiment

Experience as the basis of indigenous knowledge that is shared through performing. Magnat begins her 2011 essay, "Conducting Embodied Research at the Intersection of Performance Studies, Experimental Ethnography, and Indigenous Methodologies":

> Embodiment, lived experience and intersubjectivity are key to experimental approaches articulated at the intersection of performance and ethnography. [...] Since embodied experience eludes and possibly exceeds cognitive control, accounting for its destabilizing function within the research process potentially endangers dominant conceptions of knowledge upon which the legitimacy of academic discourses so crucially depends.
>
> (2011: 213)

Magnat demands that we take seriously not only the worldviews but the epistemologies-methodologies of "indigenous" peoples. As Manulani Aluli Meyer writes: "knowing is embodied and in union with cognition. [...] Genuine knowledge must be experienced directly" (2008: 224).

This "genuine knowledge" is the indigenous knowledge that candomblé and capoeira practitioners – and the practitioners of hundreds of other kinds of performances all around the world – experience. Is this kind of knowledge any more "genuine" that what a person learns via books, over the internet, or in any other "distance-learning" method? And who is "indigenous"? We must guard against the opposite of exoticizing/alienating/subordinating the "other." To super-value "indigenous knowledge" and "direct experience" is just as dangerous and false as to deny the such knowledge and experience. A balance needs to be struck between what people experience – everything from flying saucers and miracle cures to the ecstasy of trance and the mystery of extra-sensory perception – and what is "scientifically verifiable" according to the canons of Western scientific positivism.

And what is "indigenous" anyway? It used to be that everyone not-Western, not following the dictates of the Enlightenment, were regarded as "other," as outside the pale of "real knowledge." Knowledge itself was deemed to be Western. This conclusion went hand in glove with the work of Christian missionaries, colonialism, and plyers of sea-borne trade, including especially a massive slave trade that brought millions of people and their cultures from Africa to the Western Hemisphere. So almost from the very start of the invasion-settlement of the Western Hemisphere, "European" was "compromised," that is, fundamentally changed, by the infusion of African practices. It was true during the epoch of slavery and continues today that among the African peoples transported to new lands, embodied knowledge trumped book knowledge. First of all, the slave-owners wanted to prevent the slaves from acquiring literacy because *scientia est potentia*. Little did the owners know that oral knowledge is potent. Colonialism, so often treated as if it were an independent action, was in fact the necessary outcome and creature of missionary and trade activities. First indirect and then direct rule from the so-called European metropolis made conversion to Christianity and economic exploitation much easier. As the Continental powers declined and colonialism as such receded, the USA took up the gap. Before World War II, Japan – as part of its Westernizing process – acted as a colonial power whose field of play was the Asia-Pacific region.

These practices, if not the attitudes underlying them, changed over time. Non-Western literate cultures – those of India, China, and Japan especially – were admitted to the culturally superior "Club of Us." Indigenous peoples and their knowledges were, on the other hand, still excluded. This was so because much indigenous knowledge is expressed via orature,[3] music, dance, costume, masks, and visual art rather than in written literature and calculus. The indigenous knowledge of shamanism, for example, resides in the embodied practices of those who live according "wisdom" rather than according to so-called "rational systems of thought." With the ever-increasing scope of globalization – a circulation of ideas, objects, people, and performances – it is not possible to easily, if at all, separate out the "indigenous" from whatever we want to call what's not indigenous – the "metropolitan" maybe? That is, practices such as trance-dancing, nonlinear narration, hands-on training, etc., are as likely to be incorporated into the artworks and workshops of artists working in and from New York or São Paulo or Tokyo or Shanghai or Dubai ... and on through a very long list of metropoli ... as they are to be found in "native" cultures. In fact, the whole notion of "native" or "indigenous" has evaporated along with the notion of the "wild" or "wilderness." Everything has been mapped; all is visible via GPS; and what survives as "wild" are actually protected (or not so well protected) zones. In other words, where not so long ago places outside of human control existed, or at least outside of modern methods of control, what we now have are parks, zoos, and zones where human activity is supposedly restricted and managed. To put it bluntly, "nature" no longer exists on its own; it is dependent on one species, homo sapiens. Of course, we may be surprised one day as, for example, a great meteorite impacts earth; or some evolved virus ambushes our species in a truly fatal pandemic.

In all this dispersal of the indigenous, of embodied knowledge, a profound collaboration between performative and anthropological thought is entrained. But, for all that, is knowledge really equal? Anthropology still, and correctly in my opinion, depends on a positivist discourse. And where do we house the "truths" of religions ranging from the Big Five (Buddhism, Hinduism, Islam,

Christianity, and Judaism) to the myriad other belief systems accounting for the physical and spirit worlds? Not to mention Creationists, Scientologists, Wiccans, and hundreds of other – what shall I call them – "cults"? Is the knowledge danced at a candomblé terreiro to be given equal weight to the announcement recently by scientists working at CERN's (Conseil Européen pour la Recherche Nucléaire) Large Hadron Collider near Geneva of the existence of the Higgs boson, "a long sought particle that is a key to understanding why elementary particles have mass and indeed to the existence of diversity and life in the universe"?[4] Is the Large Hadron Collider's work and discovery less mysterious than the trance-dancing of Shango or the other orisha? In terms of people's daily lives, which has more effect? Do any of us here understand either process sufficiently to pass judgment?

Magnat is not talking about that kind of comparison. She is referring to:

> engaging the entire organism in the research process [...] the notion of "sensuous scholarship" developed by Paul Stoller who suggests that ethnographers should become apprentices to those they are studying. [...] The embodied research process he envisions values a "mixing of the head and heart" and demands an involvement in that process [...] akin to performance training, namely, an "opening of one's being to the world – a welcoming," or an "embodied hospitality" which Stoller argues is "the secret of the great scholars, painters, poets, and filmmakers whose images and words resensualize us."
>
> (Magnat 2011: 218)

The performance work Magnat and her woman colleagues undertook was in the tradition of Jerzy Grotowski's search for cultural constants/archetypes in "vibratory song" – movements and sounds emanating from, or located in, the lower belly below the navel and above the pubic bone, the chi. " [... F]or these women from different cultures and generations, who often work with ancient traditional songs, it is the power of performance, transmitted through their teaching and performing, which gives meaning to their creative work as members of a transnational community of artists" (Magnat 2011: 214). Indeed, artists more than most social scientists take seriously alternative epistemologies and methods of accessing, mastering, and using performance knowledge. A number of artists recognize, as Cree scholar Shawn Wilson says, that "from an indigenous perspective, research is ceremony because it is about making connections and strengthening them" (in Magnat 2011: 214). Or, as Hawaiian scholar Manulani Aluli Meyer asks, "Will your research bring forth solutions that strengthen relationships with others or will it damage future collaborations? [...] Knowledge that does not heal, bring together, challenge, surprise, encourage, or expand our awareness is not part of the consciousness the world needs now" (2008: 226). Or, to put it another way, as the editors of *A Handbook of Critical and Indigenous Methodologies* write in their Introduction:

> During the "Decade of the World's Indigenous Peoples" (1994–2004), a full-scale attack was launched on Western epistemologies and methodologies. [...] Indigenous scholars asked that the academy decolonize its scientific practices [...] while developing indigenous knowledges, voices, and experiences. [...] Indigenous knowledge systems are too frequently made into objects of study, treated as if they were instances of quaint folk theory held by the members of a primitive culture. The decolonizing project reverses this equation, making Western system of knowledge the object of critique and inquiry.
>
> (Denzin et al. 2008: 3, 6)

The fact is that "indigenous knowledge systems" are likely to be performative, embodied. This is what "performance as research" scholars do. This is something Victor and Edith Turner explored shortly before Victor's death in 1983:

> Anthropological literature is full of accounts of dramatic episodes which vividly manifest the key values of specific cultures. [...] When they study, say, a particular performance of a ritual, they are on the look-out for expressions of shared cultural understandings in behavior, as well as for manifestations of personal uniqueness. Nevertheless, while it may be possible [...] to demonstrate the coherence among the "parts" of a culture, the models [the anthropologist] presents remain cognitive. Cognizing the connections, we fail to form a satisfactory impression of how another culture's members "experience" one another. [...] For several years [...] we have been experimenting with the performance of ethnography [...] We've taken descriptions of strips of behavior [...] and asked students to make "playscripts" from them. Then we set up workshops – really "play-shops" – in which the students try get kinetic understandings of the "other" sociocultural groups. [...] The actors' "inside view," engendered in an through performance, becomes a powerful critique of how ritual and ceremonial structures are cognitively represented. [...] In these occasions of intercultural reflexivity, we can begin to grasp something of the contribution each and every human culture can make to the general pool of manifested knowledge of our common human condition. It is in dramatics and dynamics most of all that we learn to coexperience the lives of our conspecifics.
>
> (Turner 1986: 139–140, 153)

Edith Turner continues this work. Near the end of her 2012 book, *Communitas: The Anthropology of Collective Joy*, she writes, "Communitas – what is it? [...] Communitas is activity, not an object or state. Therefore, the only way to catch [communitas is] in the middle of its elusive activity, in process. [...] It is the space between things that makes communitas happen" (2012: 220–221). But, I ask, is this kind work "objective" scholarship? Does objective scholarship exist? Ought it to exist?

The Sources of Human Culture Are Performative

In "Drama, Script, Theatre, and Performance" (1973), I wrote about the performances in the paleolithic caves of southwest Europe. I further explored this in "Toward a Poetics of Performance" (1977). Both essays are published in the various editions of *Performance Theory*; here I am quoting, extrapolating, commenting on, and updating these writings. This train of thought is the basis of my strong belief that human culture is fundamentally, "originally" if you will, performative.

Early homo sapiens – anatomically modern humans – arrived in Western Europe about 40,000–45,000 years BP replacing Neanderthals but also perhaps interacting and even interbreeding with them. These modern humans were not farmers or villagers; they were hunter-gatherers. Their bands didn't stay rooted in one spot, but neither did they wander aimlessly. Each band had its own circuit: a more or less fixed route through time and space. This route was determined by seasonal vegetation and the movement of prey. Ceremonial centers were used over and over for vast stretches of time, millennia. Cave art evidences these centers, but maybe there were also fresh-air sites, long obliterated. The cultural level of these early modern Europeans – at least in terms of painting and sculpting – was very high: The masterpieces of the caves of southwest Europe and the mobile art of Eurasia are testimony enough. Cave art from far back exists in many parts of the world, though nothing comparable to Lascaux, Altamira, Chauvet, and the others in terms of age or artistic sophistication has yet been uncovered elsewhere.

Of course this art was not art of the type objects-to-be-collected-and-sold or "art for art's sake." The cave art, and some footprints of adolescents moving in a circular pattern, indicating some kind of initiatory dancing, is what physically remains of what were, I believe, complex ceremonial-ritual practices. That the cave art accompanied performances and was not designed for relaxed viewing as in museums or art galleries is clear from what the caves were. They were pitch-dark except for animal-oil lamps and torches; some are cold and wet. The art is often difficult to access, placed in cramped and out-of-the-way spaces – almost as if part of the "message" is the effort, almost ordeal, necessary to come face to face with the representations.

> A sunken river guards the fearsome Tuc d'Audoubert, two hundred long underground feet of which one breasts or boats upon before the first land; then comes a precarious thirty-foot steep shaft up ladders placed there and slippery pegs [neither probably there in paleolithic times]; and next a

> crawl through claustrophobic low passages, to reach the startling foot-
> prints of ancient dancers in bare feet and the models of copulating bisons,
> in clay on the floor beyond.
>
> (La Barre 1972: 397)

Certainly this is not a venue where people could stand back and admire works
the way moderns do at the Louvre.

The caves were theatres: spaces where something happened, where stories
were enacted, where people were initiated, where shamans went on vision
quests, where fertility – human and animal – was celebrated, where hunting
and/or other kinds of magic was practiced. We probably will never know with
certainty what the functions of the cave art were. Indeed, the functions may
have changed over time. We do know that the caves were important: some
were in use for millennia, active, participatory spaces. The support for this
interpretation of the caves and cave art is contained in several books, notably
John Pfeiffer's *The Creative Explosion* (1982), David Lewis-Williams' *The
Mind in the Cave* (2002), and Yann-Pierre Montelle's *Paleoperformance: The
Emergence of Theatricality as Social Practice* (2009).

Fertility is a root theme. Carvings, paintings, and stand-alone figures connect human and animal fertility. The most ancient figures are of women with
very large breasts, thighs, and buttocks and prominent vulvas depicted without
pubic hair. Figures small enough to be cradled in a hand have been found from
western Europe through to Lake Baikal in Siberia. These date from approximately 40,000 to 10,000 years BP. Although not as numerous as the women,
there are also phallic representations (rarely of entire men). J. Angulo Cuesta
and M. García Díez note that "Foreskin retraction practices, some possibly
circumcised phalli, copulative acts, onanistic gestures, instruments possibly
used for masturbation, and other scenes of a sexual nature, some of them difficult to interpret, show that the sexual behaviour of people in the Upper
Palaeolithic period was biologically and physiologically similar to our behaviour" (2006: 254).

Cuesta and Díez argue that, over time, humans became less solely concerned
with fertility and more preoccupied with sexual pleasure. Could there be a
paleolithic pornography? One has only to think of the Indian erotic sculptings
at Khajuraho (950–1150 CE) and Konarak (1238–1250 CE), where many of the
copulatory positions are also dance positions of classical Indian dance. Sexuality is the very substance of dancing. The turns-outs, lifts, and spreads of
ballet – not to mention the vulvaesque folds of the ballerina's tutu – are
sexual. And ballet is far from exceptional among dances. The links among sex,
visual pleasure, body movement, and artistic representation are obvious.
Could all representations – landscapes and portraits as well as overtly sexual
representations – not only record but also excite? Is a basic function of art to
arouse? Is it too far-fetched to regard the caves as female "penetrated" by
(probably) male artists-shamans who stroked colors and forms on the walls?

A famous item is in Lascaux near the bottom of a 20-foot deep shaft: a representation of a man with an erection facing a bison disemboweled by a spear. Near to the man a bird-head stick. Is he a shaman in trance (as Lewis-Williams thinks)? What of the sculpted-clay copulating bison or the many hand-stencils or arrangements of dotted lines which have been interpreted sexually? Yes, there are other animals – lions and horses especially – with no obvious sexual meaning. But isn't the very ability to make likenesses a cultural sexuality? The ability to create lookalikes is a way of procreating. Wasn't the invention of visual art in paleolithic times actually an emergent awareness of humans ability to make more beings? Isn't all visual art erotic?

This eroticism is not only in the making and looking. It is also in the handling. In El Castillo cave, one may see

> five bell shaped signs. They have long been recognized as representing the vulva. [...] The red female symbols and the single black male symbol are spectacularly situated within a slightly raised part of the so-called second vestibule of the cavern of El Castillo. Below the smoothened surface of the niche which they occupy is a small table-like projection of the rock, beside which fall the folds of a curtain-like formation. [...] Parts of this rock curtain show signs of having been rubbed smooth by long usage.
>
> (Giedion 1962: 190–192)

In India and elsewhere, people rub sculptings of the phallus and the vulva. I've seen people reach out in temples and in museums, making a life-taking touch. Everywhere, cult items are fondled; curing and blessing are accomplished by "laying on of hands." And, of course, foreplay is manual. What other kinds of performances may have been going on in the art caves? And why was this period of human history so important, impacting everything that followed? Lewis-Williams believes that 45,000–35,000 BP was a period of revolutionary transition in Europe, a cognitive quantum leap.[5] "Upper Palaeolithic people had a clearer, more precise mental picture of what they wanted their tools to look like, and that picture was linked to the social groups to which they belonged. [...] Society was diversifying; [...] human creativity and symbolism were linked to social diversity and change, not to stable history-less societies" (2002: 76–77). During this period people developed tools with true handles, jewelry and burials with jewelry; they engaged in long-distance trade of seashells and perhaps other precious items; there were increasing interactions among allies and lethal struggles against enemies practiced both by physical and magical combat.[6] Storytelling as a way of collecting the past and retaining collective knowledge was fused with embodied behavior: not saying what happened but showing it, dancing it, singing it. Lewis-Williams: "In Upper Palaeolithic communities, representational art and elaborate burial practices were both associated with different degrees and kinds of access for different categories of people to 'spiritual' realms (that is, realms of mental imagery) and, as such, had a common foundation in a type of consciousness Neanderthals lacked" (2002: 93–94). These core qualities of modern human cognition were marked by the interaction among "four mental modules": social intelligence, technical intelligence, natural-history intelligence (lore, storytelling), and linguistic intelligence. It is in the caves, in the making of the art and the behaviors associated with the art, that these four modules most strongly interacted with each other.

Lewis-Williams posits the "discovery" by paleolithic shamans of "entoptic phenomena," events that take place between the eye-viewing-the-world and the visual cortex: daydreaming, hallucinations both "natural" and drug-induced. These visual events

> are "wired into" the human nervous system. [...] Simply put, there is a spatial relationship between the retina and the visual cortex: points that are close together on the retina lead to the firing of comparably placed neurons in the cortex. When this process is reversed, as following the ingestion of psychotropic substances, the pattern in the cortex is perceived as a visual percept. In other words, people in this condition are seeing the structure of their own brains. [...] Subjects try to make sense of entoptic phenomena by elaborating them into iconic forms, that is, into objects that are familiar to them from their daily life. [...] In altered states of consciousness, the nervous system itself becomes a "sixth" sense.
>
> (Lewis-Williams 2002: 127–128)

The cognitive imperative demands that people interpret entoptic phenomena, have them "make sense" – as stories told, sung, and danced, or painted and sculpted in the caves.

The iconic forms are the cave paintings and sculptings; the formations of rock that, under the right light, appear as animals such as the Comarque horse. Humans both find and invent visions that take the shape of "spirits," "helpers," or "guides": non- or extra-human beings. These helpers are not only shamans' allies but, modulated into poetry, the descent of the hero-shaman himself into the underworld of the dead, as in the journey of Odysseus and later Aeneas' or Dante's sojourn in Inferno guided by Virgil (creator of Aeneas). The visions that Lewis-Williams posits the paleolithic shamans had were a kind of "swirling vortex or rotating tunnel that seems to surround them and draw them into its depths" (2002: 128–129). These entoptic visions are hypnagogic – the state between sleeping and waking – that the shamans were skilled at entering, guiding, and recalling. Many animals dream (we suppose, noticing REM sleep). But homo sapiens not only dream, but recollect, represent, and re-enact their dreams. Lewis-Williams thinks that paleolithic shamans developed "the ability to recall and socialize dreams and visions" derived from "the visual images experienced in altered states of consciousness" (2002: 192). These not-dreams/not-not-dreams were developed into "a set of socially shared mental images, which were to become the repertoire of Upper Palaeolithic motifs, long before they started to make graphic images. This prior formulation explains why the repertoire of motifs seems to have been established right from the beginning" (2002: 193) of the art-making epoch.

As for how the art was first created, Lewis-Williams has a unique explanation.

> How then did people come to make representational images of animals and so forth out of projected mental imagery. I argue that at a given time, and for social reasons, the projected images of altered states were insufficient and people needed to "fix" their visions. They reached out to their emotionally charged visions and tried to touch them, to hold them in place perhaps on softer surfaces and with their fingers [the "macaronis" so prevalent in the caves]. They were not inventing images. They were merely touching what was already there.
>
> (2002: 193)

The first two-dimensional images were not two-dimensional representations of three-dimensional things in the material world, as researchers have always assumed. Rather, they were already "fixed" mental images" (Lewis-Williams 2002: 193). "[T]hat is not a real bison: you can't walk around it; and it is too small. That is a 'vision,' a 'spirit bison.' There is nothing 'real' about it. For the makers, the paintings or engravings were visions, not representations of visions" (Lewis-Williams 2002: 194).

Lewis-Williams's theory explains figures such as the Comarque horse, which seem to be "there" in the rock, emergent when light comes from a certain angle but otherwise "not there." Even some of the paintings "emerge" from the walls more than are placed "on" the walls (as in an art gallery). Certainly, the incredible procession of animals in Lascaux has this quality of emergence.

Lewis-Williams's theory is good, as hypothesis, but impossible to prove. Furthermore, so many of the paintings and sculptings in the caves are very realistic – with a clarity of vision and an uncanny ability to depict motion, even "stop action" as in the multiple images of lions in Chauvet, that it seems highly unlikely that stoned people could make such "cool" art, such exact art.

Of course, one theory need not explain everything. The caves offer such a diversity of pictures and signs put there over thousands of years. Societies – even paleolithic societies – or maybe especially paleolithic societies – could not have been static; otherwise, "history" would have stopped at its inception. Lewis-Williams, like others writing about the caves, telescopes time. Not being able to fit eight, ten, 12,000 years into customary historical time schemes, people tend to forget how long the caves were in use. And, as a gloss on Lewis-Williams's idea, he posits that the cave-users were like Plato's prisoners in the cave who also believed that their hallucinations were reality itself.

And, don't forget, there was a lot more going on in the caves beyond image-making. The shamans were performers. They danced; they initiated the youths whose footprints are still present on cave floors. No doubt the shamans sang stories through long dark nights. As Homer reminds us: "These nights are endless, and a man can sleep through them, or he can enjoy listening to stories."[7] The ability to storytell, to weave a single narrative fabric of truths, lies, and fantasies, is one of humankind's most impressive and unique accomplishments. Part of the great cultural leap forward of the paleolithic was the integration of storytelling, dancing, and singing. This performative was embodied in a persistent (or traditional) form which was kept from one event to another: the style, if not the substance, of the narrations, choreographies, melodies, and rhythms, were known by all, makers and listeners-viewers both (if there were any spectators as such). The performances were taught by one group, or master shaman-artist to the next. As the word "tradition" denotes, performance knowledge was passed on by means of cultural trade.

Furthermore, there were scripts – not something carved in stone or scribed on parchment, but embodied "known" scenarios that pre- and post-dated every particular enactment: a what-to-do and a way to do it. Each specific evanescent performance kept and transmitted the script, which was more important than any single re-presentation. The scripts are performance knowledge, life-sustaining knowledge, knowledge that later would be called "sacred." And when, so, the performances would be called "rituals." But at first there were no such categories. People did these things for many reasons, including entertainment, which must not be thought of disparagingly. Keeping the scripts intact guaranteed the efficacy of the rites; abandoning the scripts endangered the cultural continuity of the group. And, parallel to what Lewis-Williams theorizes about how the cave artists "found" rather than "made" the paintings/sculptings, the efficacy of the performances was not a "result of" dancing-singing-storytelling but was encoded within the event. In other words, in paleolithic ritual performance, as today, doing is a manifestation more than a representation.

Manifestations were implicit, or potential, in the scripts. These very ancient performances (some more than 35,000 years BP) were products of cultures that were "aliterate," not nonliterate or preliterate. Future literacy was not implicit in the paintings, sculptings, handprints, patterns of dots, and markings found in the caves. What is immanent in these configurations are doings. What is in the caves is what remains of a much vaster constellation of performances. The making of the art itself may have been closer to "action painting" than to "gallery painting." That is, the act of making the figures, or finding them, as with the Comarque horse, was what was important. Items we today associate with signs and symbols would, in paleolithic times, be associated with doings. Talking, at least at its outset back when, was controlled meaningful breath-noise, not a translation of ideas into words. Infants acquiring speech do the same: they know what they are saying by saying.

Mostly scholars focus on the visuals – after all, the magnificent paintings and sculptings, plus some enigmatic dots and other signs and handprints, are what survives. But what happened in the caves is more important – if we can find it out – than what remains as visual traces. I believe that what actually grabbed people at the time was experiential: the sounds and movements enacted within caves, with probably an emphasis on the sounds. The visual art was part of the performance process, components of a well-developed environmental theatre.[8] As Pfeiffer writes:

> [C]aves are wonderful places for acoustic as well as visual effects. Underground ceremonies must have been designed to take advantage of and shatter the silence as well as the darkness, to bombard the ear as well as the eye with a variety of sensations planned to arouse and inform. [...] Imagine the sound of bullroarers nearby in an underground labyrinth, the sound of flutes rising high and clear as a human cry or a bird from place impossible to locate.
>
> (1982: 183)

In 2009, a bone five-finger-hole flute dated 35,000 BP was discovered in Hohle Fels, Germany; in 2012, flutes from the nearby Geißenklösterle cave were dated to 42,000–43,000 BP. Pfeiffer describes paleolithic bullroarers, and he notes that

> archeologists digging at a site on a tributary of the Dnieper River northeast of Kiev unearthed a set of mammoth bones painted red which they believe served as percussion instruments: hip-bone xylophone, skull and shoulder blade drums, and jawbone castanets. [...] The high-stepping, bison-horned man in Trois Frères seems to be playing an instrument which has been interpreted as a pipe or musical bow.
>
> (1982: 180)

There is experimental support for Pfeiffer's claims. The paleolithic artists-shamans knew that the caves as such were acoustic resources. According to Iain Morley,

> Reznikoff and Dauvois (1988) carried out an extensive analysis of the acoustic properties of three caves featuring Palaeolithic painting, in the Ariège area of the French Pyrenees. [...] They found that there was remarkably consistent correlation between the locations of the paintings and the places of particularly great resonance. Most of the cave paintings were within a meter of a point of resonance, and most of the points of resonance were accompanied by a painting of some sort. Further, they conclude that the location of some of the paintings can only be explained by their relationship with a point of resonance, as they are often not easily visible or accessible. In fact, some of the locations are marked only with red dots, where there was no room for a full figure (Reznikoff and Dauvois, 1988, quoted in Scarre, 1989). It would seem that the acoustic properties of the cave were at least as significant to the painters as the art itself,

as the position of the art seems to have been dictated by the resonance. These paintings are of the same age as many of the Upper Palaeolithic flutes and whistles [...] and it seems quite likely that the painting activities, and possibly whatever other activities were carried out in the caves, were accompanied by sound-producing of some kind.

(Morley 2003: 69)

Not only music, but dancing. In Tuc d'Audoubert, near Trois Frères:

Impressed on the clay floor are about fifty heelprints of children estimated to have been thirteen to fifteen years old. [...] They seem to start at a place deeper in the chamber, and fan out in a half a dozen rows toward the entrance, each row perhaps representing the path of a child. And why were the children walking or running on their heels? Furthermore, the chamber is so low, 5 feet high at the most and 3 feet or less in most places, that even children would have to stoop and stoop low.

(Pfeiffer 1982: 110)

Initiation rites, perhaps. Performance, certainly. Theatre in the sense that we moderns use the term?

Theatres are what Yann-Pierre Montelle thinks the caves were. Montelle reminds us that in Latin, *cava*, meaning "cave," is etymologically related to *cavea*, the auditorium of a theatre, or the theatre itself. The link is in the sense of a "cavity" or hollow space. Montelle theorizes the continuity from the paleolithic caves to ancient theatre is not in narrative patterns but in theatre architecture. Of course, the flaw in his reasoning is that ancient theatres were outdoor open spaces, and caves are concealed, dark, "indoor" spaces. But Montelle's notion that "theatricality" – rather than ritual, shamanism, etc. – is what we should be looking for in the paleolithic is worth paying attention to. Montelle says the essence of theatricality is "a space providing a locale for alterity, a site in which to frame 'otherness.' Indeed, the power of transforming the habitual into a constructed otherness seems to have been with us all along and has always been a powerful (while undeniably transgressive) tool" (2009: 3).

Montelle points out that this paleolithic theatricality, though clearly present in the European example, is seen also "in the Americas, Australia, China, India, Central Asia, and the Middle East. This global phenomenon helps confirm the emergence and ubiquity of theatricality on a global scale" (2009: 4).

In developing his theory, Montelle uses Lascaux as the prime example. Lascaux, dating from 17,000 BP, is a large cave with more than 1,500 "works" deployed in large "galleries," corridors, small chambers, and a deep pit, called the Shaft. Montelle argues for a logical spatial progression through these spaces from "The Hall of the Bulls," with its large images, some more than 15 feet. This space is for large gatherings; "there is an undeniable sense of movement in the compositions [...] towards the next section of the cave. [...] The figures [...] seem to be confronting each other theatrically" (2009: 200–201). From the Hall of the Bulls to the Axial Gallery – all names are modern, and should be used with a warning of ethnocentrism attached – participants moved in a prescribed way to the "Axial Gallery [which] was chosen as a repository of local knowledge – both ideological and mythical. [...] The Gallery was a collective inner sanctum where small-scale initiatory procedures were conducted" (Montelle 2009: 202). Montelle posits that there was an integral relationship between the knowledge "in" the visual art and what was instilled by means of performance – that the walls were a kind of script or permanent repository in reciprocity to the evanescent (if often repeated, with different initiands) performances. Montelle says that initiates were led step by literal step deeper into the cave from the familiar to the strange, the secure to the terrifying.

Next, "we" descend down an 18-foot drop at the Shaft where there is very little room for more than one or two people. The scene on the wall is of a mysterious stick figure of a dying (?) or in trance (?) bird-headed man with an erect penis confronting a disemboweled bison. Next to the man is a stick with a bird-head, a shaman's staff (?). Montelle offers this explanation:

> Perhaps what was depicted was the obscene core of the mythical discourse intentionally relocated "offstage" [*ob skene*]. This knowledge could have been the *prima materia* of the collective consensus – the unrevealed secrets characteristic of initiatory procedures. [...] The Shaft was the inner sanctum of the cave: the point of departure and the point of closure, brought together in a revelatory discourse about appearance and disappearance, birth and death [...] It seems reasonable that the scene may have been revealed to only a few selected individuals.
>
> (Montelle 2009: 205–206)

In agreement with Lewis-Williams, Montelle believes that the caves were "a mesmerizing iconographic amalgamation of polysemic messages whirlpooled" (2009: 208). For both men, the caves were sites of initiatory and/or shamanic performances, ordeals, and the seeking for and transmittal of important esoteric knowledge. This knowledge could be imprinted on initiates and shamans only by means of effective theatre – what Montelle calls "paleoperformance." Montelle thinks that the caves were selected because of their potential for theatricality. In his book, he offers detailed descriptions of three types of paleoperformances: public performances, initiatory procedures, and periods of seclusion.

> In these three short narratives, I have presented the polymorphic and performative aspects of pedagogy. What these three episodes have in common is that they occur in a deep cave, with the purpose (and pressure) of

transmitting information. [...] Theatricality emerged under the pressure of increased information provoked partially by a demographic explosion. Under this stressful socio-economic condition, sociocultural models had to be either preserved in greater secrecy or widely disseminated in order to incorporate unaffiliated elements. [...] The common denominator among these three types of palaeoperformance is that they are variable forms of initiatory procedures. In fact, in an attempt to answer the question: "what is palaeoperformance?," I would have to respond that they are the tangible manifestations of theatricality in the form of initiatory procedures. [...] "Initiatory procedures" is a generic description for a variety of performative activities – from storytelling to painful initiations.

(Montelle 2009: 217–218)

Thus, theatricality is at the core of the emergence of what on a global scale became ancient to modern cultures. Wholesale speculation, of course. But not necessarily false for being so.

The Brain as a Performance Site

Recent studies of the brain, supported by fMRI imaging, lead in two contradictory directions. First:

the case is being made for the biological basis of a wide range of behaviors and social problems once thought to be moral or psychological matters. In the law, neuroscientific knowledge is being presented as a challenge to notions of free will and personal responsibility, and biologized notions of morality are being offered through the use of fMRI in courtroom settings. In evolutionary psychology the brain has been marshaled to support conservative ideas about social roles.

(Pitts-Taylor 2010: 636)

On the other hand, "there is also much public excitement about brain plasticity. Brain plasticity or neuroplasticity refers to the capacity of the brain to modify itself in response to changes in its functioning or environment" (Pitts-Taylor 2010: 636).

Not so long ago, it was thought that the brain is "set" early in life; that neural learning was an early-life phenomenon. But now scientists know that the brain changes throughout life. Not only does it deteriorate, as in Alzheimer's and similar dementias, but, more importantly for what I am discussing, new neurons are created, new synaptic connections made, and older connections weakened or strengthened. In other words, the brain can be trained throughout life. Such training can proceed "automatically" or in response to conscious control. A brain able to learn and rewire itself challenges biological reductionism. "The plastic brain is a situated brain, culturally, biologically and socially. [...] Each brain responds to its environment and also to its own workings over the lifespan" (Pitts-Taylor 2010: 637).

To date, most neural experiments and brain studies deal with the "brain in the head," what is encased in the skull. But there is also a very important second brain, a "brain the belly." This brain is the enteric nervous system (ENS). The ENS is about 400 million neurons (about the same number as in the spinal cord) lining the esophagus, stomach, small and large intestines, pancreas, gallbladder, and biliary tree; the nerves within the muscles of the gut's wall; and the nerve fibers that connect these neurons to each other. The ENS operates more or less independently from the brain to which it is linked by the vagus nerve. Vagus (meaning "wandering," as in vagrant) goes from the brain stem through the neck, thorax, and digestive system, affecting breathing, digestion, and heartbeat. About 90 percent of the vagus nerve sends messages from the ENS to the brain informing the brain about what's going on "down there." About 10 percent of the vagus nerve sends regulatory messages from the brain back to the belly (and other organs affected by the vagus). The ENS is a complex neuronic network able to act independently, learn, remember, and, as the saying goes, produce gut feelings (see Blakeslee 1996: C1).

I learned about the ENS in relation to developing "rasaboxes," a psycho-physical training method I devised that links Sanskrit performance theory as expounded in the *Natyasastra*, a manual of theatre training from about 2,000 years ago, to modern theatre practice, and my own work in actor training. The rasabox work organically linked the ENS, Asian martial arts, and actor training. Rasa theory in the *Natyasastra* states that aesthetic experience, both from the performer's and the partakers' experience, is of tasting and sharing the flavor, the "juice" (*rasa*), of what is performed. Aesthetic experience is not so much visual as it is visceral. The Asian martial arts speak often and in detail about the region between the pubic bone and the navel as the center of the body's energy. My rasaboxes work concentrated on exploring the connections between these realms of knowledge.[9]

I wrote to Michael Gershon, a leading expert on the ENS (see Gershon 1998). He replied:

> Thank you for your letter. You touch a bit of raw nerve. You are certainly correct in that we in the West who consider ourselves "hard" scientists have not taken Eastern thought very seriously. The problem with a great deal of Eastern thought is that it is not based on documentable observation. You cannot quantify ideas about strong feelings or deep power. We therefore either ignore Eastern ideas about the navel, or take them as metaphors, which are not very different from our own metaphors about "gut feelings." On the other hand, I have recently become aware of quantifiable research that establishes, without question, that vagus nerve stimulation can be used to treat epilepsy and depression. Vagus nerve stimulation also improves learning and memory. Vagus nerve stimulation is

something physicians do and is not natural, but 90 percent of the vagus carries ascending information from the gut to the brain. It is thus possible that vagus nerve stimulation mimics natural stimulation of the vagus nerve by the "second brain." [...] In short, I now take the possibility that the gut affects emotions very seriously.

Rasabox training explores the deep empathy confirmed by the observation of "mirror neurons": when someone performs an action and/or feels an emotion, specific neurons fire, and when spectators watch performances in life, dance, theatre, film, etc., the same neurons fire in the observers' brain as in the performers'. Erin Mee reports, "In one experiment ballet dancers, capoeira performers, and non-dancers observed ballet dancers and capoeira performers. Researchers found that observation of action stimulated, to some degree, the network of motor areas involved in the preparation and execution of action in the observer, meaning that the motor areas of the brain are not only activated by performing actions, but by observing the actions of others" (2014 forthcoming). In other words, spectators perform in their imagination along with the performers they observe. This is true not only visually but also with regard to all the senses. In fact, smell and taste are more powerful and "primal" than sight and hearing in this regard. It all goes to demonstrate that emotions are physical, embodied, and contagious. I do not have the space here to go into detail about rasaboxes training. The important point is that both brains – the one in the head, the other in the belly – can be trained. What's needed are more systematic efforts at enhancing and enlarging the communication between the two neuronic systems and further explorations of our complicated neuronic networks connecting people to each other. Our bodies do not end with our skin but extend beyond into the brains of others.

Where does anthropology and performance come in? If the brain is plastic, if it is shaped by the environment and can be trained, then we can envision new ways of understanding how culture actually "inhabits" the brain. Many traditional rituals, especially those using trance, operate performatively by means of repetition and rhythm (drumming, singing, dancing). The psychotropic effects of trance are well known.[10] The paradox of trance is that for those who know or have learned how, entry into trance is willed and controlled, but once a person is "in" trance, the expected or normative trance behavior takes over. The gateways to trance – whirling, singing, meditating: there multitudinous many ways to induce trance – are consciously controlled, but once in trance a mind–brain state similar to that of dream-sleep takes over. Trance may be thought of as a kind of "lucid dreaming," dreaming where the dreamer to some degree controls the trajectory of the dream. As Richard Castillo notes:

> Parallel to the example of sleep, I suggest that trance is a behavior based on a narrowed focus of attention, which with repeated experience will result in its own unique tuning of the CNS [central nervous system] with

its own related psychophysical characteristics contrasting to those which sustain the usual experience of consciousness, and, thus, the environment and the self. I suggest this process can be intentional and based on culture-based behavioral norms such as religious practices. I further suggest that through repeated behavior, alternative neural networks can be strengthened, extended with new learning and associations (so-called "state dependent learning"), and even (at the extreme) developed into integrated, alternative conscious entities capable of independent thought and action (dissociation).

(1995: 27)

Trance, of course, is performance, a physical doing, a powerful way of injecting cultural practices deep into brain structure, actually altering the brain. Obviously, but sometimes the most powerful truths have been out there staring us in the face, trance-performing is both a cause and a result of retrained brains. Masters of trance – shamans, candomblé performers, and other traditional performers, and some artists – have trained their body-brains using traditional methods. It is time now to investigate and characterize these methods, to treat them as embodied knowledges. The old-fashioned opposition between "rational" and "instinctual" thought/action needs to be discarded in favor of holistic studies that treat master performers not as "objects of study" but as partners in research.

This approach is in harmony with rapidly developing digital technologies that are erasing what separates the "inside" from "outside," as Brian Rotman writes:

artifacts, from windowed screens to hypertexts are rewiring the very brain/minds that imagined them. In this way we are facilitating the emergence of a larger – collectivized, distributed, pluralized – "intelligence" by allowing ourselves to become more "othered," more parallelist, more multi, less individualized – able to see, think, enjoy, feel, and do more than one thing at a time.

(Rotman 2000: 74)

As you might expect, there is a counter-narrative to this neuro-triumphalism. The ultimately flexible and trainable brain can also be regarded as a neoliberal post-Fordist value-added object: "the ultimate biological resource [...] the brain is seen as a smarter, better version of any man-made high tech tool" (Pitts-Taylor 2010: 642). As in the industrial epoch when bio-mechanics translated people into machines, in our digital epoch computers and brains converge. In a time when everything biological is for sale – organs, blood, human eggs, genes, etc. – Catherine Waldby's "biovalue" (2000) comes into play. The flexibility without limits of the trained – and retrained – brain is equivalent to outsourcing, breaking up what once were unified, made-to-order or at least manufactured-all-in-one-place things into the widely dispersed multi-focused processes of post-Fordism.

In my opinion, both possibilities are actualities. The brain is trainable, and performance in its broadest sense, including indigenous methodologies, are excellent examples of such training as well as models for how-to-do-it; what is done with this knowledge is another question.

Ending

Embodiment, in the largest sense, is the underlying point of contact between anthropological and performative thought. How might the rituals/entertainment/art made in 30,000–40,000 BP link to practices today? I don't mean to just so-called "indigenous peoples," often treated as vestiges or victims, but also to today's artists and ceremonialists. In fact, the notion of an alterity gap – the separation of "us" from "them" – is outmoded. All homo sapiens have existed on the planet for the same number of centuries. There are no latecomers to humanity.

The deep fetches evidenced by paleolithic performances are what Grotowski researched during his Art as Vehicle phase from 1986 to his death in 1999. This work continues today, guided by Thomas Richards and Mario Biagini. As Dominika Laster writes, "Grotowski examined the role of the body in the transmission of transgenerational collective memory" (2015 forthcoming). In Grotowski's words:

> Memories are always physical reactions. It is our skin which has not forgotten, our eyes which have not forgotten. What we have heard can still resound within us.
>
> ([1968] 1969: 185–86)

> It is not that the body remembers. The body itself is memory. That which has to be done is the unblocking of body-memory.
>
> (1979: 133)

Grotowski devised extremely detailed and precise ways of "unblocking" body-memory. He sought collective memory in Haitian Vodou, Islamic *dhikr*, and the Baul songs of Bengal.[11] He guided Richards, whose grandfather was Jamaican, toward his Caribbean roots. Richards himself describes the process:

> What I did was to enter a process of questioning. I remember through action. It is an approach that can lead to an alive doing, because I am not trying to produce an effect, a result – also I am not trying to reproduce the effect of yesterday. [...] Grotowski often said: "You need to be looking for." To keep looking for. Even when you are finding keep looking for.
>
> (quoted in Laster 2015 forthcoming)

Richards looked in Afro-Haitian vibratory songs. Sometimes he walks holding a stick, a very old – an ancient – man; his voice is both deeply resonant and limpidly fluid.

Grotowski's life-work, if it can be summarized, is parallel to what anthropologists – in their own way, with their own methodologies – seek. As Laster notes:

> Grotowski's lifelong work was deeply engaged in the potentialities of performance as a form of embodied transmission. In attempting to decode the performative artifacts of ancient ritual practice, Grotowski sought to penetrate the embodied knowledge of ancestral traditions connected with precise structures, or yantra, which facilitate a method of deep knowing. Grotowski sought to revalorize oral and embodied transmission.
>
> (2015 forthcoming)

Respecting oral tradition, Grotowski walked the walk. Grotowski wrote very little. He spoke, and we listened. He insisted that people not audio-record or even take notes at his lectures. Grotowski explained that if you take notes, you "cannot be fully present and attentive to the moment" (Laster 2015 forthcoming). Zen.

This kind of work connects to the brain's ability to mirror and project. As James K. Rilling writes:

> Another of the remarkable aspects of human cognition is our ability to project ourselves into other times and places so that we are not limited to thinking about the immediate here and now. In other words, we can simulate alternative worlds that are separate from the one being directly experienced. We can project ourselves into the past to remember things that have happened to us, into the future to formulate and rehearse plans, and even into the minds of others to understand their mental states. How do they feel? What do they know?
>
> (2008: 22)

Grotowski believed that this "horizontal ability" to connect with others was also a "vertical ability" to connect with the past and with "higher powers." I do not share Grotowski's belief in higher powers, or even know exactly what he meant, because he was not an orthodoxly religious man. But I do respond to his sense, shared by tragedians of several cultures, that human life is to some degree "shaped" – by gods, genes, history, ecology, other human beings: who knows for sure?

Here I end, not conclude. What performance does is create worlds or – if you accept at face value what masters of sacred ceremonies aver – gains admittance to other worlds and interactive relations with nonhuman beings. What the physicists are doing at CERN is also attempting access to another world, one which these scientists believe is fundamental to, yet barely perceptible by, the world we ordinarily live in. The dancers I saw at the can-domblé near Rio in July 2012 had located their Higgs boson. Isn't our job as anthropologists and artists, as human beings with big brains, to foster actual and respectful communication between those possessed by the orishas and those possessed by the Large Hadron Collider?

Notes

1 I have developed the notion of "restored behavior" in several essays, most particu-larly in "Restoration of Behavior" in *Between Theater and Anthropology* (Schechner 1985: 35–116).
2 For some basics and some elaborations concerning performance studies, see Schechner (2012, 2013); Ferreira and Muller (2010); Phelan and Lane (1998); McKenzie (2001); Jackson (2004); Taylor (2003). And for an ongoing in-process definition-in-action, read *TDR: The Journal of Performance Studies*.
3 To better understand "orature," see Ngũgĩ wa Thiong'o (2007) and his "Oral Power and Europhone Glory: Orature, Literature, and Stolen Legacies" (1998).
4 *New York Times*, July 4, 2012.
5 I am not considering what may have been happening in Asia, Africa, Australia, or the Americas during the paleolithic era. However, until evidence shows otherwise, the cave art of southwest Europe is the oldest of its kind.
6 Shamans practiced warfare by sending their "helpers" to disable and kill enemies in ways that are parallel to the practice of the Yanomamo shaman Dedeheiwa as depicted in the film *Magical Death* (1973) by Timothy Asch and Napoleon Chagnon.
7 *Odyssey*, XV 392–393.
8 Environmental theatre in the sense that I develop it in *Environmental Theater* (1973, revised 2000).
9 For a detailed explanation of the rasa theory and rasaboxes, see Schechner (2001). This essay is included in Portuguese in Schechner (2012). See also Mee (forthcoming).
10 See Rouget (1985); Castillo (1995); Kawai et al. (2001); Oohashi et al. (2002); Schmidt and Huskinson (2010).
11 Grotowski's interest in Haitian vibratory songs is part of a fascinating network of people and practices. One aspect of this network are the Polish soldiers who were part of a force dispatched by Napoleon to Haiti in 1802 to suppress the revolution of the slaves. The campaign failed; Haiti won independence in 1804. Some Poles joined the revolution and in gratitude were offered Haitian citizenship. About 240 accepted, and their descendents are known today as Polone-Ayisyens. In 1980, Grotowski came to Haiti in search of possible relatives. He invited one man, Amon Fremon, a *houngan* (Voodoo priest), to Poland for the Theatre of Sources. For a fuller exposition of this aspect of Grotowski's Haitian-Polish connection, see Kolankiewiecz (2012).

References

Asch, Timothy and Napoleon Chagnon (1973) *Magical Death* (film). Documentary Educational Resources, Watertown, Mass.
Blakeslee, Sandra (1996) "Complex and Hidden Brain in the Gut Makes Cramps, Butterflies, and Valium," *New York Times*, January 23, pp. C1–C3.

Castillo, Richard J. (1995) "Culture, Trance, and the Mind-Brain," *Anthropology of Consciousness*, 6 (1): 17–32.

Cuesta, J. Angulo and M. García Díez (2006) "Diversity and Meaning of Palaeolithic Phallic Male Representations in Western Europe," *Actas Urológicas Españolas*, 30 (3): 254–267.

Denzin, Norman K., Yvonne S. Lincoln, and Linda Tuhiwai Smith (eds.) (2008) *Handbook of Critical and Indigenous Methodologies* (Thousand Oaks, Calif.: Sage).

Ferreira, Francirosy Campos Barbosa and Regina Polo Muller (eds.) (2010) *Performance Arte e antropologia* (São Paulo: Editora Hucitec).

Gershon, Michael (1998) *The Second Brain* (New York: HarperCollins).

Giedion, Siegfried (1962) *The Eternal Present: The Beginnings of Art* (New York: Pantheon).

Grotowski, Jerry (1969 [1968]) *Towards a Poor Theatre*, ed. Eugenio Barba (London: Methuen).

——(1979) "Ćwiczenia" [Exercises]. *Dialog* 12:12–137.

Jackson, Shannon (2004) *Professing Performance* (Cambridge: Cambridge University Press).

Kawai, Noriel, Manabu Honda, et al. (2001) "Catecholamines and Opioid Peptides Increase in Plasma in Humans During Possession Trances," *Cognitive Neuroscience and Neuropsychology*, 12 (16): 3419–3423.

Kolankiewiecz, Leszak (2012) "Grotowski in a Maze of Haitian Narration," *TDR*, 56 (3): 131–140.

La Barre, Weston (1972) *The Ghost Dance* (New York: Dell).

Laster, Dominika (2015 forthcoming) *Growtowksi's Bridge Made of Memory: Embodied memory, Witnessing, and Transmission in the Growtowski Work* (Kolkata [Calcutta]: Seagull Books).

Lewis-Williams, David (2002) *The Mind in the Cave* (London: Thames & Hudson).

Magnat, Virginie (2011) "Conducting Embodied Research at the Intersection of Performance Studies, Experimental Ethnography and Indigenous Methodologies," *Anthropologica*, 53 (2): 213–227.

——(2014) *Grotowski, Women, and Contemporary Performance: Meetings with Remarkable Women* (London: Routledge).

McKenzie, Jon (2001) *Perform – Or Else* (London and New York: Routledge).

Mee, Erin (2014 forthcoming) "Rasa Is/As/And Emotional Contagion," in Sreenath Nair (ed.), *The* Natyasastra *and the Body in Performance: Essays on Indian Theories of Dance and Drama* (Jefferson, NC: McFarland).

Meyer, Manulani Alui (2008) "Indigenous and Authentic: Hawaiian Epistemology and the Triangulation of Meaning," in Norman K. Denzin, Yvonne S. Lincoln, and Linda Tuhiwai Smith (eds.), *Handbook of Critical and Indigenous Methodologies* (Thousand Oaks, Calif.: Sage), pp. 217–232.

Montelle, Yann-Pierre (2009) *Palaeoperformance: The Emergence of Theatricality as Social Practice* (Kolkata: Seagull Books).

Morley, Iain (2003) "The Evolutionary Origins and Archaeology of Music," PhD dissertation, Darwin College, Cambridge University.

Oohashi, Tsutomo, Norie Kawai, et al. (2002) "Electroencephalographic Measurement of Possession Trance in the Field," *Clinical Neurophysiology*, 113 (3): 435–445.

Pfeiffer, John (1982) *The Creative Explosion: An Inquiry into the Origins of Art and Religion* (New York: Harper & Row).

Phelan, Peggy and Jill Lane (1998) *The Ends of Performance* (New York: New York University Press).

Pitts-Taylor, Victoria (2010) "The Plastic Brain: Neoliberalism and the Neuronal Self," *Health*, 14 (6): 635–652.

Reznikoff, I. and M. Dauvois (1988) "La Dimension sonore des grottes ornées," *Bulletin de la Société Préhistorique Française*, 85 (8): 238–246.

Rilling, James K. (2008) "Neuroscientific Approaches and Applications within Anthropology," *Yearbook of Physical Anthropology*, 137 (s47): 2–32.

Rotman, Brian (2000) "Going Parallel," *SubStance*, 29 (1): 56–79.

Rouget, Gilbert (1985) *Music and Trance* (Chicago, Ill.: University of Chicago Press).

Scarre, C. (1989) "Painting by Resonance," *Nature*, 338: 382.

Schechner, Richard (1977) "Towards a Poetics of Performance," in *Essays on Performance Theory, 1970–1976* (New York: Drama Book Specialists), pp. 108–139.

——(1985) *Between Theater and Anthropology* (Philadelphia, Pa.: University of Pennsylvania Press).

——(2000) *Environmental Theater* (New York: Hawthorn Books). First published 1973.

——(2001) "Rasaesthetics," *TDR*, 45 (3): 27–50.

——(2003) *Performance Theory* (London and New York: Routledge). This is a revised and updated edition of the 1977 *Essays on Performance Theory* cited above.

——(2012) *Performance e Antropologia de Richard Schechner*, ed. Zeca Ligiero (Rio de Janeiro: Mauad).

——(2013) *Performance Studies: An Introduction*, 3rd edn (London and New York: Routledge).

Schmidt, Bettina E. and Lucy Huskinson (eds.) (2010) *Spirit Possession and Trance* (London and New York: Continuum).

Stoller, Paul (1997) *Sensuous Scholarship* (Philadelphia, Pa.: University of Pennsylvania Press).

Taylor, Diana (2003) *The Archive and the Repertoire* (Durham, NC: Duke University Press).

Thiong'o, Ngũgĩ wa (1998) "Oral Power and Europhone Glory: Orature, Literature, and Stolen Legacies," in *Penpoints, Gunpoints, and Dreams* (Oxford: Clarendon Press), pp. 103–128.

——(2007) "Notes towards a Performance Theory of Orature," *Performance Research*, 12 (3): 4–7.

Turner, Edith (2012) *Communitas: The Anthropology of Collective Joy* (Basingstoke: Palgrave Macmillan).

Turner, Victor (1986) *The Anthropology of Performance* (New York: PAJ Publications).

Waldby, Catherine (2000) *The Visible Human Project: Informatic Bodies and Posthuman Medicine* (London and New York: Routledge).

Index